SEARCH

SEARCH

A HANDBOOK FOR ADOPTEES AND BIRTHPARENTS

by Jayne Askin

with Bob Oskam

HARPER & ROW, PUBLISHERS, New York

Cambridge, Philadelphia, San Francisco, London

1817 *Mexico City, São Paulo, Sydney*

FIRST EDITION

Designer: Sidney Feinberg

Library of Congress Cataloging in Publication Data

Askin, Jayne.
  Search: a handbook for adoptees and birthparents.
  Bibliography: p.
  Includes index.
    1. Adoptees—United States—Identification. 2. Biological parents—United States—Identification.
  I. Oskam, Bob. II. Title.

| HV881.A8 1982 | 362.8 | 81-48028 |
| ISBN 0-06-014970-1 | | AACR2 |

---

82 83 84 85 86 10 9 8 7 6 5 4 3 2 1

To my husband, Bob

Contents

Acknowledgments

There are so many people who were responsible for this book. My first thanks goes to Bob Oskam, who brought order out of confusion. His understanding of the subject and his insight into what needed to be said made him an excellent working partner on this project.

Search and support groups, regional project directors, state adoption counselors, attorneys, and legislators all cooperated, with quick responses to letters and an abundance of information. Without their help, I could not have compiled the individual state laws and learned the kinds of projects, plans, and future policies being considered.

I wish to thank the Adoption Search Institute and the Triadoption Library for their generosity with materials and files, and the Orange County, Mesa Verde Branch, and the Huntington Beach Main Branch reference librarians for their advice, help, and many hours of support.

To my children, Shan and Molly. To my mother, who supported my search and my writing. To all those family members and friends who understood my needs and respected my attempts to compile this reference material.

I wish to acknowledge my birthmother and birthfather, who gave me the one thing I never had, answers to my many questions about my beginnings and my heritage.

A special thanks to Bob, my husband, and to Linda, who were always in the trenches fighting with me.

To Josephine, who ended where I began.

—JAYNE ASKIN

My particular thanks to Rick Balkin, who has consistently been a supportive, encouraging friend throughout my career as editor and writer; to Jean Naggar, whose encouragement came at a crucial moment when I was first considering this project; to Carol Cohen of Harper & Row, whose faith in this project has been cheerfully unwavering.

A special note of appreciation to Jayne Askin, who has exercised unaccustomed patience and unstinting cooperation in the tasks shared to see this book emerge in its present form.

—BOB OSKAM

Introduction

"Where did I come from?" "Who am I?" "Whom do I look like?" "Does my relinquished child look like me?" "Do my birthparents ever think about me?" "What medical problems might I have inherited?" "Why was I relinquished?"

If you're an adoptee, you don't need an explanation of how much these questions haunt you through your life. If you're not, imagine for a moment that you've never known the answers to questions like these. Hard, isn't it? Whenever you've thought about things like this, you had someone to ask, but more than that, you had your questions answered. As a child you may not always have been given complete answers to questions you asked, but by the time you were a teenager you had a sense of your own and your family's history. You consider it yours by birthright. An adoptee has no birthright in that respect. At least the adoption laws don't recognize one.

As a birthparent you're put in a somewhat different situation, but the result is the same. You relinquished your child—often because you had no choice—and the adoption law is so structured that you never again receive word of that child. Somewhere your child comes into a new home, matures, and grows to adulthood. You know this, but never get the opportunity to reassure yourself that your child is all right. For a relinquishing birthparent, the emotions other parents can freely express are held hostage for a lifetime.

Is there any other way? After all, there's still the best interests of the child to consider. Somehow a stable, secure environment has to be provided for the child. Can you do that with birthparents in the picture vying with adoptive parents for the affections of the child? Wouldn't that cause the child conflict and insecurity? Under the circumstances, it seems logical that the relinquishing parent should step out of the picture.

That's the argument continually raised against efforts on the part of adoptees and birthparents to reconnect. But there's one thing it ignores in citing the best interests of the child: There's no child involved per se. As an adoptee searcher you aren't a child anymore. You're an adult who feels entitled to know your own background. And as a searching birthparent you're seeking contact with your child who is now an adult. This grown child is—or should be—as free to say yes or no to having any relationship with you as with any other adult.

Those in the adoption movement who are working and fighting for an opening of opportunities to establish a new connection between birthparent and son or daughter are doing so on behalf of adults on both sides. They are not working for some imagined right to interrupt the rearing of children. They claim no such right. What they do ask is why adults continue to be regarded as children, as though they were incompetent to decide whether or not to connect with another adult who is the closest of blood kin.

You may note that I haven't spoken of adoptees "finding their families." I've consciously held back from doing so. Adoptees have been taken in as son or daughter by adoptive parents who provide them a home and family where they are loved. The adoptive parents have loved and cared for the child they've adopted and have earned the right to be called Mother and Father. Those of you who are adult adoptees recognize this better than anyone else. What many people do not understand is that adoptees aren't searching for new families. Adoptees already have one, thank you. All that an adoptee doesn't have is a complete sense of connectedness with the past. There's a blank wall drawn across it. You may feel cut off from a piece of yourself by that wall. Now that you're an adult, you feel you should be allowed to look beyond that wall, to make the connection that will tell you where you came from, what set you on the road to where you are. Many of you have in fact won the support of your families in this effort—of your real families, those who provided you with a home and love you continue to cherish.

It's for similar reasons that I shy away from the term *natural parents.* That makes it sound almost as if others would then be unnatural parents. The adoptive relationship isn't that, however. Adoptive parents are playing a natural role. They are in a most fundamental sense natural parents. Where others may commonly think in terms of natural versus adoptive parents, those in the adoption movement who promote the right of search prefer to speak of birthparents and adoptive parents, each natural parents.

For many of you who are birthparents, the irony is that so often you are judged unnatural parents. Part of society habitually thinks in terms of careless, uncaring playboys and loose women. But it's not like that as a rule. Many,

many of you relinquish children you would rather keep and love, watching your child grow into adulthood. Personal misfortune, economic pressures, family pressures pushed you to do something you would rather not do. And like the natural parents you are, you hope one day to see your child grown, to know whether you might have grandchildren, to learn what your child has made of him- or herself. You're not trying to take the child away from those who have loved and provided a home for him or her.

Thus, throughout this text I will use the term *birthparent* to represent the genetic parent of a child. A brochure published by Concerned United Birthparents, called *The Birthparent's Perspective,* offers the best explanation of this term:

> We find the terms "biological" and "bio-parent" descriptive of a mechanical incubator or unfeeling human baby machine. We are neither; our continued love and concern for our birthchildren is akin to any parents' for their children. Although we do not object to the term "natural parent," we find many adoptive parents rightly resent the implication that they are "unnatural" parents, for they may parent quite naturally, indeed. Therefore, we choose the term "birthparent," one word, analogous to terms like "grandparent," "grandmother," or "grandfather." We remain the child's progenitor and thus find the term "birthparent" both accurate and sensitive to our place in the child's existence.

This book is written to present choices and alternatives available to adoptees and birthparents who wish to search. (And to adoptive families and others who support and participate—or who may simply wish to understand—the search activities of a son, daughter, or friend.)

If you are contemplating a search, the first and most important question you will need to answer is "Should you search?" The very fact that you're reading this book is an indication that you have considered—are still considering—this question. Even so, I cannot tell you that to search is or ought to be a foregone conclusion. I can only present it as a choice available to you. And I can tell you how to go about your search.

If you decide to undertake a search, you hope to find a loving, honest, healthy person (or persons) who has thought of you over the years, who will reach out to you and answer the many questions you have. You hope to locate a birthparent, a relinquished child, a brother or half sister, perhaps even a foster parent, who is like you—who may look like you, think like you. But are you being totally realistic and honest with yourself?

Can you face what you may find? A birthparent who denies your relationship? A birthfather who never knew of your birth? A grown child whose interests and lifestyle are radically different from your own, who may harbor resentment and bitterness at your "abandonment"? A birthmother who can't tell you which man of many is your birthfather? A family with an "undesirable" background? An account of conception and birth under other than socially accepted circumstances? Are you ready to risk rejection, this time with no possible flight into fantasy or rationalization to ease the pain?

Read through this book, and when you are finished, reread this introduction. If you decide "No, I'm not ready to search," consider the cost of this book well worth the conclusion reached. If you decide to search, know that all along the way there are new friends to help you and groups dedicated to opening your records. Most important, whether or not you locate a specific person—and chances are better than ever that you will—you will discover important things about yourself and who you are.

You'll probably come out somewhere between the worst and the best possibilities at the conclusion of your search. Whatever the reception you meet with, in the process of search there will have been questions of long standing answered, contacts made. And there is the possibility of a new relationship that hopefully can grow to fill a void that previously existed.

We see that although the desire to search has always been there, buried and seemingly lost except for the occasional thought, daydream, or outburst, the actual commitment to search is a special stage in itself. It is arrived at over a period of time, as the self gradually evolves from one level of consciousness to another, striving for authenticity and self-autonomy.

BETTY JEAN LIFTON, *Lost and Found*

Deciding to Search

As an adoptee or birthparent who initiates a search for those from whom you have been separated through relinquishment and adoption you instinctively feel you have a right to reach out for contact. It seems only natural that you be allowed the opportunity to reestablish the kinship connection broken years earlier. And yet when you do begin to search, you immediately come up against a system of relinquishment/adoption records administration that insists you have no such right. Frequently you face outright hostility from agencies holding records, administrations that feel you have no right to the information you're seeking.

Searchers are hard put to understand this opposition to what they consider their right to know. They generally hold onto their deep conviction that they *do* have rights, regardless of the present administrative attitudes. As the search movement grows, searchers are becoming increasingly outspoken and articulate in defense of the rights they claim. In addition, they are learning to turn to their advantage the rights that *are* accorded them as citizens, in particular the right of access to public records.

What *Are* My Rights?

Under the American system of government, citizens (either as individuals or organized into groups pursuing defined interests) can raise a challenge to any federal, state, or local statute (law) or administrative policy affecting them that appears inconsistent with the guarantees contained in the Constitution of the United States. Such challenge can be pursued through the federal court system. Since relinquishment and adoption procedures are governed by state laws, these procedures can be measured against guarantees contained in the applicable state constitution as well as the federal Constitution. On the state level, citizens can challenge any state or local law or administrative policy that appears inconsistent with guarantees contained in the state constitution. State courts can also be asked to give their opinion on whether a state law is in violation of the United States Constitution. Their ruling, however, has effect only within the state's borders, whereas a federal court ruling can apply on a broader level.

The Adoptees' Liberty Movement Association (ALMA) has instituted two class action suits in efforts to unseal adoption/relinquishment records, in New York and in California. The New York suit was filed in the United States District Court for the Southern District of New York on May 23, 1977; the California suit in the Superior Court of the State of California for the County of Los Angeles on April 3, 1981. The complaints in each case summarize the guaranteed constitutional rights that ALMA and most searchers feel are violated by current restrictions maintained on adoptees' life records. Here is the summary of violations as stated in the California complaint. ("It," in each case, is the restricting article of state law sealing the adoption records.)

  (a) it imposes on adult adoptees one of the incidents and badges of African slavery in violation of the Thirteenth Amendment to the Constitution of the United States and Article I, ¶ 6, of the Constitution of California;
  (b) it invidiously discriminates against adult adoptees in violation of the Equal Protection Clauses of the Fourteenth Amendment to the Constitution of the United States and Article I, ¶ 7(a), of the Constitution of California;
  (c) it abridges adult adoptees' liberty and property interests in their own identities in violation of the Due Process Clauses of the Fourteenth Amendment to the Constitution of the United States and Article I, ¶ 7(a), of the Constitution of California;
  (d) it constitutes an unreasonable seizure of adult adoptees' persons and papers in violation of the Fourth Amendment to the Constitution of the United States and Article I, ¶ 13, of the Constitution of California;
  (e) it takes adult adoptees' property interests in their own identities without just compensation in contravention of the Fifth Amendment to the Constitution of the United States and Article I, ¶ 19, of the Constitution of California;
  (f) it contravenes the prohibitions against laws impairing the obligation of contracts in Article I, ¶ 10, of the Constitution of the United States and in Article I, ¶ 9, of the Constitution of California, by binding adult adoptees to contracts between their natural and adoptive parents to which the adoptees never were parties;
  (g) in cases of adult adoptees who suffer crises of religious identity, it violates those adult adoptees' right freely to exercise their religion guaranteed by the First Amendment to the Constitution of the United States and Article I, ¶ 4, of the Constitution of California;
  (h) it violates the rights of privacy and personal autonomy of adult adoptees in

regard to decision as to matters of family life arising under the Ninth Amendment, under penumbras of the First, Fourth, Fifth, and other Amendments, and under the word "liberty" in the Due Process of the Fourteenth Amendment to the Constitution of the United States, and under Article I, ¶¶ 1 and 24, of the Constitution of California;

(i) it violates the "inalienable rights" which all people "by nature" have of "pursuing and obtaining safety, [and] happiness," guaranteed by Article I, ¶ 1, of the Constitution of California.

The core of the argument is based on the principle of equality that this country was established to promote and protect. ALMA President Florence Fisher probably says it best, in terms that anyone can understand. This is how she views what is fundamentally at issue:

> In the United States, the adopted adult, at any age, is denied the right to see the records of his birth and adoption. . . . The adoptee must show "good cause" why he should be shown these records. Thus far, the courts have *never* deemed a man's desire to learn "the truth of his origin" good *enough* cause! This sealing of the records of adopted *adults* is an affront to human dignity and perpetuates rather than eliminates the stigma of illegitimacy. We are granted conditional equality, i.e., the name of our adoptive parents and the right to inherit from them, while our natural heritage is buried, obliterating our rights as human beings for all time. These sealed records not only deny us our civil rights as citizens of the United States, but our human rights to know our roots! WHERE ELSE IN OUR FREE SOCIETY IS SUCH SECRECY CONDONED?

The New York suit was dismissed by both the federal district and appeals courts, which held that the New York laws cited "do not violate substantive due process because New York wanted to protect the privacy interests of the natural and adoptive parents [and] do not violate the equal protection clause of the Fourteenth Amendment, nor do the New York laws violate the Thirteenth Amendment of the United States Constitution which abolished slavery."

The California case is still pending as of this writing. California's state constitutional limits provide that case a dimension lacking in the New York case. In addition, the challenge to California practice is more broadly stated on federal constitutional grounds.

The New York ruling illustrates the courts' sensitivity to problems in the area of conflict of rights—in this case searchers' right to know versus others' right to privacy.

Searchers do not contest society's need to balance conflicting rights. However, it does seem unprecedented to those seeking to change the laws that efforts simply to establish contact with another individual—and that individ-

ual the closest of blood kin—should be seen as a violation of another's right
to privacy.

Adult adoptees and birthparents continue to feel that being denied the right
to know who the birthparents are and what has become of the children violates
basic human rights that the United States Constitution does guarantee. How
does that knowledge, in itself, amount to any violation of another's guaranteed
rights?

State Law

Adoption laws are enacted and administered at the state level—in a few
states even at the county level. Each state differs from the others in some
respect. There is no uniformity. Practice varies from relatively open records
in Kansas to difficult-to-search records in Hawaii.

In most states the law generally defines records available. In almost every
state, as birthparents you have a right to all documents issued before actual
relinquishment. You are entitled to your child's original birth certificate, but
not the amended certificate bearing the adoptive parents' names. As an adoptee
you are usually entitled to all records issued after the relinquishment. You may
receive an amended birth certificate but not the original. Upon finalization of
an adoption the original birth certificate is sealed and cannot be opened without a court order. In some states the adoption agency and hospital records are
also sealed. The purpose is to "protect" the identity of the relinquishing
birthparent, the adoptee, and the adoptive family.

In undertaking research for the reference section in the back of this book
to determine state law regarding open records, I became aware of how unclear
the situation often is, despite the general policy followed. That is pretty much
as indicated above. I'm not the only one who has discovered the potential for
confusion and frustration in state practices. A 1977 Child Services Association
publication by Mary Ann Jones put it this way:

> It should be a simple matter to determine which states have open records and which
> do not. But, it is not. Laws are seldom clear in terms of which records are sealed,
> who may have access to the records, what information is contained therein and
> what specific information is considered sealed. In addition, the effect of a law is felt
> less in its actual wording than in its interpretation and administration, which vary
> not only from state to state but within a state over time. A final problem is that
> it is difficult to keep up with new legislation in this area across 50 states. For
> instance, most articles cite Connecticut and Florida as having open records, but
> both states rescinded those statutes in 1973 (although a recent court order in
> Florida may have reinstated their open records).

Identifying Information

The general practice for states nationwide is to withhold information considered to be identifying in nature. "Identifying information" is whatever the authorities have decided might make it possible for you to pinpoint the name and address of your relinquished child or of your birthparents. Only "nonidentifying information" may be released. Here is how a 1977 Task Force on Confidentiality in the Adoption Program Report to the California State Department of Health defined what information that included:

> Nonidentifying information is to be considered any information other than that which would lead to the identification of a member of a biological family. Information such as personal, social, and medical history is normally considered nonidentifying. Examples of identifying information are names, address, and other details, such as the specific job title of a biological parent.

There is no national standard on identifying information. Depending on the state involved, interpretation may be more or less restrictive than in California. In some states the name of the hospital where the child was born and/or the name of the attorney who handled the court proceedings will be considered identifying. Other states will fairly routinely release an adoptee's first name if this has subsequently been changed.

One's race has usually been considered nonidentifying information, but in the following case this did not prove true.

Betty Chase was raised as a foster child. Her first foster parents were white, and she was considered white. At an early age her skin color raised questions, and after a time she was placed in black foster homes and raised as a black. She then culturally identified herself as black and married a man of that race.

On February 10, 1978, when Ms. Chase was thirty-three years old, county authorities responded to questions from Ms. Chase and added that her race was white: "Our records indicate that all your immediate forebearers [*sic*] were white with the exception of your maternal grandmother's mother who, it is reported, was an American Indian (no tribal identification)."

After a lengthy battle with county authorities and a difficult search, Ms. Chase finally located her birthmother. She discovered her birthmother was black and her heritage was black, Native American, and white.

In any state there will be something of a gray area between what is considered clearly identifying and what is not. State authorities and agencies licensed by the state, in drawing the identifying-nonidentifying distinction, implicitly acknowledge that you have a right to any nonidentifying information you request. You can be pretty sure that asking outright for a name and address will run you up against the brick wall established by the law. However, at times you may ask for information that you do not feel is clearly identifying and still run into the same brick wall. You're in that gray area where sometimes records administrators lean one way, sometimes the other.

In this situation, challenge the person who refuses to give you what you feel is nonidentifying information. But do so in a tactful manner. Belligerently asserting your rights to a social worker or civil servant rarely wins you cooperation. Sometimes, if you respond to a refusal to provide a point of information with a question—"Is that identifying?" "How is that identifying?"—the person facing you may reconsider and give you more details than if you just quietly accept his or her interpretation of the law. Persistence in pursuit of your rights to information can pay off. Familiarize yourself with the state adoption laws that apply to you. It is here that you will discover the distinctions between identifying and nonidentifying information. You will have a better sense of when to persevere and when to back off. I've included a summary of state laws in the state-by-state reference lists that make up the final portion of this book. However, since these laws are under review in a number of states, also check further for recent amendments or additions that may affect your rights.

Your library probably has a copy of your state constitution and an index to state laws. If not, ask for a photocopy of the pertinent material through interlibrary loan (see Chapter 4) or refer to a nearby law library. You can also ask for help from a search and support group that follows changes in state adoption laws closely.

When searching, you will be gathering information from a much wider range of sources than just those having custody of your adoption/relinquishment records. In directing inquiries to those sources, the question of identifying versus nonidentifying information rarely comes up as such. You will simply be depending on the general right of free access to public documents and publicly held records. In some cases the law or administrative code that applies may require that you state a particular relationship to a person you wish information on—there are considerations of privacy that come into the picture here and there. But many records can be reviewed more freely.

Even when searching through records to which you theoretically have a right of access, it is best to avoid mentioning adoption search as the reason for desiring information. Some records are open only to those indicating a reason seen to be acceptable, which is sometimes specified so vaguely that it becomes a subjective determination made by the civil servant you're dealing with. "Adoption search" given in response to a question on why a certain record is desired too often leads to a decision not to release information. If you cite "genealogy search" as a reason for requesting records, you will get a different reaction, even though the objective is much the same. You can also cite a need related to inheritance and estate settlement or a medical need to know (see below). The thing to remember is that when you put your request in the context of adoption search, you may in effect find yourself denied "identifying" information in a situation where normally the records administrator does not distinguish between identifying and nonidentifying information.

State Inheritance Laws

Consider the question of what rights you have under state law in the context of inheritance and disposition of your estate.

James R. Carter made the following observation in the *Tulane Law Review* about this problem:

> In some states, the decree of adoption, while almost totally severing the relationship between the natural parents and the adoptee, does not divest the adoptee of the right to inherit from his natural parents. In fact, when an adoption statute is silent on the question of whether an adoptee can inherit from his natural parents, some courts have allowed adoptees to inherit under the laws of descent and distribution. If these same states deny an adoptee the right to see his adoption records to ascertain whether he had inherited property from his biological parents, it may be argued that the adoptee is being deprived of property without due process of law.

How can one know whether or not he has an inheritance if he does not know the name of the person who is leaving an estate? How can a birthparent leave an inheritance to a child whose name he does not know?

Depending on what the law is in your state relative to adoptee inheritance rights, you may be able to cite the right of inheritance as a reason to open adoption/relinquishment records to you. That is not to say you will automatically be given the information you want. To the extent there is conflict between adoption laws and those covering inheritance, adoption records administrators may very well choose to follow the code that is most directly addressed to their area of responsibility. But in seeking out other records, it can be helpful to present your interest as based on inheritance considerations.

In the state-by-state reference lists in the back of this book, I've indicated states' replies to my question on adoptee inheritance rights. Again, doublecheck for any updating in the laws. (Adoptees of Native American [Indian] heritage should note they have certain rights of inheritance under federal law. See Chapter 4 for details.)

The Model State Adoption Act

Although the adoption search movement is far from its goal of open records on all adults, some steps have been taken. A Model State Adoption Act was proposed by the United States Department of Health and Human Services early in 1980. This model law, a draft recommendation that has been circulated for comment within the states, is now under review at the federal level. There is no telling how long it may be before the Secretary of Health and Human Services issues it as a formal recommendation to the states or if it will be recommended. Even then states will be under no obligation to follow it. However, it would add weight to growing opinion that it is time for the laws in the states to change.

As drafted, the Model State Adoption Act has this to say about open records:

> *Section 502 (d), Birth Certificates*—An original birth certificate, sealed pursuant to this section, shall at any time be opened as a matter of right to the birthparent whose rights were terminated or to the adult adoptee upon application to the Office of Vital Statistics. The applicant shall be provided a true copy of the original certificate, without official certification and bearing a notation that the original certificate has been amended.

When comments from the states were returned after the Model Act circulated, the controversial nature of this seemingly simple provision was quickly evident. There was strong opposition from a majority of public and private social welfare agencies that responded. Of eight adoptive parent organizations responding, only one favored open records. Birthparents, birthparent groups, adult adoptees, and adult adoptee groups predictably heavily favored this recommendation. Otherwise comments were mixed pro and con.

The amount of opposition to the open records provision makes it uncertain whether a final version of the Model State Adoption Act will contain the provision. The odds are probably against it.

Right now the Model State Adoption Act is only potentially an acknowledgment of adoptee/birthparent rights. Until your state legislature (or the legislature in your state of search) adopts it as law, you cannot cite it to support your claim to information. It will almost certainly be a question of years before the Model Act has a chance of becoming law in any state.

You can follow the progress of the Model Act, as well as obtain possibly helpful adoption-related information by contacting your state agency. Adoption groups are another source of information on the progress of the Model State Adoption Act.

The Adult Qualification

A considerable amount of the opposition to open records comes from those who see open records as a threat to the stability of the adoptive family. They fear open records may enable birthparents to locate an adopted child and move to take that child from the adoptive parents. Much of the negative comment on the Model State Adoption Act's open records section was along this line.

What those who follow this line of thinking overlook is that the rights that adoption groups and searchers traditionally claim is a right of adults to make free contact with other adults. The question of "best interests of the child," which is used as partial justification for sealed records, is irrelevant. Neither of the involved parties is a child.

Adoptees and birthparents have up to now overwhelmingly supported the need to consider the best interests of the child when it comes to the matter of sealed records—that is, as long as "the child" *is* a child. Those who want open records recognize as well as anyone the potential for disruption of the family environment and for resultant psychological damage to the child where a situation is created that leads to a contest for affections.

Each state must establish its own age of majority for adoptees, but in doing so must look closely at the rights of both adoptee and birthparent. While there are some birthparents who believe they should be allowed to search for their relinquished children, even if these children are under the age of majority, this book deals with adults searching for adults. It ought to be easy to establish an adult qualification in state adoption laws so that the rights of adults are not compromised as the result of concern about the best interests of the child. The Model State Adoption Act, as originally drafted, does this easily and clearly.

When it comes to the other justification for sealed records—protection against invasion of privacy—those contacted as the result of a search already have legal protection, the same as that provided every citizen. Present law actually imposes a restrictive privacy on birthparents and adoptees that many find burdensome. As the growing record of reunions shows, many, many of of those contacted in supposed violation of their right of privacy are genuinely pleased at the opportunity presented to establish some link with the family member who located them. In some cases, those whose right of privacy was supposedly being protected had themselves made efforts to locate the individual who was searching for them. What kind of protection is it that thwarts efforts by adults who are the closest of blood kin to make contact with each other?

Federal Law

Federal legislation does not grant birthparents or adoptees any specific rights to records withheld from them under state law. The states have full authority to establish policy in this area, although always subject to the limitations set out in the United States Constitution. As I mentioned earlier in this chapter, these limitations are currently being tested in the courts.

However, federal legislation does grant searchers the right to certain information kept on individuals at the federal level. Your rights here are established principally by the Freedom of Information Act (5 U.S.C. 552) and the Privacy Act of 1974 (5 U.S.C. 552a).

The Freedom of Information Act requires the federal government to release to individuals upon request material that pertains to them and is contained in executive agency or department files. Researcher Sarah P. Collins in a report from the Congressional Research Service points out: "Any person may request information so long as the request reasonably describes the information sought and is made in accordance with published rules and regulations concerning the time, place, fees (if any) and procedures to be followed." The agency referred to must decide within ten work days whether to release the information and then immediately notify the person of its determination. The agency must also specify any fee for document search and duplication.

Agencies may withhold information only in specified categories, such as trade secrets and other confidential business information, classified material, and, according to researcher Collins, "information which, if disclosed, would constitute a clearly unwarranted invasion of privacy." The Freedom of Information Act allows the individual to request the appropriate federal district court to order an agency to produce records in the event they are withheld without apparent good cause.

The Privacy Act is primarily aimed at restricting the federal government in its collection, use, and disclosure of information on individuals. However, it also allows individuals access to information the government holds on them, and so supplements the Freedom of Information Act in that respect. The provisions on access appear to be somewhat broader in the Privacy Act than they are in the Freedom of Information Act, so that in writing to an agency for information it holds on you, you may do well to cite your rights under both laws.

Examples of agencies that may hold useful information on file are the Passport Agency of the United States Department of State and the Immigration and Naturalization Service of the United States Department of Justice. The latter will be important for American citizens or permanent residents who are foreign-born, as records of entry into the United States may contain information that an adoption agency does not have or will not release. It has been reported that one adoptee discovered her original birth certificate through filing for information from the Passport Agency under terms of the Privacy Act.

For more specific details on exercising your rights under these two federal laws, check your library for books or articles explaining their workings. One excellent source is L. G. Sherick's book *How to Use the Freedom of Information Act: FOIA* (New York: Arco Publishing Company, 1978).

Native Americans

Native Americans (Indians) are in a unique position when it comes to adoption rights. They are the only group of citizens whose rights of inheritance are governed by federal law, and these rights cannot be changed in any way through adoption.

Native Americans must be able to prove a tribal affiliation in order to qualify for inheritance rights that attach to membership in a particular tribe. If you are a Native American by birth, either wholly or in part, contact the Bureau of Indian Affairs of the United States Department of the Interior (Interior Building, 19th and C Sts., NW, Washington, DC 20242) for information on how you can claim whatever inheritance rights you may have through tribal affiliation. Somewhere in that process you may also uncover leads to your birthparents. As a birthparent with a Native American background, you can press adoption/social service agencies to make it possible for your child to claim his or her federally protected birthright.

Need To Know

You do not rely only on rights established by law to justify your search efforts. You probably feel a compelling need to know. This need is usually what is behind your undertaking this difficult, often frustrating search process. Searchers are rarely pursuing their goals simply out of some idealistic sense of right. They are working to resolve an intensely personal life adjustment difficulty. Since laws—and consequently the rights established under law—are presumably based upon perception of social needs, a review of searchers' rights cannot be complete without a look at searchers' needs.

Psychological Need to Know

Self-identity and establishment of a sense of connectedness are uppermost in a searcher's mind. The remark below, from one of the individuals connected with the ALMA lawsuit in New York, reflects how deeply painful the lack of this knowledge can be:

> We are not separate or different from those born with a heritage they have always had knowledge of . . . and the freedom to investigate further if they so choose. Being denied information concerning myself that is not denied a nonadoptee is degrading and cruel, and I must fight the pain of not knowing who I am every day of my life —and that pain becomes more intense as I get older. . . . Not knowing affects me in my everyday life to the point of obsession. How long can I search the faces of strangers in the street . . . wondering . . . at times convinced that I am looking upon the face of my mother or father, a sister or brother, aunt, uncle . . . a face I think looks like mine . . . before I can stand it no longer? . . . What an invasion of humanity! . . . [to] close up a human life in a vault somewhere and say, You may not know about yourself—you have not the right even to ask. . . . Your anxieties are neurotic, your curiosity unnatural. . . .

Fortunately, awareness of the psychological need to know is occasionally seen in remarks from the bench in cases involving adoption rights. Judge Wade S. Weatherford, Jr., of the Seventh Judicial Circuit of South Carolina, presiding over a case concerning the opening of adoption records, put the issue of the relationship between needs and rights into particularly sharp focus when he stated,

> The law must be consonant with life. It cannot and should not ignore broad historical currents of history. Mankind is possessed of no greater urge than to try to understand the age-old questions: "Who am I?" "Why am I?" Even now the sands and ashes of continents are being sifted to find where we made our first step as man. Religions of mankind often include ancestor worship in one way or another. For many the future is blind without a sight of the past. Those emotions and anxieties that generate our thirst to know the past are not superficial and whimsical. They are real and they are "good cause" under the law of man and God.

It's unfortunate that up to now so few administrators, legislators, and judges have thought to look at the psychological need to know as a valid reason for opening records. But many adoptees have written movingly on this subject. Read their accounts. You'll find the titles of some of these books in the Reading List at the end of this book.

Birthparents suffer a different psychological burden, although one that is equally painful. To begin with, whatever inherent parental love they possess is totally thwarted by the present blanket censorship of records. Circumstances of relinquishment and adoption necessarily require a birthparent to step back, however painful that often is. Why do they require that in later years relinquishing parents may not know their child's adult identity, may not be assured that their child is well, may not reach out and touch that someone they gave life to?

What mother who has ever held and looked with love at her own newborn child cannot imagine the years of anguish another such mother has suffered because circumstances forced her to relinquish that child? What loving father cannot imagine the painful helplessness a man experiences at having to give up his child? Yes, reality dictates that the choice of relinquishment has to be made, that it has necessary consequences of separation. But what reality dictates that a relinquishing parent ought never to have the opportunity of personal assurance that his or her child is all right, never to experience pride in the child's accomplishments, never to share with the child any of the life experience that is naturally a part of the child's heritage? What makes the emptiness suffered by these birthparents during years of separation so desirable that they must suffer it forever? Why must they carry a life sentence without hope of parole or pardon?

Although a relinquishing birthparent is often thought of as a cold, uncaring individual, the truth is more often something else. In the words of one birthmother, "I didn't take the easy way out. I didn't lack mother love—I just lacked everything else."

Birthparents frequently have to deal with an enormous sense of guilt about relinquishing their child. And this is so even when they have been as much victims of circumstances beyond their control as is the child itself. Despite this, the present system of administering relinquishment/adoption records demonstrates little compassion. What it does instead is to reinforce the guilt, to treat birthparents as if they were enemies—lifelong enemies—of the child. What is the social advantage here, especially when the child has matured to adulthood? It may be that the child has no desire to establish or maintain any relationship with his or her birthparents. However, in that event, he or she as an adult can wield the same power that is exercised in deciding not to pursue any relationship—the power to say no. But current law deprives the child of an opportunity to speak for himself or herself. The law dictates the answer for everyone, despite massive evidence that many would, in exercising their own adult right of free choice, say yes.

It is primarily in these contexts that the psychological need to know has been expressed up to now. However, recent research findings suggest another psychological need that may come to be cited in the future—a psychological need to understand genetically influenced behavior patterns.

In a recent study of twins separated early in life, psychologists at the University of Minnesota noted some remarkable patterns of similarity. Siblings who were strangers to each other demonstrated surprising shared traits of behavior. Some turned out to share the same phobias, others a range of personal interests or habits. While the scientists involved do not feel their findings are totally conclusive, one of them, psychologist David Lykken, remarks, "What is emerging in my mind is that the most important thing to come out of this study is a strong sense that vastly more of human behavior is genetically determined or influenced than we ever supposed."

Stories of unexpected "coincidences" come up in reunions that the press occasionally reports. A *New York Post* story early in 1981 noted the case of two brothers, not twins, who had been separated for nearly twenty-five years but nevertheless shared a surprising range of specific interests and vocations. *Reader's Digest* in spring of 1981 noted a case of triplets separated at an early age who likewise shared an amazingly similar pattern of life adjustment. None of the three had ever known he was one of triplets—the reunion came about almost by accident.

It seems increasingly important that this aspect of psychological need be considered. Contact between adoptees and birthparents will allow the adult adoptee opportunity for a better understanding of behavior patterns that may be genetically influenced. Depriving the adoptee of knowledge of his or her genetic heritage, from this perspective, can be seen to deprive him or her of an important dimension of self-knowledge.

Medical Need to Know

Among the long list of ailments that have been found to include some genetic factor are allergies, arthritis, asthma, several forms of cancer, cardiovascular (heart) diseases, epilepsy, multiple sclerosis, sickle-cell anemia, and certain visual disorders. More than two thousand genetic diseases have been identified, and, in addition, many other conditions thought not to be inherited as genetic diseases do tend to occur more frequently in some families than others.

State adoption laws usually do take some notice of a medical need to know. But they are not always clear to what degree you have a right to know. Can you claim a right to whatever medical information is kept in your files—at any time? Or can you only claim that right in a situation of compelling need—that is, only when you are ill with some condition and at a point where doctors require a more complete medical background? Some conditions need to be managed or watched for before symptoms appear. And preventive medicine has come into its own in the past ten years. But how can one use preventive medicine if one doesn't know, is hindered from knowing, what to be on guard for?

I recently spoke with an adoptee who had located her birthmother. It was only through conversation with her birthmother that she discovered a history of breast cancer in her family. She related this to her doctor, who confirmed that this knowledge would make early detection of any breast cancer she might develop more likely.

One of the co-plaintiffs in the New York ALMA case relates that his adoption agency had told him that one of his grandparents had died of cancer.

> Apparently unknown to the agency were the additional facts which I have determined since meeting my natural parents and their families, that two more of my four grandparents died of cancer and that two of my great-grandparents had died of cancer. With that family history now in my possession, I am in a position to avoid carcinogens. . . . This demonstrated to me how inadequate it would have been for me to have relied solely on what is in the adoption agency's files. . . .

Courts seem to feel that releasing necessary information about medical problems from adoption records will solve the problem of a medical need to know.

Recently there has been a dramatic example of the implications of a medical need to know. From the late 1940s to 1971, more than two million pregnant women used the drug Diethylstilbestrol (DES) to prevent miscarriage. The federal Food and Drug Administration banned DES when an apparent link was established between its use by pregnant women and development of cancer in children they carried during that pregnancy. In October 1978 the United States Surgeon General issued a physician advisory to every medical doctor and osteopath, warning of the hazards associated with use of this synthetic estrogen. While the advisory warns of danger primarily to the female child, DES is suspected of having potential for damage to male offspring as well.

In certain parts of the country—New York City, for example—public awareness campaigns have urged mothers who have used DES to contact local health authorities or their doctor for information and advice on recognizing and dealing with possible health problems associated with DES. Young adult women are also the target of this sort of campaign. But what of the adoptees whose birthmothers are unknown to them? How can they determine if they are under any risk, if their birthmothers' medical records, as contained in the adoption file, are incomplete? And they probably are.

That's a common problem for adoptees. Medical information is almost always incomplete. Omissions in adoption records are often as important as what is included. And that's not necessarily the fault of the birthparents. The present system does not encourage them to maintain an up-to-date medical history in the records held by the adoption agency. Older adoption records are especially scanty on medical information. In previous decades, the genetic factor was not considered as important as it is seen to be now for predicting potential health problems. Adoptees have no source to turn to for answers to questions that may be vital to them. The birthparent who has important information cannot easily pass it on, may not realize it matters that it be passed on. The health risks that adoptees face would be much more apparent, and the parental responsibilities that many birthparents feel could be carried out more naturally and fully, if the opportunity for contact were allowed.

Recent Trends

I do not by any means wish to give the impression that there is no progress being made in recognition of adoptee/birthparent rights, that there is no consideration of their needs. There is a growing awareness of these, both among the public and among government decision makers. But as encouraging as that awareness is, right now you will still find yourself faced with a system of records administration that discriminates against you as you begin your search. The situation, as summarized in a letter (dated June 6, 1980) I received from the Illinois Department of Children and Family Services in response to one of my inquiries about open records, is this: "There are currently no statutes addressing the issue of 'open records.' There is a general feeling that legislation relating to 'open records' will be forthcoming."

There you have it. The present reality is still a restrictive one. The future looks bright—there is movement toward a system that is more flexible and considerate of rights and needs that have routinely been ignored in the past.

For those who desire a sense of the progress being made, let me quote the following excerpt from the summary to the *Report of the Task Force on Confidentiality in the Adoption Program,* prepared for the California State Department of Health in July 1977.

> During the seven months of this task force, a number of events occurred which had an influence on the group deliberation: (1) two state court decisions in New Jersey and New York strongly supported the right of adult adoptees to have information of their origin, although stopping short of opening agency records; (2) England implemented a law opening original birth records to adoptees over the age of 18; (3) the Child Welfare League of America adopted revised standards of practice which reaffirmed the value of confidentiality to parties to the adoption but at the same time urged agencies to advise that such confidentiality cannot be assured in the future; (4) major research findings of the Children's Home Society of California were published indicating that out of 1,294 respondents (adult adoptees 288, birth parents 102, and adoptive parents 904) 88.9 percent of the adoptees, 82.4 percent of the birth parents, and 73.1 percent of the adoptive parents supported the right of adult adoptees to have access to their original birth certificates; (5) Los Angeles County Department of Adoption reported that in 1976, 278 adoptees and 247 birth parents contacted the Department for information and/or assistance in seeking identifying information; (6) state legislation was introduced and passed in Minnesota which would give adult adoptees access to information from their original birth certificates if the birth parents concurred following contact by an adoption agency; (7) the California State Bar Association announced support for legislation to provide access to identifying information for adult adoptees; and (8) a bill was introduced in the California Legislature by State Senator William Campbell to establish a registration system to facilitate the meeting or exchange of information between adult adoptees and birth parents.

Encouraging? Absolutely. But now, already half a decade later, the reality is still that adoptees and birthparents wanting to make contact must do so without official recognition or support of their right to do so or of their need to do so.

Balancing Rights

In closing this chapter, I would like to point out to you the importance of balancing rights. Because when all is said and done, your rights and needs exist in a social setting that does include other people with rights and needs of their own.

As a searcher, you have to be aware of the potential for conflict between your right to know and others' right to privacy. You must set standards that guide you appropriately. With those firmly established in mind, you will be aware when pursuit of your compelling right to know infringes on another's genuine right to privacy. Take into account that often the way you pursue a line of inquiry—the people you contact, for example—can prove more an invasion of another's privacy than the actual line of inquiry itself. Setting standards here will guard you against irresponsible action that might be taken in moments of excitement, when under pressure, or at times when you don't quite know what to say.

There are no groups, professionals, or other individuals who can weigh your needs better than you can, so setting guidelines on respect for privacy must be a result of your own decisions. A pressing medical need for information, for example, can weigh differently than a need to establish a connection with a past. There are groups that say anything goes—your rights supersede all others. Present society has a tendency to state that your rights have no precedence over anyone else's—and, in practice, at times to put them in the back seat relative to others'.

You will probably find yourself somewhere between these two positions as you draw up your rules of self-conduct. Much time and thought should go into this, because time and again your guidelines will be tested as you come into contact with new people and encounter difficult situations. By setting and following standards you feel to be appropriate, and by defending your rights when necessary with a clear conscience on how they balance against rights claimed on behalf of others, you will be able to maintain your own sense of pride and dignity more certainly.

2

Getting Moral Support

Although it may be possible for an individual to undertake a search without having to deal with the highs and lows others face, I have yet to meet such an individual. You will need support from someone right from the beginning.

Why Will I Need Moral Support?

There are two factors that work together to lead even the initially casual searcher to seek out moral support. The first is the impact of directly facing the emotional stress that an adoption or relinquishment search produces. The second is coming up against the lack of consideration for the needs of searchers displayed by those who control records containing essential information. Let's look briefly at what's involved for adoptees and birthparents in either case.

The Adoptee

Although society as a whole may not seem to attach a stigma to an adoption situation, the fact is that you may be one of the many adoptees who carry a sense of stigma or emotional scarring with you. And that is often the case whether or not your adoptive parents have been matter-of-fact with you about your adoption.

As an adoptee searching for your birthparents you may be seen as a neurotic individual not content with your family. Some few adoptees may fit that image, but for the most part adoptee searchers are average citizens who function capably and responsibly in society. They are not set apart by reason of poor adjustment to the realities of day-to-day living. They are not a group of eccentrics with a radically different view on social issues from those held by the general public. The typical adoptee searcher is just a John (or Jane) Doe

—Mr. (or Ms.) Middle America. You are probably like almost everyone else, a person with emotional needs and curiosity and wonderment at where you came from. The difference that exists is not an outgrowth of the experience of unusual psychological needs. It is primarily an outgrowth of the very different circumstances surrounding your origin and the adjustments to a situation which was beyond your control. You do not know the answers to questions naturally raised by everyone—answers that most people so routinely obtain that they rarely consider how very important they are for the development of a complete sense of self-identity. For you, the absence of answers about where your roots lie results in a feeling of "unconnectedness" that the average person never has to face. This can at times create serious emotional conflicts, but such conflicts should be seen as a natural consequence of the circumstances that have deprived you of a socially conventional sense of rootedness, not as an indication of innate abnormality.

In initiating a search you are, on the whole, no more or less neurotic than the adoptee who does not choose to search. However, in initiating a search, you are ultimately confronting conflicting feelings that may be misunderstood by those around you. This kind of confrontation, I maintain, is more typical of the individual with a positive drive to self-fulfillment than a form of neurotic behavior. However, for you, the searcher, it is almost always an unsettling process, requiring adjustments that cannot be anticipated and that may prove hard to make. Many times adoptees try to explain that their search is for themselves—who they are—not for a birthparent. But in order to fill in the missing facts—to learn how you began, the factors that make you what you are—you must seek the person who has those answers. You might very well prefer to get those answers from your adoptive parents but realize this choice is not possible. You must stress, again and again, what you hope to do, what your needs are and the choices available to you. Any moral support serves to keep you anchored and focused in your day-to-day life, which must go on. It provides you an outlet for sharing or expressing emotions that otherwise could overwhelm you.

The Birthparent

As a birthparent who has relinquished a child, you are likely to be faced with a stereotyped judgment of your past actions. Society is apt to think in terms of a cold, uncaring, irresponsible woman or man who abandoned a helpless child, then went on to further escapades in life without second thoughts. All too often birthparents themselves carry the burden of a self-image that contains an element of this judgment, even though the circumstances of relinquishment will usually have been too complex to warrant this simplistic view of the actual facts.

At a recent Concerned United Birthparents (CUB) meeting, a young woman, very nervous and distressed, asked to be excused from identifying herself. After a while she entered into the conversation. No one pressed her to speak, and the moderator stated she was welcome to remain silent or say anything she wished—no one was there to make judgments.

This young woman had never been able to tell her story before and could not hold back her tears in telling it now. She had relinquished a child when she was fifteen. Her parents had pressured her into the relinquishment because it was "best for the child"; she herself would soon forget all about it. That had been six or seven years ago. Since then she'd married and now had a two-year-old child from the marriage. But the pain she'd suffered in relinquishing her first child had not dissipated. She had come to the group not in hopes of searching, since the relinquished child was still small, but to help her come to terms with a decision she now feared was wrong. She spoke of much anger and resentment toward her parents—since the birth of her second child she had hardly had any relationship with them at all. She could not forgive their attitude and the pressures that led to relinquishment of their first grandchild.

It is rare that the decision to relinquish a child is made for the sake of convenience. Usually there are considerable pressures and complicating factors at work. But because it was your decision—an extraordinarily difficult and unpleasant one in most instances—you need to recognize that you're susceptible to feelings of guilt about whether it was a correct choice.

When you embark on a search, you are inevitably confronting feelings that are deeply disturbing. These may be near the surface or they may have been deeply buried for years. In either event, having the open support of someone close to you, or at least sharing a common understanding with another birthparent who experiences the same "need to know" or reawakened sense of responsibility vis-à-vis his or her child, will make your search one less racked by guilts, anxieties, or any feeling of being "out of synch" with the world around you. Support will help keep you centered in the here and now. It will make it easier to reject any negative judgment you may feel saddled with—either by others or by yourself. It will enable you more readily to see yourself in a new—and probably more accurate—light: as a mature person who now wishes to deal differently with a problem situation than he or she did at a younger age.

Chances are, as an adoptee or a birthparent conducting a search, you will encounter a variety of frustrations as you work to achieve the goal you've set for yourself. Some of the frustrations will be minor; others will be more substantial, the kind of blockages that virtually anyone would be hard put to tolerate, let alone accept.

Take the example of Katrina Maxtone-Graham, an adoptee searcher who fought for many months against the Children's Aid Society (New York) in an effort to obtain a full record of her adoption history. The Society repeatedly rebuffed all her attempts to learn her birthmother's identity. The social workers she encountered were obstructive on almost every front. She reports on the conclusion of one visit to the Society's offices:

> As I was leaving, the social worker made the pronouncement, "Your mother has made a new life for herself. The episode is forgotten. It's all over with for your mother. It's over, and done with, and finished." I was struck by this statement. It was so inconsistent with humanity that I could not accept it.

The attitude reflected by this social worker is, unfortunately, not all that uncommon. And it takes no great imagination to see what a devastating effect this can have on an adoptee or birthparent who is only trying to gain a sense of connectedness others take for granted. As a searcher, you'll expose yourself to the experience of this frustration and humiliation, perhaps often. You may see yourself remaining steadfast and steady throughout all such occurrences, but you'll find the sympathetic support of someone who accepts your motivation and right to know an invaluable aid in keeping things in proportion. It's difficult for most people without support to maintain morale and purpose when up against a cold, bureaucratic system that denies them an element of their identity, either in the manner of treatment or as a result thereof.

Note also that the frustrations can mount beyond anything you may have braced yourself for. In Katrina Maxtone-Graham's case, for example, she eventually discovered that the policy of noncooperation on the part of the Children's Aid Society was carried out despite a notation in her file by her birthmother: "I want it understood that if Judy [Katrina's birth name] is ever in need and the . . . [agency] knows of it, they will be sure to call on me for help." Clearly, Katrina's birthmother was not all that opposed to the possibility of reestablished contact with Katrina; the agency nevertheless pursued its policy of blocking any contact. It is hoped that your search will not be met with such obstructiveness—but it may be. In any event, you'll find the expression of moral support encouraging and reassuring during the experience of similar or other frustrations. Keep in mind that as you face these experiences, you're also likely to be dealing with personal anxieties and doubts related to the decision to search. You handicap yourself from the outset if you deprive yourself of any source of support open to you.

The Stages of a Search

You may assume that once a decision to search has been made, you will plunge right into the process with an aloof, assured, businesslike manner, able to face and deal with all the conflicts and frustrations as they come up, and finish the search in the same emotional frame of mind you began it. The reality is that most searchers pass through a series of stages in their quest. The impact of conflicts and frustrations varies in each stage. But moral support is important through all of them. This is so for the broad reasons already given, but also because you yourself at times will become confused and bewildered by changes in the intensity of your own reactions to what is happening in each stage. That is to say, in addition to dealing with resurfacing or already present emotional conflicts, you might be thrown off balance by shifts in your own perspective from one stage to the next.

Let's briefly look at what typically happens in the process of search as far as the searcher's own reactions go.

Separation

In this first stage, the searcher is commonly somewhat removed from the emotions of searching. You often express the reason for starting the search in very neutral terms—you are undertaking it to make your life more interesting or out of simple curiosity, or you may cite a "medical need to know." You begin by concentrating attention on the mechanics of search; feeling no need to make a strong commitment to it. Often you respond to queries about what you are doing somewhat defensively, maintaining that the outcome is not so important to you, that if you get bored with it you can easily give it up.

This first stage does not last very long for most. And those whose support or interest is enlisted at this point may find themselves puzzled when you become progressively more involved and passionate with this quest, notwithstanding early assurances that it is only a matter of limited significance. "But I thought it didn't mean all that much to you—you said it didn't!" is a common expression of puzzlement from friends or family members.

It is the awakening of deeper feelings and needs that proves so confusing for many a searcher. In the first stage you are often quite convinced that this process you've begun is genuinely in response to an incidental kind of curiosity.

You may realize the intensity of your desire to know, but it hasn't become an essential part of your life. However, before long the intensity builds, and you are swept along into the further stages of search without quite knowing what is happening or why your initially controlled reactions seem to have snow-balled.

This also complicates things on the level of gaining support—how do you ask for understanding if you yourself don't understand what your real aims are? This understanding is often beyond the comprehension of the person who has offered to help. That person often can help and understand fully your needs only after you have sorted through your own thoughts. And yet you are likely to feel a need for support before this process is complete.

Because of this pattern, it is best to avoid stating a categorical reason for your endeavor when you first begin your search. Sure, you probably can think of a reason that others will accept without too much challenge or question. "Medical need to know" will usually serve as an acceptable reason—heredity is now a known factor of concern in relation to susceptibility to common serious health problems. As you pass from the first stage through those that follow, there will probably be a growing awareness of other, more complex motivations that can be difficult to express. What becomes apparent now as you pursue that all-important information is that you are looking into the hidden reasons pushing you to search. That is not to say that previous reasons are now invalid; rather, they were not complete.

People do respond to reasons that make sense to them. Don't necessarily hesitate to indicate the reasons for your search. Just avoid making them definitive. Be alert to the fact that they will probably undergo some kind of change; tell those from whom you seek support that such reasons as you can provide—whether logical or emotional—may gradually take on a different character. Impress upon them that it's not possible for you to know altogether exactly what you will be seeking—you wish you did. Possibly your needs have been pushed so far back into the recesses of your mind for so long that you are able to open up to them only a little at a time. Possibly there are deep hurts that cannot be faced all at once. What you hope for in having someone's support is to be able to share feelings that well up in response to each aspect of the experience as it develops. If you can express yourself in this fashion when first going into your search, others will be more prepared for the varying emotional conflicts you are likely to experience as you go through the subsequent stages of search.

When turning to someone who hasn't shared the adoptive or birthparent experience, it's best not to insist on a complete understanding of what you are going through—after all, how can those who haven't shared the experience understand it. Try rather to bring them to some awareness of how important this process is to you. Though they can never fully understand what it all means to you, you can make it clear that it is linked to your sense of who you are.

Indignation

The second stage of search is marked by an intensification of feelings. The neutral attitude typical of the first stage is dropped. These feelings commonly surface in the form of indignation or rage at the frustrations encountered in attempting to gather information rather than as anxieties, fears, or doubts connected to the personal significance of the search activity. The sentiment most expressed at this point is "How dare anyone violate my right to information that is kept on ME!"

Although the initial experience of indignation is genuine enough, don't focus on your indignation to such a degree that it prevents you from thinking about the deeper feelings that have also been awakened. This rage may act as a cover for feelings of rejection, insecurity, and guilt that have started to surface or a sharpening of them in instances where the searcher has already had some awareness of these feelings.

At this point, having someone to turn to for moral support becomes very important. You are probably confused. With support from others, you will have more courage to face the mishmash of emotions you now find rising within you; you will feel less vulnerable and alone in dealing with both the growing turmoil within and the frustrations imposed on you from without. In your search for that connectedness that has heretofore eluded you or that you have previously sacrificed, having moral support helps maintain a proper balance in your day-to-day life.

By now you may begin to understand there were deeply felt needs that prompted you to begin your search. If in enlisting the support of a family member or friend you stressed an attitude or reason that is now undergoing some change, realize that some confusion or uncertainty may attach to their reactions now. Enlist their patience in accepting your consideration of deeper, more personal motivations; be as patient as possible in allowing your supporters time and room to come to a new perception of your involvement in this pursuit as well as of your frustrations.

Obsession

There comes the time in your pursuit of information when you become more and more involved in your search—nothing or no one can deter you. All your efforts and free time are directed toward correcting a gross miscarriage of justice against you—against anyone in your position. It may become a common event for you to confront friends, relatives, and even strangers you encounter with your burning determination to set things right. You are apt to be quick to judge others for their failure to see the issues as you see them. And yet you very well may not be facing the problem realistically.

During this stage the hurts and resentments that have usually begun to surface by now will be having a more sustained and disturbing impact. Think about what is happening. Is your crusading zeal possibly designed, in part, to keep those hurts and resentments from overwhelming you? And, if they have not already been a factor by this time, are there anxieties now about what you will actually discover? Do you ever think, "What if I find something terrible?" "What if the person sought doesn't understand my need to know?" "What if the child I relinquished doesn't understand my reasons?" Does your obsessive drive to locate that baby or mother to some extent grow out of a frantic desire to have disturbing fantasies such as these laid to rest?

It may be that coming to the decision to search was so difficult that now having to face obstacles that block the progress of your search causes anger and resentment. This anger and resentment toward those that withhold information and impede your progress is understandable, but your severe reactions to those hindering your progress may be influenced by doubts as to the decision itself.

During this stage you need moral support more than ever, but the obsessive nature of your pursuit often makes it difficult for your supporters to continue their support. The constant focus on getting to the identity of your birthparent or relinquished child can create tension with someone who now at times may wish you'd forget the whole thing or, at least, that you'd keep it "in perspective." You have to accept that at times it will be difficult for your supporters to respond to your needs for sympathy and involvement as completely as you'd like. Perhaps you'll find that you do have a friend or relative who at every turn will be right there in the trenches with you, fighting for total vindication of your rights. But recognize the likelihood of uncertainty or some weariness intruding at times. Remember that this war you're fighting is at times strange to one who doesn't share the experience of adoption or relinquishment.

Suppression

Following a period of obsessive determination to achieve the search goal —and perhaps to change the system as it relates to adoption or relinquishment records as well—you may find yourself withdrawing from the fray. The reasons vary. It may be as a result of the cumulative effect of frustrations encountered, of disruption of previously established routines, of anxieties that develop, and so on. It may simply be that you feel the need for a rest. Or the halt may be called at a point where a critical piece of information has actually been uncovered.

Whatever the prompting factor, it's important to understand that this reaction represents another stage for most searchers—it's not necessarily the end. You have put your search aside. It may be that you seldom even think about it anymore—your conscious desire to go on with it seems to have evaporated. You may feel this way for a few days, a week, a month, or forever. A few individuals stop their search permanently, but you are more likely to find that you eventually move on to the fifth stage.

From the vantage point of your supporters, your behavior may again prove a puzzlement. There may be surprise and shock that you're apparently giving up on this quest which your supporters know has been so critically important to you. Or there may be relief that you've stopped, with the potential for a reaction of shock or confusion at whatever time you decide to resume searching. Whichever the case, for a moment you may once again find yourself seemingly out of step with those supporters who've been traveling the search road with you. As before, give your supporters a chance to make their adjustment to what is, in effect, your adjustment to your experience. You can't realistically expect that this adjustment will be completely synchronized with yours.

Acceptance

This stage is arrived at when you accept *whatever* it is that you've discovered. This can mean you accept that you do want to continue your search, or that you're not ready to carry it through to the conclusion you'd originally hoped for, or that you now have and want to take the opportunity to try to develop a new relationship not previously possible for you.

Now you must deal with the qualms you probably have. Preparation for a reunion is very difficult, as you don't know what you will find. Will the birthparent be receptive? Will the relinquished child (who may be conflicted about role models or a sense of loyalty to the adoptive parents) wish to talk to you? Will you find an undesirable parent or child? Will the medical histories you find bring new concerns into your life?

Realizing that you're willing to accept whatever the results of your search might be does not lessen your need for moral supporters. As your search comes to an end, and especially if the possibility of a reunion exists, you may find yourself more dependent than ever on your supporters. As much as all searchers hope this isn't the case, no searcher can overlook the possibility of rejection. If you've decided to seek a reunion you run the risk of attempting to establish a relationship, the intensity of which may run the gamut from love to hate. Whether a relationship develops or not, the entire situation is a trying one for you and for your supporters.

One adoptee I know carefully tracked down her birthmother. It was a long and tedious process, but finally a current name and address were found, and the phone call for initial contact was made. A very cheery, bright woman answered. She was astonished, sympathetic, and willing to help in any way, but stated it was impossible that she was the birthparent. After much conversation both agreed the facts had somehow been distorted and that possibly a college friend must be the mother. The woman promised to help, to relate all the facts she could remember.

The adoptee hung up the telephone devastated. She had searched so long and hard—coming up with the wrong name meant starting all over. During the next few days she retraced all her steps in an effort to discover where she'd made her mistake. Her frustration mounted at her inability to figure it out. Then, after several days, a phone call came through from the woman she had thought was her birthmother. She stated that she was in fact the birthmother, that she had realized this might eventually happen, and so had mentally prepared herself for it. However, she'd never told her husband or children about the birth, and she'd denied being the mother in order to have time to tell her family the truth. After several days of sorting out facts and feelings, she was now calling back to say she was the birthmother and that her family fully supported her getting to know her relinquished child.

This story has a happy ending, but you can imagine the value of moral support to the adoptee through those few days of seeming defeat. Her attitude of acceptance still could not prepare her for the shock of initial denial.

Even if you do not find the person sought, you will emerge from the search with a heightened self-awareness that can be channeled in a positive direction. A search should bring a sense of pride and dignity when you review the difficult tightrope that had to be walked—one of weighing your need to know against another's right to privacy.

No two people experience the stages of search in the same way. Each deals with unique circumstances and contends with very personal hopes and fears. Virtually all who search will find that the pattern of their search to some degree mirrors the general pattern—although often this is clearer in retrospect than during the process itself.

The Fear of Failure or Rejection

Many an adoptee or birthparent has been stimulated to search as a result of the publicity others have received when their search has ended happily. Pleasant reunion stories appear in newspapers and magazines every week, giving the impression that all is well when the search ends. And the idea of their own happy reunion stirs them to decide whether to proceed or not: "If the possibility of a happy reunion exists for others, why not for me?"

Even so, I doubt that *any* searcher really feels secure just in knowing that others have found a "happy ending." There are haunting uncertainties that grow as the search progresses. Of course the way you express these doubts to yourself influences exactly how disturbing they will be; some individuals will be able to handle them more readily than others. No one, however, will escape a brush with them. And when that comes, having your supporters standing by is invaluable.

Although there is always a chance you won't locate the person you're seeking, you should know that the odds are good that you will. Search techniques are more refined than ever; the network of search and support groups is constantly growing; there is at least some improvement in the general attitude toward searching; and we live in a record-oriented society, so there is a wide range of potential leads that can be pursued.

In the process of search you are also confronting deep-seated feelings about a fact of your past that has greatly influenced who you are today. This is perhaps more apparent with adoptees than with birthparents, but my conversations with birthparents reveal a similar significance to them of their search —in carrying it through, you are to a considerable extent reviewing feelings about yourself. It's noticeable, for example, that many of those who enter into a search do so at an important time in their lives—after marriage, after the birth of a child, after passage of a significant age milestone (achieving legal age, turning forty, fifty, and so on), after a death in the family. These are events that prompt many to reflect on who they are, on what their life has thus far

been and where they feel a need for change. For adoptees it means a consideration of the circumstances surrounding adoption and their impact; for birthparents, those surrounding relinquishment.

You may initially feel a compulsion to justify the rationale for your search,
but this ultimately becomes less a consideration than the experienced need to
justify actions taken through the search. It is your responsibility to set appropriate guidelines for yourself. Be cautious, as these guidelines will be tested
again and again in moments of excitement, when under pressure, or at times
when suddenly you don't know quite what to say. In effect, in searching for
someone else you pursue a course that makes it possible to discover something
more of yourself. And that, to my mind, is *not* failure, whether you locate a
birthparent/relinquished child or not.

As for the fear of possible rejection, the key, I believe, lies in accepting
whatever it is you will find. In addition, be alert to this: The initial contact you
eventually make will be a surprising, emotional event to the other person. This
person cannot have anticipated your call or self-introduction, even if perhaps
he or she has considered the possibility of it "some day." It will probably take
more than a moment just for the realization to sink in that suddenly here is
an opportunity for establishing a new relationship. It may take days or weeks
to adjust to that fact and then to act on it. Don't be too quick to assume you've
been totally rejected. Many searchers do find that acceptance ultimately awaits
them. Those few who are rejected naturally experience pain and disappointment, but recognizing and accepting the risk of rejection generally serves to
fortify them substantially. And at least they have raised the veil of secrecy that
had been drawn across an important part of their lives. The uncertainty of not
knowing has been resolved. That provides a very positive feeling for many.
Adoptees continually state that not knowing is worse than anything they might
find. Consider the gist of the remarks of one adoptee:

> One of the things that has bothered me most about the partial information that my
> adoptive parents gave me about my natural mother was the fact that she had been
> institutionalized, without letting me know in what sort of institution. Was it a
> mental institution? Was it a prison? Without knowing these things, I will constantly
> feel anxious and in doubt. I would not mind knowing what sort of institution it was,
> but being in doubt produces lifelong anxiety.

Facing the possibility of rejection is never easy, but we inevitably face that
possibility in all areas of our lives. What are the resources you've fallen back
on in earlier years? Certainly among them will be the moral support of people
who care for you or who see in you a reflection of their own experience. As

you pursue your search, during which you will wrestle with unsettling emotions and doubts, avail yourself of the moral support that is within your reach. It will make you more able to withstand whatever disappointments may lie ahead. In the face of possible rejection, it will be a vivid illustration of acceptance and caring.

Where Will I Get My Moral Support?

You need not feel hopelessly alone in your undertaking. Nevertheless, it's not as simple as just identifying the possible sources of support and then availing yourself of them. You will be reaching for support from people with their own emotional needs and priorities. These have to be considered and dealt with.

Spouse

If you are married, the first logical source to turn to for support is your husband or wife. This is the person with whom you've entered into a life partnership. It seems only natural to be sharing your feelings about whether or not to pursue a search and about what you experience during your search with your marriage partner.

Ideally your spouse will be strongly supportive. Not only will he or she take a positive interest in what you are doing and how that affects you, he or she will assist you in your search. You'll not only have the benefit of moral support, you'll find you have the full resources of two minds to draw on in tackling this problem you've decided to face. Together you'll work out whatever emotional conflicts now exist or may arise in connection with your search. And at the conclusion you'll have both the desired knowledge relative to your birth-parent(s) or relinquished birthchild and a strengthened relationship with your spouse.

Well, it can work out that way for you, but you may find the dream of immediate, unstinting support from your spouse just that, a dream. Your spouse may find the significance of the search to you hard to understand. Why do you need a more secure sense of self-identity? What makes it necessary now to come to grips with feelings of guilt and/or responsibility that have troubled you for years? It's all water under the bridge, isn't it? Again, it's that inability for someone who doesn't share your experience wholly to understand what motivates you.

In addition, you may find that your spouse views your search as a threat to your relationship—that he or she resents the time and energy expended in an activity that seems to have no immediate relevance to life at home and that can complicate life at home. Suddenly you're preoccupied with a problem and related issues that have their focus outside the marital relationship; you may seem to be putting your marriage and your responsibilities to family in second place to a pursuit that is rooted in fantasy.

Or it may be that your spouse hesitates or refuses to support you out of a sense of protectiveness. He or she may feel that you will only be opening yourself up to further hurts that will leave you emotionally shaken and scarred, and so your spouse may attempt to dissuade you from undertaking or persisting in your search.

Or your spouse may react with indifference—it just doesn't seem all that important. If you want to do it, go ahead—just don't ask his or her involvement.

As a birthparent you may find another barrier to cooperation from your spouse: an unwillingness to accept the fact of a previous sexual relationship you have had. Men typically find it harder to accept this than women, as multiple sexual relationships have traditionally been viewed as more tolerable in men than in women. A birthparent-wife may find it more difficult to admit to a previous child—and thereby to a previous sexual relationship—than a birthparent-husband.

It's impossible to give one single piece of advice that will cover all such situations. If you're faced with this problem—and you want to initiate a search for a relinquished child your spouse knows nothing about—you will need to consider your marriage situation carefully. How do you think your spouse will react? Do you carry with you a constant anxiety that he or she will find out anyway? Would whatever risk might be taken in telling your spouse be compensated for by relief from that continual fear? Is there a mutually respected and trusted third party—a family member, friend, or clergyman—who might be able to help you resolve your fears of rejection from your spouse?

Occasionally the birthparent will have shared the fact of a previous child with the marriage partner, but the fact will remain a secret otherwise—other family members and friends have no knowledge of it. In that circumstance, if you intend to undertake a search, you should realize that one result may be eventual wider knowledge of the existence of your child and of your relinquishment. Discuss this with your spouse. How many people will be told? Who will they be? How will the two of you resolve any discomfort that may arise in the face of shock or disapproval on the part of family members—in particular of your in-laws, friends, coworkers, and neighbors.

If you are experiencing difficulty enlisting the support of your spouse, it may be because you have failed to share with your spouse your feelings about your adoption or relinquishment. If your spouse is confused by your needs or can't comprehend the reason for your search, perhaps you haven't given him or her sufficient opportunity to look at the issue from your point of view. If you are considering or have decided to undertake a search, plan time for discussing and sharing your feelings with your spouse. Think about what you are going to say, about what your spouse's reactions are likely to be. Keep in mind that how you present the problem can influence how your spouse reacts to it. An announcement made in passing while dinner is being prepared might be taken less seriously than one shared during a period of quiet time that allows scope for a thoughtful discussion of issues and feelings from both perspectives. With more information about your needs, with a clearer awareness of inner fears and hopes you may not previously have admitted, your spouse will more readily recognize the importance for you of a determination to search. Understanding may still not be immediately forthcoming, but support may be there, nevertheless.

In coming to a decision to search, it may be that you are reading books on the subject. Let your spouse read them too. Point out selected passages that reflect your feelings. Making him or her aware that others have feelings like your own can aid in winning acceptance for yours. If you are in, or plan, contact with a search or support group, ask your husband or wife to accompany you to a meeting. This again provides an opportunity for him or her to see that your experience is not just some neurosis of yours that is best resisted.

You may find that, despite your most reasoned efforts, your spouse remains unwilling to be supportive. Should this be the case, recognize that just as you will experience changing feelings, so may your spouse. You may find that once you've attended several workshops, written letters, received answers, and/or uncovered new leads, your spouse may become interested and express a desire to help. As this happens, remember that your spouse will have some questions of his or her own. Be patient and open in your response to them. Curb the temptation to answer with a remark like "I thought you didn't want to help" or to revive some other quarrel about a previous lack of interest.

Occasionally you might find the support offered by a spouse (or other family member or friend) a problem. That person may go beyond the bounds of providing encouragement and/or assistance and seek to impose his or her views on the proper way to conduct your search. Should that happen, you will need to block diplomatically what amounts to an interference with the goals you have established. In a matter as personal as this, to follow priorities set by another contributes to feelings of conflict and uncertainty. Tell your spouse (or other supporter) that you appreciate the intent to help. Encourage suggestions on how an area of search might be approached; acknowledge that you value his or her readiness to listen to your expression of feelings. But be firm. Emphasize that you wish to avoid unwanted tension between the two of you, but that you must follow your own sense of priorities. Obviously, you have to deal with this problem in light of the relationship you have with your spouse.

Suppose that your spouse refuses to be supportive—what then? For one thing, it means a probable reevaluation on your part of whether you want to go ahead with your search anyway. The lack of support expressed in the form of general indifference may not give rise to any great conflict. If, however, your spouse declares absolute opposition to your proposed activity, you must reflect on what that means to you. You may go on to conduct your search in secret —you might receive correspondence via general delivery, a post office box rented near your home, or via a sympathetic friend; you may arrange calls so as to avoid any chance of interception or being overheard by your spouse. But this creates an obvious situation of tension—the fear of discovery is constant. And should your spouse actually come to a realization that you've decided to disregard his or her opposition and to search in secret, there's great likelihood of marital conflict. You have to decide what course to take and whether it's worth it to you.

The one point of advice I will repeat here is that you keep the door as open as possible to a later change of heart on the part of your spouse if at first he or she refuses or fails to be supportive. The issue has an impact of its own on the marriage partner, arousing fears and uncertainties that may take some time to deal with. If in your disappointment and hurt at your spouse's first reactions you can keep this in mind, it will prove easier later to accept a change of heart as genuine. You're less likely to get locked into your resentment that this person who is supposedly most in tune with you has not immediately realized the significance to you of what you are undertaking. (I advise the same openness where other family members or friends similarly fail to declare support at the outset of the search.)

Family

The issues here vary for adoptees and birthparents. As an adoptee you have been transplanted into a family environment other than that into which you were born. In your search for your roots, you will often find yourself dealing with the question of loyalty to your adoptive family. The adoptive parents may interpret the decision to search as a rejection of them, as a statement of dissatisfaction with the job they did in raising you. And there are also some adoptive parents who feel that the adoption itself is a secret that should remain hidden. If your adoptive parents feel this way, naturally this can place you under considerable strain.

At an early age you may have become aware that every child fears he or she is adopted and needs reassurance from the family that it is not so. But for you no such assurance could be given. It may be that the fact you were adopted and the loving reasons for the adoption are spoken of freely, but the fears and unspoken questions are never broached. It's as if you were born the day your parents walked into the room and made their selection.

Your adoptive parents may be unsettled by your decision to search. Their feelings are in a large part a reflection of a general attitude that adoption properly closes the door on a child's past history forever and provides a substitute family tree that is complete in every respect.

Many adoptive parents have introduced their children to the world of adoption through a book published in 1939, *The Chosen Baby* by Valentia Wasson (Philadelphia: J.B. Lippincott). Although it has been updated in its illustrations, cover, and print style, the story remains the same. It begins, "Once upon a time there lived a man and woman named James and Martha Brown." It ends, "James and Martha and Peter and Mary Brown are a very happy family." Your expression to your adoptive family of a decision to search may be interpreted by them as an indication on your part that you are not happy or satisfied with them as a family. They may have swallowed the fairytale that adoption, once accomplished, quite rightly wipes out a child's past—that any subsequent concern about your birthparents is perverse on your part or means that they have failed.

Suppose James, Martha, and Mary Brown were very athletic—tall and thin, agile and quick. While Mary was always playing ball or jumping rope, you would find Peter in his room drawing; he was always small and almost clumsy, and he never enjoyed sports like the other members of his family. Now Peter and Mary have grown up, and Peter still loves to draw and has chosen to make his living in a related field. He is very talented and wonders how he became so. Peter chooses to search and discover if his talent came from his birthparents. Peter's search is not a negative reflection upon his adoptive parents nor indicative of any unhappiness on his part. He is searching in order to reconcile his feelings of being different from the other members of his family. Now let's further suppose that, through it all, "James and Martha and Peter and Mary Brown are a very happy family."

In trying to win support from your adoptive parents, it is very possible that you will have to deal with their insecurities. Naturally, your first line of explanation will be that you are not looking for a new mother and/or father to replace them; locating your birthparents will not change the relationship established with them. It may help to cite a "medical need to know." As already noted, this seems to be the least threatening reason for searching. Indeed, it is a perfectly legitimate motive, but it is not the only legitimate motive. And you want your parents to be supportive as you explore those motives which lie deeper. If, through your childhood and adolescence, you've been able to share feelings of insecurity and doubt with your adoptive parents, impress upon them that you hope they will be as open to your sharing the feelings you have now. Make them aware that this affords you and them an opportunity to accentuate a relationship of closeness and mutual support. How could this kind of sharing be a threat?

Obtaining the support of your adoptive parents is important because they are your most available link to the past. Their recollections of the circumstances surrounding your adoption can provide valuable clues or leads for you to pursue as you seek out your birthparents. They may actually already have a crucial piece of information. One adoptee I know discovered his parents had a copy of a baptismal certificate that indicated his birth name.

Make an effort to broaden your parents' perspectives on your needs. Be explicit that your needs are an outgrowth of the fact of adoption, not a result of any shortcomings in their performance as parents. Ask them to read about the experience of others so that this fact will become more apparent to them. Ask them also to attend a search and support group meeting with you.

In order to avoid distressing your adoptive parents, you may choose to avoid discussing questions about your origin with them. You may feel that only upon your adoptive parents' death will you feel free of a conflict of loyalties in regard to searching out your birthparents. But then one of the most valuable sources of useful search information is beyond reach. In the words of one adoptee in this situation, "For my entire life I had been unable to approach my adoptive mother about my past, and her death made me realize that my past was now dead, too."

It may be that you find your adoptive parents absolutely unable to comprehend what your aims are in pursuing a search. The only thing they seem able to focus on is the threat of rejection or what they see as an implicit accusation that they have failed you as parents. In that event, it's probably better to pursue your need to know independently of them. Remember, this is *your* search and *your* need. While you would like support from people you love, you don't need to share this with persons who then translate your need into their hurt and fantasized failures.

Lest the focus in these paragraphs seem directed disproportionately to the possibility of a lack of support from adoptive parents, let me relate a personal encounter that illustrates a more positive reaction from an adoptive parent.

In April of 1980 I attended an adoptee/birthparent conference at the Disneyland Hotel in Anaheim, California. One morning at breakfast I found myself seated next to an attractive woman I guessed to be in her early forties. I asked whether she was attending the conference as an adoptee or birthparent. Neither, came the reply. She was an adoptive parent with three adopted children, ranging in age from twelve to sixteen. She had been reading lately about adoptees searching and felt it possible that one or all of her children might experience this need some day. She was aware of a certain inner pain in contemplating this possibility, but she recognized that her children would not actually be seeking a new set of parents and that the search would not affect feelings toward her. Even though her first reactions included fear, she discovered that facing the situation was not as difficult as she'd expected. She'd met many searching adoptees and heard what they had to say. She'd spoken with birthparents and realized that there was no real threat in the kind of relationship they hoped to establish with their relinquished children. As in helping a child through any difficult time, she wanted to be ready with meaningful support when the search question came up. I'm sure many loving adoptive parents are similarly prepared to extend moral support once their children express a need to gain a connection to their birth origin.

As a birthparent searching for a relinquished child, you will be generally less dependent on your parents as a link with the past. You have your own memory of the events surrounding relinquishment. You were, after all, a principal in the decision and its subsequent implementation.

However, to the extent that family relationships are important to you, having the active moral support of family members is equally important. This can mean having to face any lingering sense of shame that may be harbored by your parents or other family members—which will influence their readiness to consider your needs openly. If they have not faced their feelings, if the subject of your child is one that by some silent agreement is never brought up for discussion, they are apt to resist your first efforts at bringing them up now. Their concern for what the neighbors might think, or what they still view as a shameful blight on the family name, may prevent them from being supportive. The possibility of enlisting their support depends in large part on the avenues of communication that remain open between you. If you now have a comfortable relationship with your parents, chances are excellent that you will in time be able to share aspects of your search with them. Allow latitude for a period of adjustment if at first they appear unable to understand your needs in pursuing your search.

Children

Often the decision to search out the missing connection with the past comes at a point where you have a family of your own that includes one or more children. What do you tell them?

Two important factors influencing your decision will be your child's age and relative maturity. If your children are three, six, and nine, telling them will be much different than if they are twenty, twenty-five, and thirty. What is your relationship with your children? Have they asked you questions about their family tree that would provide an opportunity to introduce them to the fact of your adoption?

Children react in different ways, according to their age and temperament. A friend of mine is searching. Her two teenaged children find it very exciting and are actively participating to the extent they can. Her ten-year-old, even though she is in the room when related conversations take place, gives no evidence of interest and does not participate.

As a birthparent you probably will find the question of what to tell your children more difficult. Your relinquished child is a sibling to the children who are part of your present family. Do they know of this other sibling? How do you feel they would react—would their attitude toward you change? You will also have to consider their attitudes toward sex. Among young people there is often something of a double standard. They accept sexual openness and experimentation among their peers; they often find it difficult to accept that their parents may have indulged in that same openness and experimentation.

What about telling a small child that he has a brother or sister who was relinquished? In this case, confronting the child with an event beyond his capability to grasp would be irresponsible. It will not provide you meaningful support; it can generate unnecessary confusion or anxiety in the child. As a concerned, aware parent, you should know best when to tell your child and how to present the information most naturally. Adoption and adoption search are easily understood and accepted by children. When it comes to relinquishment, the subject is not one that is as naturally introduced or easily explained. With young children it is often advisable not to raise the subject until the time comes when they need to know what is happening, possibly at the time of a find.

Whether to tell the children and how and what to tell them should probably be discussed first with your spouse, as with other issues that affect the family as a whole. It will be more difficult to come to agreement on telling the children when your spouse is not supportive than when he or she is. If you are pursuing your search despite your marriage partner's opposition and he or she is aware of that, it may be possible for you to compromise somewhat along these lines: You will agree not to confront the children immediately about the fact of your search and the reasons behind it, but at such time as their interest becomes apparent or it seems unavoidable that they will be touched by an aspect of the search—as when a reunion is imminent—you and your spouse will tell them together in a nonjudgmental, matter-of-fact manner. Obviously the agreement you find yourself able to reach depends on the relationship you have with your spouse. If you feel obliged to search in secret, then it's evident you won't feel free to share your experience with the children in the home. Of course, the children's ages are a factor, too. If you have adult children— perhaps even teenaged children—you may not feel it imperative to "clear" what you tell them with your spouse first. Still, in most cases, I'd advise you to let your wife or husband know that you've shared this information with your children.

While I have discovered no instances of children failing to be supportive of a parent's search once they are told of it that doesn't mean it hasn't happened. Parents who are concerned that their children will not be supportive may not tell them. I have encountered many instances of parents whose children are enthusiastically supportive of and participate in their search. I have met birthparents who spoke of difficulties bringing the subject up, but who found once the subject was out in the open that it was discussed freely in the home. (Most had not told younger children until the search reached a point where a find looked near.) Birthparents with teenaged children or those approaching teens noted that it wasn't a particularly comfortable way to approach sex education, but once the subject was broached, sex education was a natural byproduct. In each case, winning the support of the children had an unmistakably positive effect on the morale of the searcher.

Friends

When trying to explain my need to search, so often the friend listening would respond with the wrong question or conjecture. For instance, while I would be talking on a level of the need to know, the friend would answer on a level of "What if the birthparents are rich and famous?"

Some people are able to grasp much of the significance of what you are doing quickly. Others can't. It is very painful for a searcher to find that a close friend is unable to lend support, can't understand, and may even disapprove, while another quickly recognizes needs within you and offers full support. Sometimes there's no alternative but to listen to a friend express an opinion that runs completely counter to your experience and feelings. In such a case acknowledge that you've heard what was said, and then proceed on to another subject.

You can keep friends who don't seem to understand updated in a brief or casual manner. Possibly, once they see the importance of this endeavor to you, they will express more interest—they will be open to a deeper sharing of feelings, to being educated in what search is all about. Some may prove unable ever to see your search as anything more than a subject that makes for interesting cocktail conversation. You will quickly get a feel for when and with whom you can truly share this very personal experience. Although it's likely that you will find yourself surprised and disappointed at the reaction of one or more close friends, chances are excellent that among your friends will be one or two who stand prepared to lend you support and aid, even if they at times find it hard to understand completely why you are so focused on what they see as a past event.

Other Adoptees/Birthparents

In 1978 the *Washington Post* estimated that there were some five million adoptees in the United States, of whom some two million were actively searching. They could not provide an estimate of the number of birthparents searching, but one reunion registry reported that applications now come through from birthparents in about the same proportion as from adoptees. This suggests a staggering total of searchers.

Look around you. Possibly you are friends or acquainted with someone else who is adopted or who is a birthparent with a relinquished child (although the latter may not as readily declare himself or herself). *All* adoptees are at least curious about their origin. And I suspect that all birthparents have occasion to wonder about what may have become of their relinquished child. If you know you share either experience with someone else, it is usually easy to introduce the subject of search. That's not to say you'll encounter immediate, automatic support. Some adoptees/birthparents will not respond or may not be inclined to be particularly supportive. I assume that to mean they are not ready to consider a search for themselves. They may still be afraid of seeming conflicts in loyalty, may be afraid to face the unknown, may feel they have an image to live up to which doesn't allow for search, or may prefer to live with their fantasies. They may be so defensive that they feel constrained to dissuade you from undertaking your search. Then again, despite their fears or uncertainties, they may watch you pursue your search with a pointed curiosity that betrays an inner longing on their part to resolve the same unanswered questions.

Reaching out for support in this context does not require that adoptees match up with other adoptees only or that birthparents link up only with other birthparents. Adoptees and birthparents can provide each other genuine support that can at times be even more meaningful than that offered by someone engaged in the same search. Adoptees see in the searching birthparent an encouraging example of concern and caring that they hope to find in their own birthparents; birthparents similarly see in the searching adoptee an example of a relinquished child who sincerely longs for some contact with the parents who gave him or her up for adoption. The aim of the search/reunion is the same for both; the process of search is very similar; the fears that each encounters will be much the same. Motives may differ—for example, a need to gain a sense of connection with one's birth roots versus a need to resolve past guilts or failings with a new openness to responsibility. But these motives are largely complementary—there's no conflict between them. And the many similarities that exist make possible a broad sharing of experience and perhaps even a pooling of certain resources.

Approach your adopted friends; establish contact with a birthparent who has relinquished a child. You may be surprised at the reaction, even if up to now the other person has never dared consider the possibility of searching. You may find a person like yourself, feeling a need but unsure how to proceed. Using a "buddy system," you may both find you now have the necessary courage to undertake a search, something you hesitated or feared doing on your own.

Search and Support Groups

I have referred and will refer repeatedly to search and support groups. There is a variety of them. Some groups will work for adoptees and birthparents alike, others for one or the other. Some groups concentrate on aiding actual searchers, others focus on efforts to influence legislation—most do both. All have their origin in the uniting of people determined to promote the rights of adoptees and/or birthparents seeking information relative to their birthparents or relinquished children. They provide individual searchers with a network of support and resources far beyond that of anyone searching alone. They are established in every state in the Union; there are even a few links to similar organizations outside the United States.

Because search and support groups are composed overwhelmingly of people who have in the past responded or are now responding to the same need to know that pushes you, they constitute a source of genuine understanding. Yours may be a case where they are the only source of understanding you feel comfortable in relying on. I attended a group meeting at which a divorcee with no other children than her relinquished child told of her relief at finding the group. "I thought I was all alone, no one to help me. I couldn't believe the first meeting I attended, the friends I made." And I've witnessed similar reactions over and over again. It is so heartening to find that others have gone through the same experience you are going through, have faced the same fears, have worked out similar problems.

Search and support groups are usually activist groups seeking to change attitudes and laws relating to adoption, relinquishment, and the right to know. They work actively for reform, but they do not enlist searchers as banner-waving members to be mobilized on behalf of the cause. The interaction with searchers is on an individual, sharing level. Their aim is to provide you support, not to recruit you into a movement. Your participation is welcome; it is not demanded. Your privacy is respected fully, and you are not pressured into supporting group policies or programs. Naturally, you will be invited to contribute so as to enable the group's support activities to continue. But the extent to which you participate in any group activities is up to you. You are almost always welcome to observe a meeting if you are unsure whether you are ready to reach out for the support the group can provide you.

Search and support groups do not seek to take the place of any individual supporter you might otherwise reach out to; their purpose is to make additional support available, not to substitute for other available support. At one birthparent group I attended, I heard an embittered birthmother lash out against those who had disappointed her with their failure to be supportive. Her husband didn't understand, her best friend thought she was crazy, her parents were resentful that she was bringing up an old issue. Her only support came from the group. She went on to report that recently she'd spoken angry words to her friend and hung up the telephone without saying good-bye. The group suggested that maybe she had not given her family and friend the appropriate input and chance to support her. She felt so grateful to be with people who did not think her strange, neurotic, or crazy that she was willing to consider what the members of the group said. Their focus was on how to assist her in establishing the supportive links she so yearned for with those who were otherwise close to her.

Some groups make it possible for two searchers to join together in a mutually supportive buddy system. They are able to put people who don't know each other but are in a position to help each other into contact. Suppose you live in New York, while I live in California. You need records searched in Los Angeles, I need them searched in New York City. Through a contact arranged by the group, we are put in touch with each other. I then search for you while you search for me.

Another variation in approach works like this. Through the group you spend time searching in New York on behalf of someone, while another person searches for you in Los Angeles. What happens in this case is that you are donating hours in return for hours spent on your search. The group coordinates. In a group I've been associated with, one adoptee was searching for her birthfather. She'd learned he lived in a small town in the Midwest, but she could get only telephone directory information, which was insufficient. She mentioned this at a meeting. After the meeting a woman approached her and said she had helped a birthparent with her search; this birthparent lived in the area mentioned. She gave her the birthparent's address and told her to write and request help in finding out the information locally. The birthparent was more than happy to help; she felt she was starting to repay a debt.

There is much more to be said of the work that search and support groups do and how you can avail yourself of their help. See Chapter 7.

Professional Counseling

Some adoptees and birthparents develop feelings that are so conflicting, emotions that are so unsettling, that they must refer to a psychiatrist, psychologist, or other professional counselor. It is never easy trying to live with guilts or needs we don't understand, and counseling or some form of therapy may prove beneficial.

I am not qualified to tell you when you need professional help, but I do urge you to keep in mind that it is available. One thing I do sincerely believe: The experience of a need to know is not of *itself* an indication that professional help is necessary. And yet you may find that friends, social workers, record keepers, and others around you may continually suggest this type of support. It may be that events that led to your decision to search (mid-life crisis, divorce, death) may be the reasons that cause turmoil in your life. The search itself may be of no contributing factor, but others may focus on this as the cause of your turmoil.

The idea that you are abnormal in wishing to know about your origins— in wanting to know something of your relinquished child—is alien to me. You may, however, find yourself confused about an issue related either to your adoption or relinquishment. It can happen that the emotions stirred up during a search threaten to overwhelm you despite what moral support you have— or because it has not been forthcoming from people you have counted on. In those cases you will do well to recognize that professional help is available. But to seek counseling before you are aware of why you are seeking it, or before a problem threatens to become unmanageable, can be costly and nonproductive. Only you can know when the moment arrives that this kind of help is desirable or essential. If that moment comes, don't be afraid or ashamed to reach out for help.

If you do feel a need to refer to a professional, consider carefully where you will go. Many adoptees and birthparents have discovered that counseling they've received has not been directed toward their needs. When choosing your counselor or therapist, look for one who has some familiarity with needs commonly experienced by adoptees and/or birthparents. Ask questions. Has the counselor worked with other adoptees and/or birthparents? Is he or she familiar with papers being published on this subject? Can the counselor recommend someone who has experience with adoption- or relinquishment-related emotional trauma? Many search and support groups will recommend a counselor used by a group member. This might prove an excellent way to locate one who can help you.

What If I Don't Get the Moral Support I'm Looking For?

There is virtually always a source of moral support available to you, especially in light of the search movement's spread across the country. But it is possible you'll be refused support from a source you feel is essential to you —a spouse, parents, friends. Then what do you do?

You ultimately have to make your own decision here. Dig deeper. Look back on your life. Did your spouse, parents, friends always give you the support you felt you needed in all situations? Probably not. Your answer at times has no doubt been to accept the disappointment and go on. Your sense of priorities led you to continue. And on other occasions you may have given in and discontinued whatever you had hoped to pursue. What made the difference? Does it make the difference now? If you receive no support from your spouse, family, or friends, weigh how important your search is to you. The answer may be that it is important enough to continue without support —in some cases without further mention of it. Only you can provide that answer.

However, don't get discouraged that no source of support exists for you. You may find that those close to you will eventually respond more positively. Even if they don't, you won't need to search alone. The existence of specially established groups makes it virtually certain that there is a source of support within your reach. Once you recognize the avenues by which support can be obtained, you will find that it is available to you—you only have to turn in the right direction to get it.

3

What Will It Cost Me?

Gather together your typing paper, carbon paper, envelopes, stamps, and library card, and you have the basic search tools at hand. That sounds awfully simple for getting into a process that has the potential for complication that this one does. After all, on many levels you're undertaking to play the role of private investigator, tracking down one or two people lost to you somewhere among millions. How can it be anything but a complex, expensive experience?

There are those within adoptee/birthparent circles who will readily tell you of the great amount of time and money they spent on searching. It's true that one can spend into the thousands of dollars on search efforts. But in most instances that isn't necessary, and you should realize that a good deal of the talk you may hear of great sums spent will fall into the category of one-upmanship. For some there seems to be a sense of status attached to how much money was required to conclude a search. I would like to show that great expenses need not necessarily be the case.

To begin with, it is simply not true that the solution to a complex problem involves spending great deals of money. Attention to detail and organization are more important here. The truth is, without attention to detail and organization, a large part of any monies expended is very likely to be wasted. The organized person working on a shoestring budget has a better chance of success than the disorganized person whose way of dealing with the problem of complexity consists of throwing money at it.

With the basic search tools mentioned above, and a careful approach to circumstances requiring an outlay of funds, you can be sufficiently thorough as a searcher to assure yourself an excellent chance of success.

Budgeting

It is only through organization that you can assure yourself control of costs. A fundamental organizational tool is the establishment of a search budget. International conglomerates, local businessmen, and families all work within a budget, reviewing monies available and setting limits to expenditures in a diversity of areas, depending on money available and the sense of priority that attaches to whatever a particular budget item may be. You can and should do the same. Only you know how much money you can afford to set aside for this project. Don't be discouraged if your resources seem modest. Don't assume a small budget rules out completion of your search. With careful planning, you can often achieve the same results and in the same time as a person with unlimited funds.

Let me give you a simple example of how this can be done.

Searcher A sends away for a birth certificate, marriage certificate, and death certificate on a given person. At this point, what he is really looking for is military information. He pays $4.00 for each certificate, plus postage.

Searcher B, looking for the same information, sends a letter to the Vital Statistics Office in his state. He asks for copies of forms used in requesting the same three certificates and also asks for whatever form is used to request divorce records. His cover letter asks what information will be given on each certificate, the charge for searching out whatever information is not completely given, and what other records the office holds on file.

When the Vital Statistics Office replies, Searcher B discovers he need only apply for the death certificate to receive the desired military information. However, he has the additional forms for possible use at a later date, and also a summary of what information the other certificates will provide.

Searcher B sent two letters altogether, plus $4.00 for the death certificate. Searcher A sent three letters, plus $12.00 for three certificates, only one of which he really needed for his present purposes. While the difference in this instance may seem modest—$8.00 and one first-class stamp—multiplied over the course of a series of instances, the difference can mount substantially.

Note also that Searcher A spent money with no certainty he'd get the information sought. Searcher B submitted a fee only when he knew it would win him the desired information. In another circumstance, Searcher A might spend money without getting anything of substance in return. Searcher B, by virtue of a more organized approach, would lose only the cost of a first-class postage stamp.

Be like Searcher B. Organize yourself to hone in specifically on the information you require. Follow through with one try at that, rather than with random efforts to obtain whatever seems as though it might be useful some time. Meanwhile, keep a file of notes or information that will be useful when later following up on other leads.

Searchers with limited funds will need to spend more time planning. Wait until you have some reliable information before jumping in and sending away for every booklet offered, for every certificate you can lay your hands on. Why spend even 75 cents for a pamphlet on divorce records when you're still searching for a marriage certificate or even a birth name? Just make a note that the pamphlet's available. Then if you find you need it later, you'll know how to get it. In the meantime, conserve your resources.

I would like to present an example of how far you can go with about $15.00 when starting your search. The list is general and would need to be adapted to suit your own needs. However, it is a reliable indication of what can be done with limited funds. Please understand that this $15.00 represents only a start, but see for yourself what a good start it is. Note that the fees and charges indicated are those that apply to my state at the time this book was published. Your charges may differ somewhat, but the difference is not likely to be substantial.

Recording family information	⸺
Collecting documents on hand	⸺
Cost (fee plus postage) to obtain birth certificate	$4.20
Cost to notarize request letter for birth certificate at my bank	⸺
Cost (fee plus postage) to obtain court records	$4.20
Cost to notarize letter requesting court records at my bank	⸺
Letter sent to acquire state adoption laws	$0.20
Letter of inquiry to genealogical library (with SASE)	$0.40
Letter to register with index match-up (with SASE)	$0.40
Phone books for area of search and state capital	⸺
Waiver of confidentiality sent, certified mail, return receipt requested	$1.53
Telephone call to adoption agency, out of state (20 minutes, reduced rate)	$4.00
	$14.93

You may have only a given amount of money you can set aside each month. Perhaps that amount will be as little as $10.00. You can still search, but you must plan your search carefully.

Of course there are no guarantees that your search will not eventually involve more money than you wish to spend. Some searches are very difficult and go from state to state. Some require a mass mailing to all persons with a given surname in a large city. Some lead from one dead end to another. But even so, an organized approach taken with an attentive eye regarding budgetary limitations will prove most cost-effective.

You will probably realize that budgetary limits aren't only set by what you can financially afford. If you have a family, you may have to deal with the fact that your values and ways of seeing things often aren't the same as those of your spouse. Besides considering just how much money might conceivably be available for your search, you should review priorities with your partner. How valuable does your spouse see this search? What other wants and needs exist that might lay claim to shared resources? Some compromise may be necessary when deciding on budget limits, depending on how perspectives coincide or differ. Of course these can be reviewed periodically. And with the information in these pages, you can demonstrate to a partner concerned with costs that they are manageable. You don't have to keep pouring money into a deep, dark hole in your efforts to reestablish that connection that was broken so many years past.

Expense Factors

Are there necessary further expenses to be aware of? Yes. There will be unavoidable expenses. To a great extent your search will hinge on the unearthing of records kept in official and private files. You will have to pay fees for copies of some of these. Postage expenses can run beyond the roll of first-class stamps you have on hand. You may find yourself making long-distance telephone calls. There are possible membership dues for groups you may feel impelled to join so as to have group support resources available to you. At times you will have photocopying expenses. Now and again you will need the services of a notary public.

However, the essential expenditures here are all quite modest. If you rely on a sound plan of approach, the costs involved will probably fit easily within your budget.

Now let's look at the various expense categories you'll need to fit into your search plan.

Public and Private Agency Fees

Fees to various public agencies and archives can mount up quickly. Some expense here will be unavoidable. You will require at least some documentation to establish or confirm facts of the relationship you are investigating.

You will have to pay for copies of official certificates of record held by state governmental agencies. A death certificate can cost $2.00 in one state and $6.00 in another. Some states charge a search fee in addition to charging for the actual certificate. You may also be searching through marriage records, divorce records, birth records, property ownership records, and so on. Depending upon the circumstances facing you, you may need only one of these documents, or you may need several. The key to controlling costs here is to pinpoint only those records absolutely essential to establish a significant item of information. (Note also that at times there is a lower fee for obtaining a copy of records in person than there is for obtaining that same copy by mail.)

A few private agencies charge to open and review your files. One such agency in New Jersey charges $25.00 every time a file is opened. To reduce repeated file-opening when requesting information from such an agency on your adoption or relinquishment, prepare a lengthy, thorough, and well-planned list of questions. You will probably have to consider several avenues of questions; dealing with possibilities one at a time in this case will occasion multiple visits that otherwise could be avoided.

Only a few hospitals, from which you'll be seeking birth-related information, will require a fee to release your medical information. Ask for a notification of charges on records when you first write. Here again expense can run up if you have to pay an additional fee because you neglected to ask all the questions you might have at one time.

Archives and public libraries usually charge a fee for photocopying records and other material in their collections. The cost is usually 25 cents per page copied. If the surname you're researching is Smith, you can imagine the expense of copying phone listings for a five-year time period. Some public record-keeping agencies will charge an extra fee for certain popular surnames. Use your judgment when deciding on information in public records to be photocopied.

Postage

Mail service can run expenses up more quickly than you may realize. For occasions when a postal card is as effective as a letter, use stamped postal cards from your local post office. Also consider using the double postal card that has a perforated line, permitting the receiver to detach and reply on a separately stamped, self-addressed section. For example, if you were trying to locate a relative in Los Angeles with the surname Askin, you might need to send out thirty letters to all those with that name listed in the Los Angeles telephone directory; your message might be as short as a line or two, asking anyone with information on the person indicated to contact you by returning the attached postal card. If you are sending many such letters consider using the double postal card instead of sending a letter with a self-addressed stamped envelope.

Other services provided by the United States Postal Service you will want to be aware of in addition to first-class mail are certified mail, registered mail, and express mail, with the feature of return receipts available in each case.

Certified mail provides you a mailing receipt, which constitutes proof of mailing. Upon request you can also obtain a return receipt, which will show either (a) to whom and the date your letter was delivered or (b) to whom, the date, and the address where your letter was delivered (important in the event mail is forwarded). Determine the current fees at your local post office.

Registered mail offers maximum security and protection against loss of your letters. This service is usually recommended only when mailing items of value. The cost varies according to the value listed. Return receipt services are available, as for certified mail, at the same additional charge, and restricted delivery service is also available.

If you wish an address correction for letters forwarded by the post office, the post office will bill you, in the form of postage due, when the return receipt is sent to your address. The cost varies. This service can be very valuable to searchers when a person sought has moved.

On rare occasions you may want to utilize express mail service, ensuring delivery of a letter or package the next day. This is an expensive service and not available in all areas. Rates are according to zone. Return receipts will add another, small cost. Restricted delivery service is not available with express mail.

Your post office will provide a General Delivery service at no charge. This service enables you to receive mail addressed to you care of General Delivery, the post office, and the address of the post office.

When corresponding with agencies and individuals, list your address as General Delivery, the post office, the city, and the state. Mail will be kept at the post office for thirty days and then returned to the sender. You may stop by the post office at your convenience and pick up any mail you may have received. There are no restrictions to where you receive your mail; you do not need to live in the town where you receive mail through General Delivery. This is the easiest way to assure privacy and avoid being detected if you have chosen not to tell others of your search.

Each of these special services can be valuable to you. Awareness that they are available from your post office is important whenever it seems advisable or necessary to establish proof of mailing, proof of receipt, name of receiver, and/or address correction. Control your expenses by a realistic evaluation of needs in these areas.

Telephone Service

To the extent practicable, use the mail instead of telephoning long distance. This is particularly advisable when requesting information it will take time for someone to get together anyway. Keep in mind as well that the mail offers some advantages when you want or need documentary proof that you've been in communication with any agency or person.

If you've tried to elicit information via the mail without success, it can prove worthwhile making a phone call. You can sometimes get information this way when a letter or series of letters was ignored, or when the reply returned was that the agency to which you were writing was not allowed to give out the information requested. But remember, this can work to your disadvantage, also. A reply by an agency receiving your letter requesting information on the basis of "judicial need" is based on the information pro- vided only in your letter. If you call, the agency personnel can ask you to explain, and doubts existing in their mind may not be resolved in your favor.

Take advantage of time zone differences and special rates whenever possi- ble. If you live in California and are calling the East Coast, call early in the morning. People in New York and Atlanta are busy at work at 9:30 AM, but your time of 6:30 AM offers you a reduced rate. If you live in the East, calling just after 5:00 PM will find people on the West Coast still at work—it's just after 2:00 PM, their time. In Chicago it will be just after 4:00 PM, and you can still catch people in their offices there, too, although they'll be getting ready to leave for the day within the hour. Wherever you call, try not to call at a time when the person you wish to speak to is likely to be at lunch or just getting ready to leave the office.

As with the post office, your telephone company has a variety of services to offer. Your knowledge of what services exist and how best to make use of them will help you keep telephone costs to a minimum.

Although person-to-person rates are higher than station-to-station rates, calling person-to-person can, in many cases, be less expensive when seeking to locate someone specific. Here is an example of how this can work. You have reason to believe your birthmother came from New York City. Your birth name is Askin. There are five families listed in the New York area with that last name. However, your birthmother probably no longer goes by that name. You don't know if any of the five listed individuals are family members; you have no way of knowing if your birthmother is still living. You can narrow down the possibilities by calling each listing person-to-person, asking to speak to the name you have for your birthmother. The receiver's reaction can provide a clue of relationship. Statements such as "Operator, that's my sister's name," "Operator, she's no longer living," or "Operator, that was another family that lived here years ago" will all be cause to thank the operator and immediately to call the person back using unassisted, station-to-station rates. (Or, if you'd feel more comfortable doing so, write a letter instead.)

Under all circumstances, keep track of each person you call and speak to. In the case above, the person receiving the call might be a teenager or the spouse of a relative. An unexpected call requesting information on someone from the past might not immediately jog the memory. When dealing with agencies, keeping track of whom you've spoken to provides you a record that makes it possible to refer to that individual in any future exchange. That can often save you the time of having to re-explain yourself in every detail to a second or third person to whom you are a completely new experience. Even when you have to deal with a second or third person, the mention of information or a promise of information provided by an individual helping you previously may prompt this other person to be more forthcoming.

If you are searching out of your immediate area, your local telephone directory will not list the numbers you need. By calling your telephone business office, you can order one or more outside directories for your use. Tell your business representative the city needed. The phone book will be delivered to your home. Usually this is a free service, but some telephone companies will impose a slight charge. Ask when placing your order. You may also want to request a directory for your state capitol city—it will be an aid for any calls you may need to make to state governmental agencies.

The telephone company also makes it possible for customers who live in one city to list their name and phone number in another city directory. This service is billed to you from the business office in the city where your new listing will appear. Call your local telephone office to subscribe. Ask about charges (which are usually modest) and payment. Your listing can appear under your present name, under a maiden name, or under a birth name—whatever would allow potential family members proper recognition.

Searchers invariably check the telephone directory first when trying to locate a missing relative. How nice to provide this listing in the town of your adoption/relinquishment, in case you also are being sought. This can be especially useful to birthparents as an aid in searching for a relinquished child.

Membership Dues

If you decide to join an adoption, genealogical, or historical group, there will undoubtedly be a membership fee. Membership dues vary. Concerned United Birthparents charges a $15.00 annual membership fee. The Adoptees' Liberty Movement Association has a membership charge of $30.00. Other organization fees range from $12.00 to $50.00; most are in the range of $15.00 to $20.00. Do keep in mind that these fees are subject to occasional revision.

You will need to decide if a group fits your needs. The costs to join must be justified by the rewards to be gained. Attend a meeting as a visitor— virtually all groups allow this—to determine what the groups in your area have to offer, how you can benefit, and whether you wish to join.

There are also a number of private and state-run reunion registries, which may or may not charge a fee for your registering with them. Basically these services maintain a record of adoptees, birthparents, or other blood relatives who have indicated their desire to be listed in a reunion registry. Once someone is listed, a cross-check is run to ascertain whether the party being searched for has also registered with this service. As the reunion registry network expands, the potential for establishing contact in this fashion increases. Even if no immediate match is found, your name remains on file.

The few existent state-run registries (see Chapter 8) are either free or have a minimal charge. In general, membership fees for private search and support organizations—for example, Adoptees' Liberty Movement Association and Orphan Voyage—include a listing in the reunion registries they maintain.

Newspapers and Magazines

If you've narrowed your search down to a particular area, you may decide you want to subscribe to a local newspaper in order to catch any possible notice of persons who may prove to be related or who may be likely to provide you a lead to contacts in the area. This is generally not practical in large cities, but in many rural and suburban areas a local newspaper carries reports of births, deaths, weddings, and other doings of established residents. However, you should think carefully about monies spent on newspaper subscriptions until you are quite certain you've pinpointed the correct area of search and have some clear indication of names to be on the lookout for.

Newspapers can be helpful in another fashion. Some searchers have had success running an ad and have found information from unusual or unknown sources. The cost of such an ad varies widely from locality to locality. When you have the name of a newspaper in your area of search (see Chapter 4), write and ask for ad rates, day published (not all newspapers publish on a daily basis), geographical area covered, and costs to subscribe. When writing to any newspaper always include in your letter a statement asking where their old editions are stored. This may save you time when at a later date you wish to review past newspapers from a given area.

Your ad can ask for any information you wish. Some searchers have run ads asking for information about births at a particular hospital on a particular day; others use a more genealogical approach, stating they are looking for a missing family member. One searcher asked to receive information on the whereabouts of an old school friend, and yet another asked for information regarding births at a particular maternity home.

The wording and placing of ads should be very carefully thought out, to eliminate any embarrassment to the person sought. Try to imagine what actions may result from your ad. The idea, for example, is to find information, not to expose a birthmother to her community if she does not wish this.

Two magazines published to provide genealogists communication with each other and to answer questions relating to research on family backgrounds are *The Genealogical Helper* and *The Family Finder.* Ads can be placed in either magazine for aid in locating persons still alive. I'd estimate the average cost is from $10.00 to $12.00 for an ad running about forty words. The ads make contact possible between individuals who may be researching the same family. Current subscription costs are $14.50, or $4.00 per copy, for *The Genealogical Helper;* $2.00, plus postage (about 50 cents), for *The Family Finder.* (Further information on genealogical resources can be found in Chapter 4.)

Open A.R.M.S Quarterly, a newsletter geared to aiding searchers, began publication in 1981. At this writing it charged $6.00 for a one-year (four-issue) subscription. For $10.00 you can receive a one-year subscription, with your ad running in all four issues. (Chapter 4 contains more information about *Open A.R.M.S Quarterly.*) Note that there may be other publications periodically issued in the area of genealogy or adoption research that will provide some information helpful to you. Some are published only within a limited local area. Your state archives or library can tell you what publications are offered and what areas they cover. You can then contact them directly for a clarification of information offered and the costs of subscription or purchase.

Note that your expenses in this area are largely optional. It may be that at one point in your search you find that using ads placed in a newspaper or a periodical such as *The Family Finder* is advisable. If you are working on a limited budget, wait until other sources have been used before you take a course of action that requires such an outlay of money.

Consultants

Although the word *consultants* immediately brings to mind professionals hired at considerable cost, the fact is that adhering to a strict budget will not exclude your referring to consultants. For one thing, every search and support group has volunteer consultants to aid you in your search. And I have yet to see a group of genealogists that doesn't include at least one kind and helpful person who is willing to share information and advise you on refining your search techniques.

Be aware that your public library has an entire staff of consultants you can refer to at no cost. Your reference librarian will be invaluable as a source of information and aid on the use of the many research resources available through either your local library or interlibrary loan. Think of your local library staff first when you reach out for consultants' assistance.

Keep in mind that you can also refer to your state government for free information on state laws relating to adoption. Your state legislator can serve as a consultant to inform you of any bills pending, in committee, or recently passed in this subject area. State legislatures commonly have a reference service that will provide gratis copies of laws and information that explains the purpose and specific applicability of laws and leads to other government literature in any particular subject area.

Notaries and Photocopying

You *will* need to have papers notarized. Many states will not release your birth certificate without a notarized letter of request. As a rule, hospitals require a notarized letter before they will release medical information that pertains to you.

Your local telephone directory will offer a listing for notaries. These individuals will charge a fee for each letter notarized. However, many banks and savings and loan societies will provide notary services free of charge to their customers. Check with your bank or savings and loan to discover whether such complimentary service is available to you. You can also check with your local real estate offices.

Documents, newspaper articles, pages from telephone directories, and so on will need to be photocopied. As mentioned previously, most archives and libraries have facilities for photocopying materials in their collections. Often they have a photocopying machine available for general public use, but rates will usually be higher than through outside photocopying services. (If the material to be photocopied can't be checked out of the library, naturally you'll have to pay the library's charge.) The charges for independent photocopying services vary. Copy services tend to be more available, with more competitive rates, in more populated areas.

4

Reference Resources

Western society is highly record-oriented and has been so for many, many years. The practice of maintaining records is so long-established that in some cases people have been able to trace family history back hundreds of years. Virtually everyone born in North America or Europe (and in many areas of Latin America, Asia, Oceania, and Africa, too) is immediately put on record at birth, and a host of life situations and events affecting each person are routinely entered in some ledger or file—medical records, educational records, marital records, property and tax records, voter registration records, military records, passport and travel records, licensing records, litigation and court records, membership records, death and inheritance records. Depending on the individual, some or all of these—and/or others not included in this broad list—will exist somewhere, a web of information defining the position the person holds or has held in the community. Adding further detail are the individual's own records, either held as letters and documents in personal files or scattered among family and friends, depending on the circumstances. There's hardly a person alive for whom some sort of documentary record doesn't exist, at least in this part of the world.

When you begin your search, you may be convinced that you face an impossible task. Tracking down one person out of millions may seem like trying to find a needle in a haystack. But each existent record serves as a thread leading back to that figurative needle, and dozens of threads radiate out through the haystack, some extending out beyond the haystack's perimeter. If you can locate one or another of these through sharp-eyed research, that can eventually lead you to your needle. Because the nature of our society is such that we tie numerous record threads to each person, separating the needle from the haystack often proves a much more manageable task than you might imagine.

Consider also that you probably have some threads in hand—the records of your own birth and adoption or of your child's birth and relinquishment. These indicate dates and places that tie into the life history of the person you're seeking. They may be very fragile threads, but there's an excellent chance they'll at least start you in a direction toward others that may be more securely tied to the object of your search.

There is a wide variety of reference resources you can turn to as you develop and track down leads to the relinquished son or daughter or to the birthparents you're trying to locate. In this chapter I'll introduce you to those that searchers have repeatedly found valuable, and to some that searchers have occasionally found useful.

Libraries

If I were able to give but one point of advice on tuning in to reference resources, it would be this: Get to know your local reference librarian. More than anyone else, this person will serve as a ready source of aid as you locate and search through various directories and other reference guides and materials you'll need to consult in the course of your investigations. Explain what you are doing, and ask what information she or he might have or be able to direct you to. Librarians are characteristically staunch fighters of information censorship. As a rule they welcome and enjoy the challenge of tracking down and isolating desired points of data that together build into a solution to a puzzle that's presented them.

You can consider yourself lucky if you have access to a large city library, a good college or university library, or to the Library of Congress, where you find much material available. But even if you live in a rural community and must rely initially on a modest county or branch library, you will probably find it a surprisingly fertile source of information.

Before your first visit, compile a list of what information you will need and of books you may wish to check out or order through interlibrary loan (see below). Then spend a day or afternoon gaining as complete a sense of what information service is available at your library as you can. A sample list of considerations might include the following:

1. The reference librarian's name and hours of availability.
2. Maps—old and/or current—for your area of search.
3. Address of your or your child's adoption agency (if you know the agency involved).
4. Address of the birth hospital (if known) or of hospitals in the city of birth (if specific hospital is not known).
5. The name and address of your local or nearest genealogical society, and the date and time of their next meeting.

6. The name and address of any special libraries you might need to refer to—law, genealogy, religious.
7. The name and address of past and current newspapers published in your area of search.
8. A copy of your state's adoption laws.
9. The name and address of an adoption/search and support group in your area. (Is your librarian aware of any other searchers?)
10. The name and address of a historical association in your area of search.
11. Availability of telephone directories from your area of search, and useful numbers contained in those.
12. Books on adoption that are available.
13. Magazine articles on adoption listed in *Reader's Guide to Periodical Literature.* Which are available in the library? Can your librarian help you get copies of others?
14. Availability of photocopying service at the library for duplicating material you can't check out.
15. Additional suggestions the librarian may have.

Your search will lead you in many directions. You alone are in a position to know what you will need, so always remember that you must draw up *your own* list of considerations when exploring your library's resources.

If you feel the need for better research guidance than your librarian is able to provide you in one or two visits, turn to one of the several excellent library-use guides that are available. Three titles that I have found helpful are *How to Do Library Research, Guide to Reference Books,* and *Finding Facts Fast: How to Find Out What You Want to Know Immediately.*

When using library (or any other) resources, make it a habit to note exactly where you found any information and the type of information the source you've used offers. Record the exact book or article title and the author's name, the publisher, the date of publication, and the page(s) where you located useful data. Also jot down in what library you found the book or article. In doing research you may not always immediately recognize the importance of some information you've read and, as a result, may find the need to go back to a reference source you've previously reviewed. It can be frustrating to know you've once before come across the fact you're looking for now but can't recall where. Good notes make it possible to pinpoint information quickly a second or third time and can save you hours of aggravation.

Interlibrary Loan

Even though your local public library may be small, it will generally have access to a wide range of material not contained on its shelves. This is because public libraries, almost without exception, are part of an interlibrary loan system. Translated, this means your local public library can request from any of a host of other libraries materials not held in its collection. Most libraries offer this service to lenders at no charge, but a few will request you pay a small fee. Ask your librarian about your library's policy.

It's easy to order materials through interlibrary loan. In a matter of minutes you can order a book from the Library of Congress or microfilmed data from the National Archives. Your librarian will supply you with the forms and help direct you to the proper source. Inquire whether your nearest law library, genealogical library, or other special interest library participates in the loan system. To find out precisely what libraries exist in your area, refer to *The American Library Directory* for the addresses of national, state, county, and city libraries in the United States; refer to *The Directory of Special Libraries and Information Centers* to locate university, genealogy, law, religious, public administration, and state libraries. Your library probably has a copy of both these volumes in its reference section.

The Library of Congress

The Library of Congress, created in 1800 when President John Adams signed legislation authorizing its establishment, now serves as a central information source serving the needs of the whole country. Today it is the largest in the United States and among the largest in the world. Its holdings include more than seventy-four million items. In its own words, "The Library of Congress stands ready to lend to libraries for your serious research much of the material in its general and highly specialized collections when needed items cannot be located at the local, state, or regional level." Although this is but one function of this great library, it is the one that will most concern you. Don't let the lack of reference resources at your local library deter you. All libraries have access to the Library of Congress, and through them you'll have access to information you require for your search.

The Library of Congress can be valuable to you for its thousands of indexed items relating particular family histories and recording family members. If you are using genealogy in your search, contact the Library of Congress to see if there is a book published on your birth family. If it is under copyright, order the book through interlibrary loan from your library locally. If not, ask the Library of Congress to duplicate it for you. (But be aware of the expense involved. Find out the number of pages and the duplicating cost per page before you place a duplicating order.) Ask if the book has an index. If it does, request only those pages relating to the name you are interested in. You will need to submit form #25-15 (Order for Photo-Duplicating) from the Photo Duplication Service, The Library of Congress, 10 First St., SE, Washington, DC 20540. Ask for this form when you send a first letter inquiring what references this great library can make available to you in the area of family history.

For more information on the holdings of the Library of Congress, for microfilm copies of materials on file, or for details on general services available to you, write to the Information Office, The Library of Congress, Washington, DC 20540.

Law Libraries

The law library nearest you (check *The Directory of Special Libraries and Information Centers*) can help you to locate past or presently practicing attorneys in the United States. You'll be looking for the attorney(s) involved in your relinquishment/adoption. Ask the librarian to direct you to the *Martindale-Hubbell Law Directory.* You may find a current edition of this reference at your local library, but past editions must generally be sought at law libraries. Each edition lists practicing attorneys for a given time period.

Naturally, you're looking to discover your attorney's current address. If there is no present listing for him or her, check back editions to find the most recent listing. See if perhaps another attorney now occupies the old address or served as partner with the previous (your) attorney. In this manner you may be able to discover where the records on your case are kept or where to write your attorney privately, if he or she is now retired. If a firm refuses to release current address information, ask if it will forward a letter from you to the lawyer's residence.

There are other things to check for at the law library. It's an obvious place to find out all you can about state adoption laws. You can check books that provide sample legal forms of the sort you may want to utilize. If, in reviewing the record of your court proceedings from years ago, you need to have a legal term defined or explained, what better place to discover the definition and to review its implications?

Many law libraries charge a fee to become a member. These fees vary, but in my case I found it less expensive to photocopy information I needed at the law library than to join it and obtain full borrowing privileges. Ask what the membership charge is and what qualifies a resident borrower. If you live near a law school, find out what use privileges you can obtain from the school's library.

Basic Reference Guides

When you are trying to discover what books are available in any subject area or what books are available by a particular author, or if you are trying to track down a book for which you have only a title, your best reference resource is *Books in Print,* published annually by R.R. Bowker Company and organized in separate volumes by subject, author, and title. These volumes are updated by interim supplements that appear regularly during each year. Back volumes will help you discover books previously published that may now be out of print. (The fact that a book is out of print means that it is no longer available from the publisher—it may be readily available for borrowing at a library.) In addition to being available at virtually all libraries, *Books in Print* is also available at larger bookstores.

The Cumulative Book Index is a single-volume author-subject-title international bibliography of books published within a given year in the English language. Published annually by the H.W. Wilson Company, it can be used for the same purpose as *Books in Print.* Your reference librarian should be able to help you use it.

The *Reader's Guide to Periodical Literature* is an index for magazine articles published each year. It too is organized by subject, author, and title, so that you can locate articles of interest in any of three ways. You can also refer to *Access: The Supplementary Guide to Periodicals* for direction to magazine articles of interest.

For articles published in academic or professional journals, check the *Social Sciences Index.* Such articles tend to go into more depth on whatever aspects of a subject they treat than would a comparable magazine article written for a popular audience. Through review of an adoption-related article in a law journal, you could well learn more of nuances in the law or of new trends in court rulings than you would through general-interest periodicals. The possible disadvantage for you in turning to academic or professional journals is that they frequently use academic or technical terms the average reader is often not familiar with. They also often assume familiarity on the reader's part with the subject matter covered.

Except for a few nationally influential newspapers, newspaper articles are not indexed as a rule. *The New York Times Index,* however, can direct you to any article published by the *Times* since before the turn of the century. For a report of major news developments, this is probably your best source of information. Most large libraries and college or university libraries will have back copies of *The New York Times* available on microfilm.

However, searchers more usually find themselves trying to locate local or regional newspapers from their area of search. To discover what newspapers are in existence, consult *Editor & Publisher International Yearbook,* the *Ayer Directory of Publications,* or *Ulrich's International Periodicals Directory.* These books will give you the address, when publication began, and whom to contact for newspaper information. Naturally, you have to deal with the possibility that a newspaper published in your area of search at the time of your adoption/relinquishment is now out of business. In that case, you will have to seek out back volumes of one or another of these references. It may be worthwhile to contact a newspaper serving your search area now for information on what happened to a competitive or predecessor publication that has since disappeared from the scene. You might also try contacting libraries in your area of search to learn if they store old copies of now defunct local newspapers.

Once you've tracked down a newspaper you want to check, you'll have to inquire whether and where back issues are available for review. If they are available, you'll have to pinpoint the time period for which you want to review issues and then try to arrange access to copies on file. It's highly unlikely you'll have the benefit of an index to work with. There's a good chance you'll have to refer to county or state archives for possible issue availability. Many local newspapers are very haphazard about keeping a complete file of back issues.

The Encyclopedia of Associations can be a very useful guide. This lists religious organizations; labor unions; sororities and fraternities; and trade, business, and commercial organizations. Each of these as a rule maintains a roll of memberships, current and past. One of your search leads may point you toward one or another such organization. If you want to obtain an out-of-state Chamber of Commerce address, this is also the place to look. Most searchers will find sooner or later that they need information on some social welfare, cultural, veterans', athletic, or genealogical organization. These too are listed in *The Encyclopedia of Associations.* Take the time to become familiar with this book. You might want to photocopy the table of contents for reference should future clues direct you to an area in which one of the organizations listed is operative.

If you're on the trail of a business, industrial, or commercial concern, or if you're trying to track down a professional reference, the *Guide to American Directories* can prove helpful. This lists the hundreds of directories published to provide information for businesses and professionals in almost all areas of commerce, service, and manufacturing.

As I've said before, utilization of available reference resources starts you on the track of a lead that connects to your past at the point of separation from your child or birthparent(s) (or sibling, if you're searching for a lost brother or sister). And there are still more places to investigate.

Government Information Sources

You may feel that since it's government policy that keeps your adoption/relinquishment records sealed there's no point in looking to government agencies for help in your search efforts. Well, the government won't help you search as such (although note the exception for those registering with the Minnesota Reunion Registry—see Chapter 8), but there *are* various government references resources that you can use freely. One or more of these can prove important in developing or pursuing a lead to the person(s) you're seeking.

In the United States there are three layers of government—national (federal), state, and local. Those laws governing adoption/relinquishment procedures and mandating how records shall be administered are state laws. By and large, the federal government does not concern itself with specifics in these areas, although naturally all state law must be consistent in intent and administration with the fundamental principles laid down in the Constitution of the United States. However, because the federal government does interact directly with citizens on many other levels, which results in records being filed on individuals in one context or another, the federal government is often as valuable a source of information as any state office might be.

Basic Reference Aid

There are a number of good reference books published to help you through the maze of government bureaucracy. The *United States Government Manual* lists the names, addresses, and departmental affiliations for all federal government agencies. *The Official Congressional Directory* lists the names, addresses, and responsibilities of all who work in or for the United States Congress.

Sometimes just identifying the proper agency or department to direct yourself to can be a problem. In that case, ask your librarian for help in locating the appropriate government address. You can also call the U.S. Government Information number, which you'll find in your local telephone directory, for assistance. Keep in mind that a call to the office of either of your state's United States senators or of the congressman for your district can also win help in the task of orienting yourself to the complexities of the federal bureaucracy.

To find your way through the maze of state government, refer to *The Book of the States,* which lists all state agencies and their addresses, or to *The National Directory of State Agencies. The State Information Book* can help you locate a court administrator, as well as law libraries, tourism departments (for obtaining maps), and other possibly useful state information sources.

Again, ask your reference librarian for assistance in tracking down a state agency if necessary. If you're still having trouble locating a particular address or official, write to or call the government information center for your state. (The address and telephone number are given in the state-by-state reference lists in the back of this book.) It may also be helpful to call your state senator or assemblyman's office for assistance.

Since local government is structurally dependent on the state government, guides to state agencies will generally provide you an eventual lead to a local agency, where that turns out to be the appropriate point of reference. It may be a matter of having to direct a first inquiry to a state agency. However, your local telephone directory will be a prime source for county/municipal agency references. Just look in the white pages under the name of your county or municipality. (Some telephone directories have a separate "blue pages" section for government listings.) For local offices of state agencies or federal agencies, check the listings under the name of your state or under United States government, respectively.

The National Archives

The National Archives is the central repository (storage agency) for all public government documents on the federal level. The material held on file dates back to the days of the American Revolution, and every day more material is added—census records, military records, government reports/studies, indexes of all kinds, and innumerable other types of records.

This great archive is administered by the General Services Administration. There is a central repository at the National Archives Building on Constitution Avenue in Washington, DC. In addition, there are eleven branches located throughout the country. The most complete explanation of the services of the National Archives is contained in the pamphlet *Guide to the National Archives of the United States.* A second pamphlet, *Regional Branches of the National Archives,* available at no cost, details which records are held in common and which are specifically maintained by the individual branch archives. Both pamphlets are issued by the National Archives and can be obtained through them or from a Government Printing Office bookstore.

The branches of the National Archives are located at the following addresses:

Boston	Federal Archives & Records Center 380 Trapelo Rd. Waltham, MA 02154 (617) 223-2657
New York	Federal Archives & Records Center Building 22—MOT Bayonne Bayonne, NJ 07002 (201) 858-7252
Philadelphia	Federal Archives & Records Center 5000 Wissahickon Ave. Philadelphia, PA 19144 (215) 951-5591
Chicago	Federal Archives & Records Center 7358 South Pulaski Rd. Chicago, IL 60629 (312) 353-0161
Atlanta	Federal Archives & Records Center 1557 St. Joseph Ave. East Point, GA 30344 (404) 763-7477
Kansas City	Federal Archives & Records Center 2306 East Bannister Rd. Kansas City, MO 64131 (816) 926-7271
Fort Worth	Federal Archives & Records Center 4900 Hemphill St. P.O. Box 6212 Fort Worth, TX 76115 (817) 334-5525

Denver   Federal Archives & Records Center
                        Building 48, Denver Federal Center
                        Denver, CO 80225
                        (303) 234-5271

San Francisco   Federal Archives & Records Center
                        1000 Commodore Dr.
                        San Bruno, CA 94066
                        (415) 876-9009

Los Angeles   Federal Archives & Records Center
                        24000 Avila Rd.
                        Laguna Niguel, CA 92677
                        (714) 831-4220

Seattle   Federal Archives & Records Center
                        6125 Sand Point Way, NE
                        Seattle, WA 98115
                        (206) 442-4502

You are most likely to refer to records in the National Archives if you are pursuing your search through genealogical records. (These are explained below.)

If you plan to visit the National Archives or one of its branches, be prepared. Your visit can result in total confusion if you don't plan ahead. Each branch has an archivist to assist you and answer questions you may have, but because of the many people using the archives daily, the time the archivist will be able to devote to you will be limited. Some knowledge of what records exist, of what indexes are in print, and of how to use the Soundex coding system (explained at the end of this chapter), together with a list of questions you need the most help with, will work to make your visit productive.

There are several pamphlets and books that will help you understand how to get to what the archives have to offer. Two that may be of help are *A Guide to the Genealogical Records in the National Archives* (list price $2.50) and *List of National Archives Microfilm Publications* (free upon request). Order directly from the National Archives, General Services Administration, Washington, DC 20408, or through a nearby Government Printing Office bookstore.

The United States Government Printing Office

The United States government, through its hundreds of departments, agencies, and offices of every description generates a tremendous volume of printed materials, all of which is available through the United States Government Printing Office (GPO). The GPO is run by the government to inform the public on its many undertakings; thousands of pamphlets are supplied to private citizens each year. Many of these can be had just for the asking. All can be ordered through the Superintendent of Documents, U.S. Government Printing Office, Washington, DC 20402. They are also available at or through the several GPO bookstores located around the country. (See below.)

To find out what material is printed by the government, look to one of several excellent sources of reference. The *Index to U.S. Government Periodicals* lists magazines, newsletters, monthly reports, and other publications issued on a regular, periodical basis. The *Guide to U.S. Government Publication* is a two-volume reference. Volume I lists current agencies and the publications issued through them. Volume II lists agencies that are no longer in operation and the publications issued through them in the past. *The Monthly Catalog of U.S. Government Publications* alerts you to books, pamphlets, and so on published recently and provides an order form by which you can order material you want.

You can now use MasterCard and Visa credit cards when ordering books and other items from the Superintendent of Documents or the regional GPO bookstores. To order directly from Washington, DC, you may phone (202) 783-3238 between 8:00 AM and 4:30 PM, Eastern Time, Monday through Friday. Or you can call the number given for a nearby regional GPO bookstore.

If you live near a GPO bookstore, it may be of interest to browse through what is available to you. You could come across a publication that may be helpful. One I found valuable was *Where to Write for Marriage Records, United States and Outlying Areas,* which cost me $1.50. This booklet lists, state by state, the addresses of vital statistics offices, the fees charged for searching records and/or providing duplicate copies, and indication of dates for which records exist. (You might note, however, that you can call your nearest U.S. Government Information telephone number to receive the same information.)

GPO bookstores are established at the following addresses:

Atlanta
Room 100, Federal Building
275 Peachtree St., NE
Atlanta, GA 30303
(404) 221-6947

Birmingham   9220 Parkway East-B
                      Roebuck Shopping City
                      Birmingham, AL 35206
                      (205) 254-1056

Boston   Room G-25
                      John F. Kennedy Federal Building
                      Sudbury St.
                      Boston, MA 02203
                      (617) 223-6071

Chicago   Room 1463, 14th Floor
                      Everett McKinley Dirksen Building
                      219 South Dearborn St.
                      Chicago, IL 60604
                      (312) 353-5133

Cleveland   Federal Office Building, 1st Floor
                      1240 East Ninth St.
                      Cleveland, OH 44199
                      (216) 522-4922

Columbus   Room 207
                      Federal Building
                      200 North High St.
                      Columbus, OH 43215

Dallas   Room 1050
                      Federal Building
                      1100 Commerce St.
                      Dallas, TX 75242
                      (214) 767-0076

Denver   Room 117
                      Federal Building
                      1961 Stout St.
                      Denver, CO 80294
                      (303) 837-3964

Detroit   Patrick V. McNamara Federal Building, Suite 160
                      477 Michigan Ave.
                      Detroit, MI 48226
                      (313) 226-7816

Houston	45 College Center 9319 Gulf Freeway Houston, TX 77017 (713) 226-5453
Jacksonville	Room 158 Federal Building 400 West Bay St. P.O. Box 35089 Jacksonville, FL 32202 (904) 791-3801
Kansas City	Room 144 Federal Office Building 601 East 12th St. Kansas City, MO 64106 (816) 374-2160
Los Angeles	Room 2039 Federal Office Building 300 North Los Angeles, CA 90012 (213) 688-5841
Milwaukee	Room 190 Federal Building 517 East Wisconsin Ave. Milwaukee, WI 53202 (414) 291-1304
New York	Room 110 26 Federal Plaza New York, NY 10007 (212) 264-3825
Philadelphia	Room 1214 Federal Office Building 600 Arch St. Philadelphia, PA 19106 (215) 597-0677
Pittsburgh	Room 118 Federal Office Building 1000 Liberty Ave. Pittsburgh, PA 15222 (412) 261-7165

Pueblo

Majestic Building
720 North Main St.
Pueblo, CO 81003
(303) 544-3142

San Francisco

Room 1023
Federal Office Building
450 Golden Gate Ave.
San Francisco, CA 94102
(415) 556-0643

Seattle

Room 194
Federal Office Building
915 Second Ave.
Seattle, WA 98174
(206) 442-4270

Washington, DC

Government Printing Office
710 North Capitol St.
Washington, DC 20402
(202) 275-1091

Room 1604, 1st Floor
U.S. Department of Commerce
14th and E Sts., NW
Washington, DC 20230
(202) 377-3527

2817 N. Lobby
U.S. Department of State
21st and C Sts., NW
Washington, DC 20520
(202) 632-1437

Every state, like the federal government, has a central location for storing historical records of all descriptions. These include state documents, county records, local and state histories, newspapers published within the state, even old telephone books for listings in the state from the past. And there's more.

Write to the address given in the back of this book for your state's archives (or those in the state of search), asking what material is available, whom to contact for different types of material, whether there's a historical society located in your area of search, and so on. You may be dealing with several states. Keep in mind that each may have different policies and procedures.

One word of advice: In writing for assistance, indicate that you are undertaking genealogical research, rather than searching for a relinquished child or a birthparent. (This goes when seeking aid at virtually all government levels, except when you are working directly to open records sealed to you.) State archives have been helping genealogists for years. Their staffs are experienced in this area and know where to find needed references; they know where to locate whatever state census records exist, and they'll be able to direct you to old voter registration lists.

State archives are a prime source of information for searchers. It's likely you'll have occasion to refer to this source at some point in your search.

Genealogy Resources

Genealogy is the study of family history—tracing one's roots. Obviously the search for a relinquished child or a birthparent is in a very real sense a form of genealogical research, although a distinction of sorts is commonly maintained between search and genealogy. Genealogists and adoptee/birthparent searchers have the same goals: reconstructing the past, locating missing relatives, and completing a family line. Many searchers find that genealogy in the broader sense provides an added dimension to their search, as well as aids in development of general search techniques.

Then consider this: If you are a birthparent, what nicer gift to give your found child (now an adult) than a detailed biological family tree? You might have information available from family members that would prove impossible for your child to obtain.

Consider also spending time collecting background data on your child's other birthparent. This does not mean you have to open direct contact with that person if he or she is someone with whom you no longer maintain any relationship. Pursue this task via open public records. If you were an unwed birthmother, you may be the only one who knows your child's birthfather— his name may not even appear on the original birth certificate. In this case, you will be the only person who can lead your child to a discovery of his or her full birth heritage.

Adoptees can begin to construct a family history once they have just one family member's name—a birth name of their own, a birthparent's name, a grandparent's name. Few people can imagine the feeling an adoptee experiences the first time he or she enters a name on the family tree. I recall the tremendous joy and encouragement I got from even the smallest notation on a work sheet or family history chart. What inner excitement when, for the first time, listening to others discuss their cultural background, I could smile and refer to my English-Scottish birth heritage.

Basic Reference Aids

I won't go into depth here on genealogy—there are already a number of good reference sources you can turn to for a comprehensive overview of this field of study. *Discover Your Ancestors: A Quest for Your Roots, Simplified Genealogy for Americans,* and *Family History for Fun and Profit* are three books that serve as good introductions.

There are several periodicals specifically aimed at those interested in genealogy. *The Genealogical Helper* is a magazine issued bimonthly by Everton Publishers, Inc., P.O. Box 368, Logan, UT 84321. One feature of this magazine is a regular column called "Missing Folk Finder." The editor describes this column as a section "devoted to modern genealogical families. It includes helpful information and requests for information on persons presumed still living." And isn't that what you want?

Another magazine for genealogists is *The Family Finder,* which describes itself as "a query magazine designed to help you find others researching the same family lines as you." It is published by a division of Anderson Publishing Company, P.O. Box 31097, Omaha, NB 68131. Check a periodicals directory at your local library for other magazines or newsletters that come out in the area of genealogy. Other genealogists will also be able to tell you of additional helpful material of this sort. Costs for running ads in *The Family Finder* and *The Genealogical Helper* can be found in Chapter 3.

There are several genealogists who have compiled lists of those known to have been on orphan trains that came across the United States in the late 1800s and early 1900s. Interested persons should write to either Orphan Registry, 5843 Grant St., Omaha, NB 68104, or S.W. Adult Adoptees Association, Rt. 2, Oak Crest Estates, Rogersville, MO 65742.

Ask your local librarian when and where the nearest historical or genealogical society meets, or have him or her point you to the *Directory of Historical Societies and Agencies.* Then attend a meeting and find out what the group's focus is when it comes to historical or genealogical research activities. You may find a group very helpful to you—I have always found genealogists very helpful and willing to share advice. Most genealogy groups periodically present beginning genealogy workshops. These will help you with research techniques that will prove of use in your present search as well as equip you to become an amateur genealogist.

You can also write to the American Association for State and Local

History, 1400 8th Ave. South, Nashville, TN 37203, for the name of a historical society near you. The AASLH also offers for sale several inexpensive
pamphlets that might prove of use. *Genealogical Research: A Basic Guide* and
Methods of Research for the Amateur Historian are two you may want to
acquire. The cost, at this writing, is $1.00 per pamphlet (or 75 cents if you are
an AASLH member). You might also note the *Indexing Local Newspapers* and
Using Consultants Effectively pamphlets available from the AASLH at the
same cost.

In addition to the above-mentioned genealogical resources, I've recently
learned of a new publication called *Open A.R.M.S Quarterly,* which began
publication in 1981. Its purpose is to present a newsletter to those involved in
a search. This is an interesting publication and valuable aid.

You may place ads in this newsletter listing the information you seek, in
the hope that other searchers across the nation may have a source of reference
you would find useful. These ads are broken down into two types: Search Ads,
which are listed under the specific month the adoptee or relinquished child was
born, and Name Search, which lists ads for specific names.

At this writing a $6.00 charge covers a one-year subscription (four issues).
A $10.00 charge covers the same subscription, plus your ad run in all four
issues. Query letters or subscriptions should be addressed to Open A.R.M.S,
P.O. Box 1522, North Platte, NB 69101, Attention Publisher-Editor Bob
O'Dell.

Census Records

Most searchers will not have to use extensive genealogical research to
locate current relatives, but some will have to go quite far back in time in order
to arrive at a present name and address. One adoptee I know discovered the
name of a great-grandfather—he was a minor celebrity in a small town. She
searched through census records to discover his children's names, and through
more current records traced her family to its living members.

Before you try to review census records, learn something about them.
Check out several books on genealogy and read through the sections explaining
census records. Your local historical/genealogy society may also have material
that can help here.

Federal census records are housed in the National Archives, with copies
in each of the branch archives. Anyone may examine these records after a
seventy-five-year time lapse. Census records have been maintained for every
decade since 1790. Except for the 1890 census records, which were destroyed
by fire and water damage in 1921, all are still on file. Copies are also available

from state archives in many cases, and at libraries established by the Church of Jesus Christ of Latter Day Saints (the Mormon Church).

Many genealogists and states have published indexes to sections of the federal censuses (and to censuses on the state level). Check your genealogy library to see if there are any available there for the state and the time period sought. Genealogical magazines will advertise individuals who have indexed certain records and will provide you that information at a slight charge.

An index for the federal census record will list the roll of microfilm needed for a given person in a given town. Some indexes will list all information found on the film. You may view these films at many state archives, all federal archives, or at Latter Day Saints (LDS) Church libraries. You can also ask for film to be made available to you through interlibrary loan. You can even purchase copies of film from the National Archives at a cost, at this writing, of $13.00 per roll. If you have the roll number you need, write to the National Archives or one of its branches (see the address list earlier in this chapter). If you wish only the single entry from a roll of film, this can be ordered for $2.00, using form GSA-7029.

You can also send in an Application for Search of Census Records (form BC-600) to the U.S. Department of Commerce, Bureau of Census, Pittsburg, KA 66762. The fee to search, at this writing, is $7.50 per name, and there's an additional $1.00 charge if the person is found and you want a copy of the census record sent you.

Do not neglect state census records. Many states have compiled these in years between federal censuses. For a record of those taken, order a copy of *State Censuses, 1790–1948* from a GPO bookstore. *State Censuses: An Annotated Bibliography of Censuses Taken after the Year 1790 by States and Territories of the United States, Index to Census Schedules in Printed Form,* and *Search & Research* are other reference guides through which you can discover records held on the state level.

The Church of Jesus Christ of Latter Day Saints (the Mormon Church)

The emphasis that the Mormons place on the documentation of family lines has resulted in vast genealogical holdings. The Salt Lake City Temple headquarters of the LDS Church contains the largest collection of family histories in the world. They have more than one million rolls of microfilm, and the Temple computer file index has more than thirty-five million names recorded.

There is an LDS branch library in every state. These libraries are open to everyone, LDS Church members and nonmembers alike, and there is no charge to visit and use materials kept there. There will be a volunteer ready to help you make effective use of the library's resources. I have yet to hear of any discriminatory treatment between LDS Church members and nonmembers, either at a branch library or in correspondence with Temple headquarters.

Your local LDS library will have rolls of microfilmed genealogical records available for review there. These will only partially duplicate the massive collection housed at Salt Lake City. However, any roll available at Temple headquarters in Salt Lake City can be ordered on loan at a cost, at this writing, of $2.25 per roll. When the film you request arrives, you can view it at the LDS branch library through which you ordered it. Branch libraries will also order census records from federal or state archives for you. The cost to order these is 75 cents each.

Each LDS library will have Temple Ordinance Indexes Request forms available. These forms request information from the Temple files, the computer file index, and family group archive records. There is a $1.00 fee to check each name. If the name you need is on file, for this fee you'll receive any information held by the LDS Church. You might receive details on census records, family histories, or references occurring in any published book or survey. Whatever the information that is forthcoming, it may provide you a useful lead to pursue further.

If you find you need or want to pursue your search at least in part via genealogy, the resources of the LDS Church can prove enormously useful. Unfortunately, LDS branch libraries do not participate in interlibrary loan with public libraries, so you will have to visit the LDS branch library to make use of its resources.

Special Sources for Native Americans

When Native Americans are adopted, they do not lose their tribal rights, which the United States government recognizes as their right of inheritance. Membership in a tribe is established by an individual's lineage. Eligibility varies from tribe to tribe, but persons of Indian descent, and this includes Aleuts and Eskimos, should check their tribal roll.

For the purpose of establishing tribal affiliation, Native American adoptees come under federal jurisdiction. U.S. Public Law 95-608, Title III—*Recordkeeping, Information Availability, and Timetables* clearly states that adoption decrees shall show tribal affiliation and name of tribe of the adopted child.

Section 107, Title I, of this same law declares, "... any Indian who has reached age 18 who was the subject of an adoptive placement, [is entitled] to find out his or her tribal affiliation and any other information that might be necessary to protect any rights flowing from that affiliation."

Further, U.S. Public Law 95-608, Title III, Section 301(a), "requires the State court to provide the Secretary [of the Interior] with a copy of the final decree or order of adoption of an Indian child plus information about the tribal affiliation of the child, the names and addresses of the biological parents and adoptive parents, and the identity of any agency having files or information relating to the adoptive placement. This information is not to be subject to the Freedom of Information Act."

To become aware of your rights as an Native American, you should contact The Bureau of Indian Affairs, Interior Building, 19th and C Sts., NW, Washington, DC 20242, and ask for a copy of the Indian Child Welfare Act of 1978 and any amendments or other laws which may have been enacted since this writing.

Special Sources for Black Americans

There are now many books and catalogues published to aid blacks with genealogy. In the past searching through genealogical records was difficult for blacks because materials were hard to obtain or information had not been compiled.

The National Archives publishes a catalogue, *Black Studies,* which includes actual letters, educational reports, land titles, marriages, and much more. There are many names and families listed in this study. Contact the National Archives and request information about RG 105, Bureau of Refugees, Freedmen, and Abandoned Lands. Ask them to send you the following: *Documents Pertaining to Black Workers Among the Records of the Department of Labor, Black Servicemen, Free Black Heads of Families in First Census of the United States,* and any other related documents.

Depending on what information you seek, *Index to the Compiled Service Records of Volunteer Union Soldiers who Served with the U.S. Colored Troops and Negroes in the Service of the U.S., 1639-1866* may be of interest to you.

Your library will have several genealogy books with chapters devoted to black Americans. Certainly Alex Haley's *Roots* (New York: Doubleday, 1976) would be a valuable and interesting text to read. *How to Find Your Family Roots* by Timothy F. Beard and Denise Demong (New York: McGraw-Hill, 1978) lists several societies devoted to black genealogy.

Special Sources for Mexican Americans

State census records can be of special value to Mexican Americans. Contact your state archives to discover the years censuses were taken and if Spanish and Mexican censuses were compiled in addition to state censuses.

Federal and state census records use the Soundex Coding System. This is especially valuable to Mexican Americans, as it provides a solution to the problem of variant spellings and similar-sounding names. A more complete guide to understanding the Soundex Coding System is below.

In addition to those information sources mentioned throughout this book, Mexican Americans should take special note of Catholic Church records. These records were often well kept and can be easily found by today's searchers. If you know the area of your search, it would be advisable to make church contact on a local level. Your private, state, or governmental agency will tell you the church affiliation of the birthparents and the adoptive parents.

Soundex Classification

The Soundex classification system is one used by the National Archives and numerous genealogical libraries. It is also used by a number of reunion registries, notably the International Soundex Reunion Registry (see Chapter 8).

The Soundex system codes names alphabetically by initial letter and by sounds following. The code comes out as one letter followed by three numbers. The letter is the first letter of the surname (last name); the numbers represent the sound combinations of the following letters in the name. This system provides a way around the problem of variant spellings and similar-sounding names, which otherwise often confuse genealogists. Many libraries will require you to code the name(s) you are looking for before material is given you. Here is a guide to Soundex coding for you.

Soundex Coding Guide

Code Number	Key Letters and Equivalents
1	b, p, f, v
2	c, s, k, g, j, q, x, z
3	d, t
4	l
5	m, n
6	r

The letters *a, e, i, o, u, y, w,* and *h* are *not* coded.

The first letter of the surname is retained—it is *not* given a number code.

A name yielding no code numbers is coded with three zeros following the initial letter. If it yields only one code number, then that is followed by two zeros; two code numbers, by one zero. (See examples below.)

Prefixes to surnames (such as Van, Von, Di, De) are frequently disregarded in alphabetizing and coding.

Regardless of length, each name has one letter followed by three numbers. For names with more than three codable letters following the first letter, only the first three are coded. (See the examples below.)

When double letters appear—or letters bearing the same code number appear together—the two are coded as one letter. (See the examples below.)

Here is a number of sample coded names.

ASKIN	A225
BERKOWITZ	B623
CARON	C650
CLATTERBUCK	C436
DAUB	D100
DAVIES	D120
HANLON	H545
LEE	L000

As you can see, the number of reference resources you can draw on in your search is considerable. During the course of your efforts you will find that some do not provide you assistance in developing or tracking down a lead. But as you sharpen your search techniques and follow the leads that do develop, you'll almost certainly find reference resources that are immensely useful, probably some that are not fully anticipated in discussion here. Each search takes its own path. Except in rare instances, there's inevitably a trace or several traces that you can follow back and then across intervening years to some present connection. There's no guarantee you'll be reunited with a joyous, expectant relinquished child, birthparent, or lost sibling, but the odds are excellent that through your efforts you'll gain more of a sense of connection than exists for you now. And odds are in your favor that you will at least learn the identity of the person or persons separated from you who are your closest blood kin.

5

Beginning to Search:
Primary Sources of Data

Throughout this book it may appear as though particular attention is paid to the location of birthmothers by adoptees, and the location of birthfathers may appear to be treated incidentally. The problem that exists in many cases is that it proves possible to locate a birthfather only after locating the birthmother—and sometimes it's impossible. The fact is that the birthmother had the baby. Her name may appear on hospital records, the original birth certificate, and court records. She necessarily, unavoidably played a part in the relinquishment proceedings. The father, on the other hand, may not be identified in these records. He may not even be aware that he has fathered a child.

Because of the differences between the situation of father and mother at the time of birth, it's easier for the birthfather to escape or miss being identified in the records. Since this is so, if you are searching for your birthparents, you will probably find that there are more leads to the mother than to the father. Sometimes the birthmother will prove the only birthparent you can locate. However, where the records on birth and relinquishment and related information give as complete an indication of the birthfather's identity as of the birthmother's, it may be easier to locate the birthfather, as his name will not have been changed by marriage. The general process of search is the same for both.

Setting Guidelines

Where do you start your search? First, consider what the guidelines to follow in pursuit of information will be. Second, consider how to organize the information you will assemble.

I believe *all* searchers should enter into the search with guidelines individually set. Your plan must begin with an idea of how you will conduct yourself during the entire search. You are undertaking a process where you will inevitably face some conflict of rights. You will have to weigh respect for others' right of privacy against your own right to know. Setting moral guidelines enables you to balance priorities when you're confronted with this conflict.

Getting Organized

It is very important that you be organized in recording and collecting information during your search. You want to take maximum advantage of each fragment of information obtained.

There is excitement and frustration in searching. Almost everything comes in bits and pieces. There may be data that do not provide any clear view of the whole picture alone, but eventually may fit together with other data to provide something of that picture. The more organized you are in recording and collating these bits of data, the more assured you will be that a picture will begin to emerge as soon as possible.

One important organizational tool is a diary of your search. Naturally, you ought to record every piece of information you obtain. This recording is best done in a single notebook in which you enter *every* detail of your search and the results of your discoveries. Make note each time of the date you speak to someone, identify the person clearly by name and position, and write down what this person tells you *and* what he or she refuses to tell you. Jot down what specifically it is that you are asking, whether the person is helpful, and whether this is a source that might be tapped again later. Don't immediately make judgments on what is or is not significant—sometimes the most unlikely fact provides a meaningful lead, although you may not immediately realize that. Also make notes of research you do (this is described in Chapter 4, on doing research).

Your search is likely to be a months-long process, and it's through your search diary that you'll develop a sense of direction on where to turn for the next piece of information you feel you need. Periodic review of seemingly unrelated bits of fact can reveal some kind of pattern. Keeping all papers together in one convenient diary minimizes the risk that important details will be overlooked in any such review. And being as detailed as possible about dates, names, addresses, positions, and so on facilitates reestablishment of contacts or development of alternate contacts as either proves necessary. There's nothing quite so frustrating as knowing you've been in contact with someone you'd some weeks later like to speak to or write again but don't recall how to get in touch with.

Maintain a complete, organized document file. This will save you many hours of rummaging through scraps of paper kept here and there—you'll be able immediately to locate documents needed for further reference.

Make copies of all letters written. Use your copy to make notes about the reply or about a follow-up letter or telephone conversation at a later date. Use a section of your diary for a calendar of correspondence, noting the date, name, and purpose of each letter. This provides you a convenient checklist of sources solicited and of responses still pending. When a letter is answered by letter, file the reply together with your original letter and enter the date, name, and substance of the response on your checklist. When dealing with an organization or agency, be alert to the name of the party responding. Is that person's title or address different from the one you used?

In addition to letters, you'll be dealing with official documents. When you obtain certified copies of these for yourself (as opposed to photocopies that are not certified), treat these with the same care you give to other official documents in your possession (birth certificates, stock certificates, deeds of title, and so on). I recommend storage in a secure location, such as a safe-deposit box. Make photocopies to hold in your home files. You can annotate, underline, or otherwise highlight information on these, without risk of defacing a document you may later need to produce for official purposes.

Virtually all official documents include an identifying docket, file, case, or record number. Get in the habit of noting such numbers for your records. The same numbers may tie into another relevant document at a later date, serving as the crucial data that link you to an important name or person.

Much of the correspondence you initiate will relate to locating and obtaining documents that provide vital leads to the person you wish to locate. Your attention to organizational details can to some extent ease gaining access to these. Certainly your approach to bureaucrats and others charged with administering or safeguarding documentary sources should be carefully considered as well. Throughout this and other chapters I have provided sample letters and forms to be used as guidelines in composing letters specifically directed to serving your information-gathering needs. Recognize that these must be adapted to your particular situation—you will have to alter elements of content to reflect what you know and/or what you hope to learn. Simply copying the letters provided here, omitting changes that would make them apply more specifically to you, can defeat the purpose for which they are intended.

Always write your letters, even to hospitals, courts, and agencies, with the idea of finding a helpful source. The same holds true when phoning. When you locate a sympathetic person, ask if he or she knows anyone else who may prove of assistance. Leave an opening for individuals to contact you. This means spending time on your letters, making the effort to anticipate reactions, and considering all circumstances. Would a clerk be more helpful if asked for aid in a naive or knowing fashion? Do you need to have your letter notarized? Should it be sent by certified mail, return receipt requested? Is a check or money order necessary? Would a typewritten letter appear too formal or a short, handwritten letter too informal?

Rochefoucauld once said, "Some disguised falsehoods represent the truth so well that it would be bad judgment not to be deceived by them." Keep this in mind. Most of your letters will be written with the intention of proving a relationship with a member of your birth family. You may want to include in your letters meaningless statements that appear to affirm such a relationship —"I had three brothers and one sister"; "We were all born in another state"; "My grandmother said she came from Virginia"; "My mother would never tell us her age, so I don't know the year of her birth." Statements along these lines aren't required for obtaining certain records, but they may serve the useful purpose of presenting an impression that you know more than you do.

At times it can help to play dumb. When you are asked for a date of death and insert the response "not living," a clerk may laugh and comment to a colleague on your ridiculous answer, but may then also provide the information himself or herself.

When writing to a private, religious, or governmental agency or individual, try to put yourself into the position of the person receiving the letter. You know that person will feel somewhat constrained by the limits the law imposes on release of information. Consider whether a generalized request for information may gain you more than one that is narrowly specific and leaves less room for interpretation. Also keep in mind that some letters may win more attention if typed and put in proper form, while others may be more effective if kept brief. These are the only guidelines I can offer. If your letter is requesting only information, keep it simple and write it by hand. More formal or notarized letters should be typewritten and include all the information you need. Try not to mention searching unless you have to. When asking for nonidentifying information ask for more than you plan to get; ask for everything you can think of.

If a letter doesn't produce the information desired, you may wish to try again at a later date with a different type of letter. Perhaps the same letter addressed to a different person or title might achieve more results. Try to get a feel of your state and the policies of the private, religious, or governmental agency involved. Use your instincts. Consider whether it's best to push with a demanding inquiry or to back off a while. Will you get further claiming an urgent medical need to know, or would a chatty, informal genealogical search request be more productive? In most cases there is no one right letter. The sample letters are only departure points, pointing you in a direction for obtaining records and facts needed.

When it comes to following up leads or making a second or third try at obtaining information that isn't readily forthcoming, your search diary and document file will prove invaluable for clues on which way to turn next. In any case, the degree to which you organize yourself, coupled with persistence and imagination, will prove important in obtaining records and other data needed.

Recollections

Once you've organized yourself—set your guidelines, developed a systematic approach to information gathering and evaluation, and alerted yourself to the problems that can arise when seeking information—you're ready to begin the actual search. That beginning is best made with a concentrated effort to recall and sort out any information that may be stored in your own mind. Sit down and list any bits of information you can recall. What were you told over the years? What possible telltale comments do you remember having been made to you or within your earshot?

Since you don't know at this point what information will help you and what won't, *list everything.* Trying at the beginning to separate fact from fiction can only be speculative. There's no guarantee that any recollection will produce the lead to the individual(s) you are seeking, but you have to start somewhere, so you begin by using the scraps of data you already have.

What kind of recollections should you tune into? Anything that possibly relates or refers to a connection with the person sought. You may, for example, have heard casual remarks along the lines of:

- Your mother was a college student.
- Your father worked for the state highway department.
- You came from a good Baptist home.
- Your child went to a couple with a college education.
- The child's adoptive father was a doctor.

These can all be clues. Work to recall simple and seemingly unconnected statements. Even if they don't immediately put you on the track of a substantive lead, they can be useful as pieces of the puzzle you're working to solve.

Look back also into your memory and impressions of what was happening at the time of adoption or relinquishment. Do you remember names of people around you that were in any way involved? Would friends you are no longer in touch with or family members you've lost contact with have some memory of events at that time? Naturally, if you were adopted as an infant, you won't have a personal recollection of the circumstances surrounding your adoption, but dig in your memory for family friends and relatives that were part of your life as a child, whom you've since forgotten. When were you last in touch? Is it possible to contact them? Birthparents or adoptive parents, in addition to turning to their own memories, will want to take the same approach to relocating key people from the past. Try to reconstruct events and conversations. Besides family and friends, was there any involvement on the part of a doctor, attorney, social worker, nurse, or clergyman?

If you were adopted as a young child rather than as an infant, you may retain some impression of events at the time, even if there are no focused memories. You may recall some image of a person you can't fully identify or associate with a specific event or place. Make note of your impressions. Complementary details may come to mind subsequently to fill in a vague image more clearly. You may be able to validate an impression as others provide you related pieces of information. Do you remember a hair color? A scent of perfume? Singing or music?

Of course, the more others can help you with their recollections, the more of a foundation you have for developing a sense of direction in your search. Again, note all details, whether they seem immediately valuable or not. Chance remarks about something recalled may come only once, particularly since that something is part of a chain of events that may be decades past. As an adoptee, if your adoptive parents are to be told of your search, you should have a long talk with them. If you are a birthparent, perhaps your parents will recall important details. Record any names they might remember. Ask specific questions. (I've provided a list later in this chapter of questions you might want to list when speaking with a social worker. You can use that same list here.) Help them jog their memory. Adoptive parents are frequently given some information about the home their child came from, and birthparents about the home their child went to. Much of the information given at the time was correct. The problem may not be in the information given—it may be in the information *not* given.

Often adoptees find their adoptive parents reluctant to remember the past. Only when the adoptee comes upon information do the adoptive parents suddenly remember. In one case reported to me, the adoptive parents were left alone for a few minutes by a social worker coordinating the adoption formalities. During his absence, both quickly scanned the relinquishment papers left lying on the desk, discovering the name of the birthmother. Once outside, they both separately wrote down the name, then compared them to be sure they had the exact spelling. Both had copied the same name. They kept the vital information and never mentioned it until their son had initiated his search and began asking questions.

Most adoptive parents will not have this information, but some do, and many will have other pieces of useful information. One searcher discovered a name given and changed in court proceedings on her adoption. It turned out to be the last name of the birthmother. The searcher then learned her adoptive parents were told at the time of adoption that the birthmother was attending a local college just before the birth. By checking past student records of this last name for several years, the birthmother's full name was discovered. It proved simple to locate the birth family, who still resided in a nearby community. Through the birth family, the birthmother was located.

As a rule, recollections from the past provide the most leads to learning a name. For that reason it's important to gather all recollections available to you. If you've saved correspondence from the past—or someone in your family has—it may be worthwhile reviewing those old letters for mention of people who could be of further aid. Do you or does someone else have a diary from previous years that may record an impression or details now forgotten? The more you can learn from an effort to recall the past, the more surely you are on the road to the identity of your relinquished child or birthparent.

Adoption/Relinquishment Papers

The process either of adoption or of relinquishment is an important one to the parents involved. It may be that adoptive parents have somewhere retained a copy of the court proceedings finalizing adoption. Or you as a birthparent may have retained a copy of your relinquishment papers—or, if you were a minor at the time, your parents or guardian may have these records. If these documents are not in your possession, ask whether your parents have them. (They may also have copies of correspondence with an attorney, hospital, or maternity home; a copy of your baptismal certificate; and/or on very rare occasions even original birth certificates.) Ask for whatever they have.

As an adoptee, your adoption papers will be the official court proceedings about your case. In many states, the copy that is available to you will have sections blacked out to conceal "identifying information." In others there is a chance that your birth name may be indicated. For example, some proceedings include a legal change of name, in which case the name at birth may have been recorded in the proceedings. There's a slight chance that it may not have been blacked out or has been only partially blacked out. In other instances, however, the change of name may be recorded as from "baby girl/boy" to the name given by the adoptive parents. Still, you should ask for a copy, as there are instances where highly valuable information will be disclosed. If your court proceedings do list your birth name, you can then write for your birth certificate in that name. A few adoptees have, in this way, by mistake—that is, in spite of official obstacles—received their original certificates identifying the birthparents.

A note of warning on birth names: Under law you may give your child any name you wish, whether you are giving the child up for adoption or not. Usually the first name is given for sentimental reasons, and the last may be either the birthmother's family name or the birthfather's family name, even if they are not married. It can also be a variation on the spelling of either parent's last name; it can even be completely made up.

One adoptee was told by her adoptive parents that her birthmother came from a small town outside Tulsa, Oklahoma. This searcher had also obtained her birth name from the adoption papers. She searched through telephone books and old city directories for all outlying areas during the years immediately preceding and following her adoption. The indicated family name was not listed, but she picked up on a variant spelling of it that always appeared where the spelling she was looking for should be. She took a long shot and contacted several people with that name and was, as a result of this clever deduction and with the admitted aid of luck and a sympathetic blood relation, able to track down her birthmother.

Besides the possibility—if a vague one—that a critical name reference will be given, you *will* find other important information. You will be able to note a docket or case number, which can tie in with other records held elsewhere. You will see the lawyer's name who was involved with the adoption, the name of the presiding judge, and an identification of any private, religious, or governmental agency involved as intermediary in the adoption—which will include reference to any private, religious, or governmental agency that may have had custody of you in an interim period between relinquishment and adoption. Each of these references is a potential link to the individual you are hoping to identify.

In addition to the actual adoption decree, the courts may have a separately filed petition to adopt, an interlocutory decree, or an independent petition for name change. Consequently, you may in your request for court records want to indicate your desire for obtaining all records available relative to your adoption and change of name. (In the case of a private adoption, there may also be a court investigator's report or home study.)

Relinquishment papers do not usually prove as helpful a source of new information as adoption papers. They will not have any information on the child's new name or about the adoptive parents. They are signed and filed *before* the adoption takes place, and what information is given is almost always exactly what the birthmother or birthfather knew and told the agency. But relinquishment papers do list names and dates, and docket/case numbers that are helpful for cross reference. Only birthparents have a right to request copies of the relinquishment papers. Adoptees/adoptive parents, who would be the most served by the information given, do not have access to them.

When writing for copies of adoption or relinquishment papers, always send your letters notarized. Each state will have a charge for providing the document(s), so you will probably need to write or call to find the fee amount. Note that sending a certified check subjects you to less delay than sending a personal check. Never send cash. The appendix at the back of this book indicates the court of jurisdiction to address yourself to in your state (or the state of jurisdiction, if you've since moved) for requesting court documents.

Birth Records

Birth certificates are valuable documents for searchers, because they specify all the particulars of birth, most importantly the names of the parents. But it gets complicated for adoptees, because all adoptees have an altered birth certificate (called an altered registration or given some other official name in certain states). The original certificate is sealed away when the final order of adoption is issued. Until then a birthparent may routinely request a copy of the child's birth certificate. After relinquishment, the birthparent will find it difficult to obtain this, as the original copy is separated from the general registry file and sealed. The birthparent will rarely have any idea of the name on the new, altered certificate replacing the original in the general file and is not entitled to a copy of the altered certificate.

In spite of the difficulty, birthparents should be aware they are entitled to a child's original birth certificate. If they did not request it at the time of birth, they can do so now. If they are initially refused by the vital statistics department, as more than likely they will be, they should appeal to the court of jurisdiction. (See state reference list in the appendix.) I have provided a sample

SAMPLE 1

LETTER FOR BIRTHPARENT REQUESTING
CHILD'S ORIGINAL BIRTH CERTIFICATE

Date

Court of Jurisdiction
Judge (if known)
Address
City, State

Regarding: Release of original birth certificate of relinquished child.

Your Honor:

I did not request a birth certificate at the time of the birth of (give name listed on original certificate). I would now like to request a full transcript of this document.

I am not asking for the amended birth certificate, nor for any identifying information—only the original certificate. If I am refused, please cite the specific law that prohibits the release of this certificate. (1)

    Birthparent: (Give name used on relinquishment papers.)
                Relationship to relinquished child:
                Date of relinquishment: (if known)
    Birth child: (Give name listed on original birth certificate.)
                Date of birth:
                Hospital (or maternity home):
                City and state: (2)

Sincerely,

(Your signature)
Address
City, State

Have a notary public certify your signature.

Other Possible Inclusions:
    1. *Add:* I am requesting this document for judicial needs. I am in the process of making out a will and need this information. (You may list any reasons you find acceptable.)
    2. *Add:* Any other identifying information you have.

Note: This letter must be personalized to fit your particular case.

letter that birthparents can adapt for requesting an original birth certificate (Sample 1). That certificate will not be particularly helpful in providing leads to the relinquished child, but it is an essential proof of parentage that a birthparent may at some later date be required to supply. It proves a link exists, even if it doesn't locate the individual sought.

One additional note to birthparents. Even if a reunion takes place and all parties are legal adults, many states require a court action to obtain an original birth certificate. Adoptees may be unable to open their records and thus obtain their original certificate. What nicer gift to the adoptee than a certified copy of the original birth certificate? One birthmother received a copy of her relinquished child's original certificate and, along with a letter explaining the circumstances surrounding the birth, sealed this information in a letter. She then wrote the adoption agency, including a waiver of confidentiality along with the sealed letter addressed to her relinquished child. In this way, she hoped, if any inquiries were made, the agency would pass on the necessary information.

As an adoptee or adoptive parent, you are in most states legally entitled to receive only a copy of the altered birth certificate. Altered means exactly that. The birthparents' names will have been deleted and replaced by the adoptive parents' names. However, you can rely on certain facts of your birth to be accurate—that is, in most cases: sex, race, date of birth, hospital, place of birth. But it is not unheard of for adoptees to discover a two-, three-, or four-day difference between the actual birth date and that recorded on the altered certificate. Keep this in mind if, in relying on a date correlation with other records, you find yourself dead-ended. Also familiarize yourself with the applicable state laws, as the practice of alteration varies among them. In Georgia, for example, you may find virtually everything altered—hospital, attending doctor, town of birth. Fortunately, most states avoid this extreme.

If you've tracked down your birth name, you can make a stab at sending away for your birth certificate in your birth name. As much information as possible should be included in your letter of request—this is true whether you are requesting an original or altered certificate. States will want an indication of your full name (adoptive or original, depending on the circumstances), sex, race, parents' names (adoptive or original), date of birth (month, day, year), community of birth, hospital, statement of purpose for which the certificate is needed, and your relationship to the recorded person. I've included here a sample letter for those who are writing in their birth name and have very little information (see Sample 2). Obtaining the altered certificate should be routine for the adoptee. In either case, when writing always ask for a certified, full copy of your certificate.

SAMPLE 2

LETTER FOR ADOPTEE REQUESTING ORIGINAL
BIRTH CERTIFICATE USING BIRTH NAME

Date

Department of Vital Statistics
Address
City, State

Records Clerk:
   I need to obtain a copy of my birth certificate. I was born as (give birth name) at (name and address of hospital) on (give date of birth). (1–4)
   I am enclosing a check (or money order) in the amount of (amount stipulated by the state).

Sincerely,

(your signature, using birth name)
Address
City, State

Other Possible Inclusions:
   1. *Add:* My mother's name was (if known).
   2. *Add:* I was born at (give time if known).
   3. *Add:* I weighed (give weight if known).
   4. *Add:* Due to a separation in our family, I am unable to supply you with all necessary facts.

Note: This is one letter you do not want to present in a legal or formal style. It is a "shot in the dark" and more than likely will not produce the desired results. It is used in the hope that your birth certificate was not sealed or that a mistake will be made in allowing its release. Keep it simple, and insert only the information needed. You may want to consider writing this letter by hand rather than typing it.

Many states, if not most, require the individual requesting a birth certificate, whether altered or original, to be the person listed on it, with some allowance made for parents. A notarized signature must be presented. When I and my husband, who is not adopted, applied for a copy of our birth certificates in order to obtain a passport, we both had to request the certificates in person or have our signatures notarized (for California and Tennessee, respectively). However, when I requested the birth certificates for my children, then both minors, I did not have to present their signatures (California).

   Because it is occasionally possible for an adult to request a birth certificate for a parent, I've provided a sample letter for that eventuality (see Sample 3).

SAMPLE 3

LETTER FOR ADOPTEE REQUESTING BIRTH CERTIFICATE
FOR A BIRTHPARENT

Date

Department of Vital Statistics
Address
City, State

Dear Registrar:

I need to obtain a full copy of the birth certificate for the following. (1)
Name: (full name plus race and sex)
Born: (month and day if known), City of _____, County of _____, State
    of _____
Mother/Father: (include this information if known)
Residence: (include this information if known)
Relationship to the above: (as it is)
Reason for request: Judicial need (2, 3)

Enclosed is a money order (or certified check, personal check) to cover the amount stipulated. (4)

Sincerely,

(your signature)
Address
City, State

Other Possible Inclusions:

1. *Substitute:* My sister and I require a *full transcript* of the record of birth of our (mother, father).
2. *Substitute:* I am starting a genealogical search and need the aforementioned certificate as part of my family record.
3. *Substitute:* I am documenting my genealogical family tree for membership in the Daughters of the American Revolution.
4. *Precede this line with:* I am unable to supply exact data with respect to the above birth, due to family separation in my early infancy.

Note: Many states will require this letter to be notarized, and some will require that you establish proof of relationship.

You may need to request this information on a form provided by your state department of vital statistics. If so, write and request this form and any that may be needed to request information on marriage, divorce, and/or death.

The birth certificate in this case will be useful in confirming birth name and birth date of the parent, two pieces of information that are often essential when working to trace an individual via other officially maintained records.

When writing for birth records, address yourself to the bureau of records or vital statistics indicated in the appendix for your (or your child's) birth state. (You can also request the pamphlet "Where to Write for Birth and Death Records, United States and Outlying Areas," published by the U.S. Department of Health and Human Services and available from the Superintendent of Documents, U.S. Government Printing Office, Washington, DC 20402, or from a U.S. Government Printing Office bookstore in your area. The code reference number is PHS 80-1142, and the charge, as of this writing, is $1.50.) States will indicate a charge for providing the birth record, which you should pay by cashier's check, money order, or personal check.

Agency Records

If your adoption/relinquishment was handled by a county agency, private agency, or religious agency still in operation, your records should be housed at that agency. If you know the name of this private, religious, or governmental agency, you should be able to locate the address and a telephone number through the local telephone directory or long-distance directory assistance. You can also contact the appropriate state agency (see appendix) for information on where your files are kept and whom you should contact regarding information contained in those files.

If your adoption/relinquishment was handled by a state agency, a private agency that is no longer in business, or privately through a doctor or attorney, your files will be at the state level. To direct your letter of inquiry to the individual in charge of the proper state department or bureau, check a current *Book of the States* or other state informational reference available in your local library to discover the name and title of the person to contact. You can also call whatever information number is listed in your local telephone directory, either for the state government as a whole or for the particular department. It is not necessary to address your letter to an individual; if you use the state agency address given in the appendix, the information will be directed to the adoption counselor in charge. Sample 4 is a letter requesting assistance from a state department, for getting in touch with whatever agency it is that actually holds your records.

There will be many questions you will want to ask of your private, religious, or governmental agency, or of the state adoption records administrator.

SAMPLE 4

LETTER FOR ADOPTEE REFERRING TO A STATE AGENCY FOR AID IN LOCATION OF LOCAL OR PRIVATE AGENCY RECORDS

Date

Post-Adoption Consultant
State Agency
Address
City, State

Dear Consultant:

I need to discover the name and location of the agency that handled my adoption. Please include information if this agency is still in operation and, if not, where my files may be found.

Name: (give adoptive name)
Date of birth: (as you know it)
Sex and race:
Name of adoptive parents:
Court record number: (if known)

I appreciate your time and effort on this matter.

Sincerely,

(your signature) Also known as: (list maiden name if married female)
Address
City, State

Note: You may wish to enclose a photocopy of your amended birth certificate.

After all, you've been wondering about your adoption or your child's post-relinquishment history for a long time. Organize your approach to the information you want to get. Are you really concerned only about medical information, or do you want to know everything—names and dates if possible, and whether anyone else has been in contact with the agency regarding your file?

Most private, religious, or governmental agencies follow the policy of prohibiting release of what is termed *identifying information.* This, as we've observed in Chapter 1, is any specific information that leads directly either to a birthparent or to a relinquished child—particularly names and addresses. However, there's considerable room for interpretation on what amounts to identifying information, with some agencies or individual social workers holding back information as "identifying" that others will more routinely release.

What's the best approach to use when first contacting the private, religious, or governmental agency? My feeling is that you should take an open approach, stating you wish all information that is in their records. If you are making your request in writing, you should indicate in your letter what you want to know, but be general. Ask for all information. Identify yourself as you are now known. Since the files will be cross-indexed, not knowing your birth name or your child's adoptive name—and you probably won't—should present no problem.

Start out slowly; let yourself get the feel of your social worker. Most likely you will have more than one contact with this social worker, so it's essential you not alienate him or her at the beginning. You don't have to mention any ultimate plan for reunion—start with specifying you want all information. Put the social worker in the position of making the decision on what is or isn't identifying information—don't make it quick and easy for him or her by self-censorship.

If you do not receive everything you want, write again. This letter should ask for everything you can get. Of course, some of your questions will be denied. Try a variant. Ask for names. If you are refused, ask for initials. Is R.A. identifying information? Is there only one R.A.? Couldn't this apply to thousands of people? Ask your social worker to remain silent if a question is true and reply if it is false. A lot can be learned from refusals to answer questions. Be as reasonable in tone and attitude as possible—you want to keep your relationship with your social worker as friendly as possible. But be persistent.

A friend of mine was born in a private maternity home in central Los Angeles. Her adoptive mother could not remember the name of the maternity home, so she requested it in a letter to the state agency holding her files. The agency refused her this information, citing it as "identifying." My friend's adoptive mother (her adoptive father was dead) then wrote again, similarly requesting the name of the maternity home. Again a refusal. Finally my friend sent a "demand letter," asking the agency to cite the applicable law forbidding release of the requested information and restating a request for access to all medical information. At long last the information was released. This indicates to what degree the subjective interpretation of "identifying" can block a searcher and provides an example of how persistence and standing up for one's rights can be important in obtaining data.

The following is a list of questions that can prove valuable in themselves or for stimulating more pointed questions of your own. Be sure you list your own questions. Be guided by what you know and what you want to know.

Adoptees

What were my birthparents' first names?
Were they both living at the time of my adoption?
What was the reason for the relinquishment?
Were my birthparents married to each other?
Was either of them married to someone else?
What medical information is listed?
Has any medical information been updated?
What was the age of my birthparents?
Were there siblings?
What state were my birthparents from? What city?
What was their educational background?
What were their occupations?
Was my birthfather in any branch of the service? What branch? What rank?
What was the order of birth of my birthmother and birthfather?
Were my birth grandparents alive at the time of my birth? What was their attitude?
   Did they participate in the relinquishment/adoption proceedings?
Was either of my birthparents still a minor in age?
What was the coloring of my birthparents' eyes? Hair? And so on.
What was my birthparents' nationality?
What was their religious preference?
Is there anything else you can tell me?

Birthparents

What name—first and last—was given the child?
What type of home did he or she go to?
What was the occupation of the adoptive parents?
How long had they been married?
Were they from the local area?
Were there other children in the family?
Has there been any update on the file?
Were other children adopted by this family? When?
Was the adoption finalized? When? In what court?
Was the child ever in a foster home? When? How many homes?
Were there any other court actions taken regarding this child?
What reason did the adoptive parents give for wanting to adopt?
Have they contacted the agency since finalization of the adoption?
Will your agency or the state recognize a waiver of confidentiality?
Will the state effect a reunion if the adoptee also requests one?
Is there anything else you can tell me?

The list can be virtually endless. When you ask these questions and others, whether by telephone or in person, keep notes. Ask for spellings of names and towns. This will be an emotional time for you, and by recording all facts the likelihood of forgetting or confusing information is minimized. Even if the answering social worker adheres to a narrow interpretation of regulations on identifying information, you stand a good chance of learning something that will prove valuable to your collection of data. Your search diary is important for keeping an organized record of your visits to or calls to the involved agency.

Birthparents are traditionally given much less information about their relinquished children than adoptees are about their birthparents. But it is still, if not more, important to be persistent. For example, you can indicate you wish a letter to be placed in your child's files in the event he or she as an adult decides to research the circumstances of relinquishment. Wouldn't you naturally want to address the child by name?

One birthmother persisted on that course—the letter would be much nicer and more personal if addressed to a person rather than to "baby boy" or to a name given at birth to which the now adult person would have no connection. She was able to obtain the first name—John. The social worker's reasoning was that John by itself wasn't identifying information. The mother later obtained the last initial from the social worker in compliance with a request to remain silent when a statement was true. Valuable information, and yet you can also see that it is nonidentifying—first name and last initial are still only pieces of the puzzle to the identity of one individual out of many John Xs scattered almost anywhere.

In seeking answers to questions, many searchers have learned to ask for assistance from alternate social workers when the person they begin with proves unsympathetic and insists on rigid interpretation of identifying information. Agencies are aware of this, and some have responded by trying to be more specific—and in consequence usually more narrow—in guidelines set for determining what is or is not identifying information. Nevertheless, if the first social worker proves difficult, ask for a different social worker to assist you. Maybe that other social worker will be more sympathetic. Attitudes are changing. Note this comment from former social worker Annette Baron:

> I sat behind the desk facing adoptees scores of times during the past years, and I honestly admit that I cringe now as I recall my attitude and behavior with them. That they remained polite and controlled is an indication of how pitifully eager they were for even the little I told them. I know now because of the many adoptees I have spoken with during my research. They have described their intense anger at that woman, me, who had the power to keep their records from them. The stranger, me, sitting there deciding what facts of their lives she would permit them to know.

Naturally, as long as the laws are restrictive, any social worker or civil servant concerned with established regulations—and each must be—will be constricted. And though some attitudes have very noticeably changed within the past few years, most of the law hasn't. Therefore general policy of administration hasn't either. This remark made by Francis E. Lewis, executive director of the Children's Bureau of South Carolina, in a presentation to the adoptee search group Triad on August 16, 1980, pretty much sums it up:

> Now to the question that is foremost in your minds today. Is Frank Lewis going to be easier to get information out of than was Jo Cannon? The answer is simple ... no. The law of South Carolina has not changed, and no policy of the [Children's] Bureau has changed, and the process for obtaining the nonidentifying information is being carried out in the same manner at this time. The one exception is a procedural change which allows the Bureau to provide the information which a person may request who lives out of South Carolina. The request should be submitted in writing, and we will provide the information in writing to them.

The question of whether information is identifying or nonidentifying will still determine whether individuals writing get answers to the questions they ask. The procedural change requiring submissions of questions in writing eliminates a lot of the flexibility that is possible in telephone conversations. (I recognize that allowing submission of questions in writing is still an advance over allowing no questions at all from out of state.)

Whether your private, religious, or governmental agency proves forthcoming or not, there is one very positive step that you can take to break through the wall of secrecy around your files: Supply the agency involved with a waiver of confidentiality to its records as they pertain to you in the event the child or birthparent you hope to contact is also trying to contact you (see Samples 5 and 6). As the adoption search movement spreads, there is a growing, if still slim, possibility that the person you are seeking will be trying to find you. In your waiver (see the sample provided) you can specify what information is to be released and to whom. Do note that insertion of the waiver into your private, religious, or governmental agency file will not always guarantee information being passed on to your child or birthparent, should he or she be in contact with that agency, too. Many states' laws may fail to make any provision for recognizing the legal effect of a waiver in this situation, so some agencies may not honor it either. Research the situation as it applies to the agency of your adoption/relinquishment. However, as there is a growing awareness of the rights of searchers, there is increasing reason to hope these obstacles will soon disappear.

SAMPLE 5

WAIVER OF CONFIDENTIALITY
AUTHORIZING RELEASE OF INFORMATION FROM
AN ADOPTEE'S AGENCY FILE

This Waiver of Confidentiality Applies to the Following: (1)
Birth name: (if known)
Adoptive name: (list both married and adoptive name if applicable)
Date of birth:
Hospital of birth:
City and state of birth:

To Whom It May Concern:
I wish this letter to be placed in any file(s) held by your agency concerning my adoption and used as authorization to waive the confidentiality guaranteed me under law. This includes the release of any agency records, hospital records, court records, and records surrounding my birth and adoption, including "identifying information." (2)

Further, upon request from either of my birthparents (or siblings, grandparents, or other requesting relatives), I wish a photocopy of this letter sent or given to (him/her/them) and recognize this letter to be my consent and authorization thereto. (3)

Please send a letter informing me of your agency's intent to recognize this waiver and, if I am refused, please cite the state law that prohibits such recognition. (4)

Signed

(your signature)
Address
City, State

Have a notary public certify your signature.

Other Possible Inclusions:
 1. *Add:* This Waiver of Confidentiality applies to the following information as I know it to be true.
 2. *Add:* . . . but excluding any papers listing my adoptive parents' names.
 3. *Add:* I request notification should one or both of my birthparents request this information.
 4. *Add:* If your state requires a specific form for this waiver, please include all necessary information.

Note: This letter may be written to state that you wish for notification of your birthparents' names but you exclude release of yours by the agency if a contact is made from any interested party. You might want to consider sending this letter certified, return receipt requested.

SAMPLE 6

WAIVER OF CONFIDENTIALITY
AUTHORIZING RELEASE OF INFORMATION ON
BIRTHPARENTS TO AN ADOPTEE FROM HIS OR HER
AGENCY FILE

This Waiver of Confidentiality Applies to the Following: (1)
Name: (give name used on relinquishment papers)
Present name: (if name changed by marriage)
Relationship to relinquished child:
Date of relinquishment: (if known)
Court record number: (if known) (2)

Concerning:
Name: (give name listed on original birth certificate)
Date of birth:
Hospital or maternity home and address:

To Whom It May Concern:
I wish this letter to be placed in the adoption file of the above-mentioned relinquished child and used as authorization to waive the confidentiality guaranteed me under law. This includes the release of any agency records, hospital records, court records, and records surrounding the birth and relinquishment, including "identifying information." (3)

Further, upon request from the relinquished child, I wish a photocopy of this letter sent or given to (him/her/them) and recognize this letter to be my consent and authorization thereto. (4)

Please send a letter informing me of your agency's intent to recognize this waiver and, if I am refused, please cite the state law that prohibits such recognition. (5)

Signed

(your signature)
Address
City, State

Have a notary public certify your signature.

Other Possible Inclusions:
1. *Add:* This Waiver of Confidentiality applies to the following information as I know it to be true.
2. *Add any information you may have that will help identify the relinquishment.*
3. *Add:* . . . upon request from the relinquished child or the adoptive parents.
4. *Add:* I request notification should a request be made for this information by the birth child or the adoptive parents.
5. *Add:* If your state requires a specific form for this waiver, please include all necessary information.

You might want to consider sending this letter certified, return receipt requested.

Hospital Records

The hospital records you are primarily concerned with here are those relating to birth. These records serve to confirm a stated date of birth; they should indicate relevant information on medical background of the birthparent(s) and some medical information on the newborn child's state of health; they routinely identify the doctor in attendance during delivery and/or subsequent complications that may have arisen; they will also contain incidental information on the birthparents that may help in any effort to locate either or both of them. The name(s) will, of course, be indicated in the hospital's records, but you may not be allowed to know them, as they constitute "identifying information." Naturally, the records will be more complete on the birthmother. There may be little if any information on the birthfather in cases where the child was born out of wedlock.

For birthparents seeking to trace a relinquished child, there is little information contained in hospital records that might contribute to identification and location of the child in his or her adoptive environment. As with birth certificates, these records will tell you what you essentially already know. However, I encourage all birthparents to obtain a copy of the hospital records relating birth particulars of the relinquished child. There is a slim chance the records will contain a fact relating to the circumstances of relinquishment that you've forgotten. Whether or not this is the case, these records, together with medical information on any health condition affecting you that may be genetically influenced, will be important to your relinquished child. Even if you have no lead toward the identity of that child, you can ask to have the information inserted into his or her agency files in the event he or she seeks information there.

If you are a birthmother, you should request the records pertaining to the birth of your child in the name you used at that time—the birth is, after all, a part of your medical history. Since hospital records are only released to the individual to whom they pertain, birthfathers will find it difficult to obtain them.

For the adoptee, hospital records can provide both important leads to the identity of birthparents and valuable health-related information. Obtain any health-related information you can to alert you to possible health problems to which you may be genetically predisposed. The name of the hospital where you were born should be listed on your altered birth certificate or in the private, religious, or governmental agency papers. In most cases, the name of the hospital will be released to you.

Most hospitals will have your records listed only under your birth name.

Your adoption, after all, took place after the fact of birth. If you have your birth name, send a letter requesting hospital records in that name (see Sample 7). Your letter will need to be notarized, as the hospital may not release records to anyone other than the patient or his or her designated agent (see Sample 8). If the hospital where you were born proves reluctant to release the information, ask your doctor to request the records. If all else fails, you can send a letter to the hospital administration which, when signed by the hospital, serves as formal confirmation of the refusal to provide you with your birth records. Include in the letter a statement that says, "I take full responsibility for not releasing medical information to (your name) and am aware that, if I withhold this information and the aforementioned suffers health problems, I am open to legal action." Send this letter via certified mail, return receipt requested. Keep in mind that this is a letter of last resort. You should not include any threats in your first request. I've prepared an alternate sample letter you can

SAMPLE 7

LETTER FOR AN ADOPTEE REQUESTING
RECORDS FROM THE HOSPITAL OF BIRTH

Date

Hospital
Address
City, State

Attention: Medical Records

I need to have *all* my medical records forwarded to me as soon as possible.

Please include the following: nursery, admission, discharge, and delivery room records, and any other records kept by your hospital recording my birth.

What types of records do you keep, and what are they called? Please list them so that my doctor may review the list and, at a later date, ask for more detailed information.

Name: (give birth name if possible)
Born: (give date)

Thank you for your time and consideration.

Signature: _____ Dated: _____

This letter will need to be notarized.

Note: You may wish to include any personal questions that pertain to your search—time of birth, weight at birth, height at birth, parents' names, name(s) of doctor(s) in attendance, or any other facts that may be on the record.

SAMPLE 8

FORM AUTHORIZING RELEASE OF MEDICAL INFORMATION

I, (give name), hereby authorize my attorney, (give attorney's name), or his agent to inspect, copy, or photostat any and all of my hospital and medical records, and I authorize you or any hospital, doctor, or nurse to supply (him or her) with all information concerning treatment for injury or illness or examination for determination of my general state of health or any other information related to my state of health or that may be contained in my medical record. (1)

_____

(signature)

Address
City, State

This form will need to be notarized.

Other Possible Inclusions:
  1. *Add:* This authorization shall be in effect from (give date) and remain valid through (give date).

Note: If you are designating someone other than an attorney as your agent, your form should reflect authorization to that person as your agent.

Source: From the book *Handbook of Law Office Forms* by Robert Sellers Smith. © 1974 by Robert Sellers Smith. Published by Prentice-Hall, Inc., Englewood Cliffs, New Jersey 07632.

also adapt to your use in the event your hospital refuses you any cooperation (see Sample 9).

Don't assume a hospital will have only one record file on you. Many keep separate nursery, delivery, admission, and/or discharge records. Be sure you ask for all records, under whatever classification they are held.

Your altered birth certificate (if you are an adoptee) or your hospital records or memory (if you are a birthparent) may provide you the name of the attending physician. Many doctors stay in the same area for their entire practicing life, but others relocate. One way to find a current location is to contact the licensing board in the county you are searching. It will release information on the current address, if he or she is deceased, or any revelant information it may have. Another source for locating a practicing physician is the American Medical Association. The local offices will supply you with the same information as the licensing board. Check your local phone book or ask your information operator for the telephone number needed.

If you were adopted as a young child rather than as an infant, check

SAMPLE 9

LETTER TO A HOSPITAL ADMINISTRATOR RE-GARDING NONCOOPERATION ON RELEASE OF MEDICAL RECORDS

Date

Hospital Administrator
Hospital
Address
City, State

Regarding: Release of medical information

Dear (give administrator's name if possible):
    Your hospital has refused to release to me any medical information pertaining to my birth. As you are the person responsible for policy, I am hereby requesting you to alter the previous decision and release *all* medical information kept by you in order to ensure that my future medical treatment will be handled with full facts available.
    If you authorize the withholding of *any* records, please note that your refusal to release such records could cause damage to my future health and may result in legal action against you and this hospital.
    I am hopeful that this letter will lead to the release of the needed records so that no further difficulty need arise between us.

Signed: _____ Dated: _____

    I, (name of administrator), do hereby swear all medical information on (give your name) has been or is now being released to ensure proper medical treatment in the future. *No* medical information is being withheld.

Signed: _____ Dated: _____

Title: _____ Witness: _____

Have a notary public certify your signature.

Note: If you prefer, have an attorney draw up this letter. Use it only if information is withheld, not as a first attempt at trying to elicit records.
    You may wish to include in the letter a reference to copies sent to your attorney, doctor, or the State Attorney General.

whether there are other medical records on you. Did you undergo tonsillec-tomy prior to your adoption? Were you treated for any childhood or other disease? Remember only you can obtain this medical information.

Foreign Birth Records

For adoptees who are United States citizens through their parents' citizen-ship, but who were born outside the United States, the birth should have been registered with a United States consulate in the country of birth. To obtain a copy of the birth registration, write to the Authentication Officer, U.S. Depart-ment of State, Washington, DC 20520, and ask for the Consular Report of Birth, form FA-240. You will need to submit a signed statement identifying the person whose birth record you are requesting. The cost, at this writing, is $3.00.

Adoptees who were born outside the United States of foreign parents and who have been adopted by United States citizens can obtain copies of their altered birth certificates from the Immigration and Naturalization Service (INS), U.S. Department of Justice, Washington, DC 20536. Birth information is required to be kept on file with the INS in order for your adoption to be legal. Request Form G-350. At this writing, a $5.00 check or money order must accompany the completed form before you can receive a copy of your birth certificate.

If you require a birth or death certificate from a foreign country, write to the Office of Special Consular Services, U.S. Department of State, Washington, DC 20520. This office will provide you information on how to go about obtaining these documents.

For additional information on births or deaths abroad or for information regarding births or deaths occurring aboard a vessel at sea or on an aircraft, you will need to obtain form HRA 77-1143. This form requests records of United States citizens who were born or died in foreign countries. It can be obtained from the Superintendent of Documents, U.S. Government Printing Office, Washington, DC 20402, or purchased from a regional Government Printing Office bookstore for 50 cents, at this writing. For information on individuals abroad who aren't (or never were) United States citizens, you must rely on records being made available to you by the foreign government having jurisdiction. The Office of Special Consular Services is again your best first reference for an indication of whom to contact and what procedures you should follow.

Adoptees who were born in a United States territory or dependency can direct inquiries to the proper government agencies there for obtaining birth information and/or confirmation of death. Here is a list of addresses for the appropriate agency in each case.

American Samoa Office of the Territorial Registrar
Government of American Samoa
Pago Pago, American Samoa 96799

Canal Zone Panama Canal Commission
Vital Statistics Clerk
APO, Miami 34011

Puerto Rico Division of Demographic Registry and Vital Statistics
Department of Health
San Juan, Puerto Rico 00908

Trust Territory of Clerk of Court of the district in which the birth or death
the Pacific Islands occurred. To discover the district, write to:
  Director of Medical Services
  Department of Medical Services
  Saipan, Mariana Islands 96950

Virgin Islands (U.S.)

  St. Thomas Registrar of Vital Statistics
Charlotte Amalie
St. Thomas, Virgin Islands 00802

  St. Croix Registrar of Vital Statistics
Charles Harwood Memorial Hospital
St. Croix, Virgin Islands 00820

For searchers trying to locate information on persons in Australia, New Zealand, Canada, or Mexico, there are search and support groups established in those countries that may be of assistance. Direct your inquiries as follows.

Australia Jigsaw International
P.O. Box 1352
Darwin, N.T.
Australia 3794

New Zealand Jigsaw International
P.O. Box 47090
Ponsonby, Auckland, New Zealand

Canada Parent Finders
National Headquarters
1408 W. 45th Ave.
Vancouver, BC
Canada V6M 2HI

Mexico Mexico Reunion Assistance
Rio Atoyac 69-2
Mexico City, 5DF, Mexico

United States search and support groups with a national membership will be able to advise and direct you toward help when searching out of the country. Refer to Chapter 7 for those addresses.

Records for Black Market Babies

It's a tragic fact that a black market has long existed to supply babies to childless couples desperate for children in their lives and homes. Different motives lead such childless couples to resort to illegal rather than legal channels.

There are several books and articles that discuss baby selling at more length than I can here. In these few pages I want simply to point to the difficulties that arise for searchers adopted under such circumstances and to suggest a line of approach for pursuing a search.

As an adoptee, you have commonly experienced the same sense of disconnectedness that other adoptees report. The problem that arises for you, in addition to possible emotional shock, is that you may find yourself unable to pursue a search with assurance of any likelihood of success. Information you were told about your background, if you were told anything, might be the same story related to your adoptive parents in order to place a premium value on your adoption. What records do exist may have been falsified. What chances might otherwise have existed for you to learn eventually your birth heritage may have been obliterated. There may be no way to trace back to the desired connection.

In some cases, however, it happens that the adoption of a child for money took place between people who knew each other. Only your adoptive parents can provide the key and, in this situation, they will understandably be reluctant to encourage inquiry into the circumstances of your adoption. You may be able to identify and locate an intermediary to your adoption, but his or her cooperation is hardly to be expected. The person—possibly an attorney or doctor—will usually prefer to keep any involvement in this kind of transaction unknown.

Corrupt agencies may be involved in arranging black market adoptions. Where that is the case, it remains possible that important agency documentation of your birth identity remains unfalsified. But the opposite is just as possible. A notorious agency in Tennessee, the Tennessee Children's Home Society, operated on a "commercial basis" for fourteen years before being shut down by the state in 1951. One state investigator's report noted that TCHS made no investigation of the background of the children. Often they destroyed what information they did have and in many cases falsified the child's background to adopting parents. The task facing the adoptee searcher with that kind of agency background is considerable.

As a birthparent who relinquished a child to the baby black market, you face a near-impossible task, too. Records, most likely, have been deliberately falsified or destroyed. You may have dealt with an intermediary who never divulged where your child went. However, since you know the identity of the intermediary, it may prove worthwhile to try to trace the transaction. As in the case of the adoptee, the intermediary is hardly to be expected to provide voluntarily details on any transaction handled. And you, the birthparent, will usually recognize that you are in an awkward position, too. Who really wants to admit, even years later, to having been involved in an illegal, potentially scandalous set of circumstances of this nature?

However, not all adoptions in which money exchanges hands are black market adoptions. Some are what are termed gray market adoptions, which are carried out perfectly legally. Fees may legitimately change hands as long as they fall into allowable categories, are properly documented, and stay within any limit prescribed by state law. Gray market adoptions may take place within an extended family or between unrelated families. They may be arranged by the birthparent(s), a family doctor, a private attorney, or a friend of the family, always according to law, naturally. Here is California's statutory provision on what fees are allowable and how they must be documented.

> Civil Code, Section 224r: *Report of petitioner's expenditures: Who must file.* The petitioners in any proceeding seeking the adoption of a minor child shall file with the court a full accounting report of all disbursements of anything of value made or agreed to be made by them or on their behalf in connection with the birth of the child, the placement of the child with the petitioners, any medical or hospital care received by the natural mother of the child or by the child in connection with its birth, any other expenses of either natural parent of the child, or the adoption. . . . The accounting report shall be itemized in detail and shall show the services relating to the adoption or to the placement. . . . The report shall also include the dates of each payment, the names and addresses of each attorney, doctor, hospital, licensed adoption agency, or other persons. . . .

Black market adoptions work *outside* prescribed laws such as this and are arranged expressly for the purpose of making money. The best interests of the child are not a consideration.

If you find you are a black market baby and nevertheless wish to pursue a search, what could you find that would be so terrible—assuming you can determine your origins? Many adoptees have long suspected that their birthparents were not happily married and might not come from an ideal back-ground. Black market transactions may involve children who were never freely relinquished, babies born in prisons and institutions for the insane, or babies born as the result of rape or incest. None of this is a reflection on the now-adult child's integrity, and to be such a child should not be seen as any reason for loss of self-esteem. Even so, you would probably still find that this knowledge requires a difficult emotional adjustment on your part.

If you decide to go through a search despite a black market baby back-ground, you will undoubtedly be concerned to know where you can turn for support and assistance. The best first contact in this context will be a search and support group or one of the adoption resource libraries identified in Chapter 7. They will be most likely to provide you direction to information or persons with experience in this situation. There are search and support groups established with the sole purpose of helping adoptees and birthparents involved with a specific problem agency. Maybe you'll locate a group along these lines that can help you with your search; maybe you'll be led to a consultant who specializes in black market adoptions. Just to discover a fellow searcher who shares your situation may be enormously helpful to you.

If you are a black market baby who is determined in spite of all these problems to trace your birth heritage, you have made a difficult, courageous decision. My hat is off to you.

Foundlings

We have all read stories about the baby found on the doorstep, in a park, or even in a trash area or wooded area. These are foundlings, with the most difficult of all searches to complete. You may not know you were a foundling, and it's possible you may not uncover this fact. However, if you are told, here are a few suggestions to help you conduct your search.

A visit to the local newspaper that carried the story might be useful. Possibly there is someone still working there that would remember the event and add some fact to the few published.

Another possible source of information will be police records. Abandoning a child is a crime, and a record of the involvement by the police force will be kept.

Foundlings, along with black market babies, will need much help in track-ing and tracing their birth families. Birthparents who are searching for an abandoned child will also find little cooperation and few facts to aid them. I strongly recommend seeking help from one of the many groups across the country that offers search help.

Group Support

A number of search and support groups have been established in the United States. These search and support groups aid you in your quest for information that can lead to identification and location of birthparents or relinquished children. The appendix at the back of this book lists groups operating in each state. You'll find a fuller discussion of group support in Chapter 7.

Keeping Busy

The process of search is an extended one, and the fact that so much time is involved frequently leads to discouragement. You will have sent off letters asking all the questions you want to know. You will have made some initial contact, perhaps with a private, religious, or governmental agency. You will have compiled all the recollections available to you. It may seem that most leads have trailed out to a vague nowhere, except in instances where they run into an obstacle, such as an agency or individual who will not provide you information they hold on you. At times you may be discouraged. Don't give in to this discouragement. But don't expect that your first round of search activity will be rewarded if you just sit back and wait for answers to flow in. While there are times when you will have to wait for a particular response before you can pursue a related lead, you can constructively direct your energies in other directions. It may prove helpful for you to take the time to read the account of another's search—several good ones have been published. You may want to familiarize yourself with genealogy, a very related interest for searchers. You may want to attend a meeting on adoption search or get in contact with other individuals who are engaged in this same process. Direct yourself to one of the national organizations for information about your area.

You can also begin plotting out further areas for research. Check at your library to find a map of your county of birth. Locate the newspapers published in the area of your birth. A good many adoptees have found a record of their birth through old newspaper archives. A local newspaper may have reported the births of four baby girls and six baby boys on a given day. This could provide a lead to tracking down your birth name. If you have your birth weight and height, look to see if that is given for an infant reported born on a particular day. The *Ayer Directory of Publications* or *The Standard Periodical Directory* will give you current names and addresses to contact. Editions of these same reference books from around the time of your birth will alert you to what newspapers then published have since gone out of business. Old copies of those newspapers may be housed at the state archives.

You get the idea. As a searcher you can to some extent depend on good fortune, but the informed, persistent searcher who seeks out all the options for obtaining information is ahead of the searcher who is haphazard and uninformed in pursuit of this goal. During any period when you are waiting for responses to queries you've sent out, make the effort to become more informed. If you seem blocked on all sides, unable to get beyond basic scraps of information you cannot organize, avoid dwelling on what you don't have—that's obvious. Concentrate instead on how you might get what you need. Take the time to look for additional moral support.

Just a few years ago, the average search took from one to three years. Now, the search organizations tell me, the average length of search is from three to nine months. Of course there's no guarantee that your search will be concluded within that time period. But your chances of achieving your goal are better than they were before. Even so, your success is largely dependent on your determination and the amount of thought and energy you invest. You as a searcher must take full responsibility for your search. You will get out of it what you put into it. Certainly there will be times when you'll feel the need to take a break, and you will probably find that the concerns of day-to-day living on occasion force you to direct yourself toward other priorities. There is no reason for self-recrimination in either event. If you are truly a dedicated searcher, you will find that your momentum continues on a certain level anyway, and building back to a full momentum will occur naturally.

The bottom line in your search project is you. How much thought are you willing to invest? How clever can you be? Can you develop an aptitude for picking up on leading statements? Can you sharpen your instincts on how best to deal with people and situations? As you enter into the search that you've decided you want to pursue, learn to be as good a listener as you can be. Organize yourself so as to maximize the benefit of any piece of information you obtain. Persist in following the leads that open up to you. With the sources of information, the tools of research, and the support networks that have developed within the past few years, there is more reason than ever for optimism that you will locate that important missing link to your past that has eluded or puzzled you for so long.

As the Search Progresses: Alternate Sources of Data

You may find that a determined effort to uncover information opens up enough leads to put you securely on the track of the person you hope to locate. However, you may find this doesn't fill in enough of the blanks. Recollections are vague. Birth records are unavailable. Agency and hospital records remain sealed. No one seems very interested in helping you develop the leads you need to achieve your goal.

Perhaps you find yourself in this situation. Despite energies spent getting yourself organized, and after a variety of efforts along lines recommended for approaching individuals and agencies, you still have only an altered birth certificate and a short letter notifying you that your adoption agency closed its doors years ago. It may have taken you two months to learn virtually nothing. One option is to call off your search. But if your decision to search came after years of agonizing questioning and doubt, giving up now condemns you to living with those unresolved feelings. The truth is, there are still many avenues of inquiry you can follow to learn who and where your birthparents are or where your child is. Even with a limited budget, but with a bit of imagination and a lot of persistence, chances are good you can achieve your goal. To help you to that end, in this chapter I've pulled together information on alternate sources of data that you can turn to when the primary sources covered in Chapter 5 prove inadequate, whatever the reason.

One word of caution again before going into these alternate sources: You're unlikely to get all the information you hope for from any one of these. Rather, you will probably find you can only get bits and pieces of information at a time. It's not until you've assembled enough of these pieces of information, relying on a variety of sources, that an entire picture begins to emerge.

One of the great frustrations you may encounter is that sometimes it seems that in order to find someone, you first have to know where he is. It's a real "catch-22" situation. You may not be able to make the best use of some potentially helpful sources of information until you have at least a few facts to work with. That is why imagination and persistence are so important. You may find sharing the experiences of people who have searched or are searching valuable at this time.

You may come up against the situation where you're missing one key detail you need in order to take advantage of a source to uncover another key detail. View this as only a temporary setback. Occasionally you may find that, even though you're missing a seemingly essential piece of information, you can finesse another bit of information without it. Unfortunately, there's no rule of thumb I can offer to guide you here. You need to cultivate a certain intuition, taking a chance on things occasionally. How you get to a certain record and what you can obtain from it varies according to the state you're searching in, how you express yourself, and it is often influenced by how cooperative a clerk or social worker is willing to be. When you first begin your search, you'll inevitably be awkward or unaware at times. Gradually, however, you'll find yourself developing a feel for what you're doing and how you should go about it.

Privileged Information

This is often one of the first sources of frustration you'll encounter. Although you might spend days arguing the justice of it, the fact is that certain people have easier access to information about you than you do yourself. Fortunately, in a few cases you may be able to use that fact to your advantage.

Hospital and medical records may very well be released to your doctor even though refused to you. Consider asking your doctor to write for *all* hospital and medical records pertaining to you if you're having difficulty getting them on your own. Your doctor is not bound by law to keep them confidential from you. Often psychiatrists and psychologists are willing to provide aid in this manner as well.

Insurance companies often require medical and family history records to determine whether or not you are an acceptable risk. Approach your insurance agent and ask that your insurance company request your medical and hospital records. After all, it's logical for the company to need those records. Your agent may only need to consult the company's computer memory bank if the information was already routinely gathered.

Many times people who seem to have some official authorization are granted privileges you as an average citizen will not be accorded. Some searchers have found that a document designating someone else to act as their agent or granting another a limited power of attorney can impress a records administrator into releasing information that was refused them. Although there's no binding legal distinction here from a third party's point of view, the officialness of the document prompts more ready cooperation. Most stationery stores carry a form for use in granting power of attorney. I've also provided a sample form here for your reference (see Sample 10).

A press pass can be valuable, too. Recently I needed to go to a nearby library for information relating to past local history. The history room is locked except for days that someone from the local historical society is there for several hours in the afternoon. I went to the reference librarian, showed her my press pass, said I needed to copy two references for a free-lance story on county history, and would she please allow me access. She did, left me alone in the room (which is not usually done), and asked several times if she could

SAMPLE 10

FORM GRANTING
LIMITED POWER OF ATTORNEY

I, _____, of _____, do hereby appoint _____, of _____, my agent, for me and in my name to (1, 2) _____

_____

_____

and generally to do and perform all things necessary in or about the premises as fully in all respects as I could do if personally present. (3, 4)

Signed this _____ day of _____, 19____

_____
(signature)

_____

Sample Inclusions:
    1. . . . apply for and receive any vital records of my birth, my health and hospital records, or court records that pertain to me, . . .
    2. . . . apply for and receive any official or personal record of medical information that may have any bearing on my health and well-being, . . .

Other Possible Inclusions:
    3. *Add:* The date of this limited power of attorney shall begin on __(date)__ and be valid until __(date)__ , and on that date shall end.
    4. *Add:* No other powers than those mentioned shall be empowered to __(name)__ .

Note: A printed form of this document can be purchased at most stationery stores for 50 cents or less.

be of further help. Possibly I could have gotten the information I wanted without the pass, but I knew it would be considerably easier with it. For some reason, the pass gave me a validity and allowed me privileges others would not have.

Press cards can prove helpful for opening doors, and you can obtain one relatively easily. You won't get access to sealed records, but many times otherwise uncooperative or uninterested civil servants or professionals will respond with a more positive attitude when confronted with a press pass. Since interpretation of regulations by the records administrator often controls whether or not any information is released, it can pay to impress him or her with some sort of official-looking authorization or credential.

Suppose you're an adoptee who wants to search old probate records. If you come in and just express a vague need to review records available, the clerk may point over to an area of the room and say, "The records are over there." And with that, you're on your own. You have to figure out how records are coded and organized. You may miss an index you could refer to for a quick overview of what is contained in them. Now suppose you come in with a grant of power of attorney or a press pass. (You may have made out the power of attorney to yourself, using your current name over your birth name.) You show the clerk your "credentials." The clerk may very well respond by taking you in hand, leading you to the index, even actually searching the records with you. Your review of the records is accomplished more speedily and with more assurance you've gotten all you can out of them.

One business that has advertised press cards for free-lance writers is City News Service, P.O. Box 1589, Albany, OR 97321. Their ad in the April 1981 issue of *Writer's Digest* indicated that, for $6.50, you could get a press pass with your name, news agency (if any), ID number, and an expiration date indicated. A photo of yourself (head shot), forwarded by you, would be sealed with the card in clear plastic. Check more current issues of *Writer's Digest* or similar magazines for updated details, or try an inquiry to the address just given. You don't need to be a member of a press corps—you just indicate you're a writer. And isn't there always the possibility you'll want to write an account of your search to submit to a magazine or a local newspaper for publication?

Marriage Records

Once your search uncovers a name or an estimated date of marriage, you may be able to develop further leads through publicly kept marriage records.

Marriage certificates will provide you with the names of the couple, the site of the intended ceremony, indication of the type of ceremony, and the name of the person officiating at the marriage. The exact form of the certificate varies from state to state, and in some states even from county to county.

Many states have past marriage records indexed. The indexes are open to the public and very easy to use. Depending on the practice in your area of search, you may be allowed direct access at no charge or be required to pay a search fee and have a clerk pull the records for you. For more individual state information, consult the appendix at the back of this book.

Other sources to check for marriage records include newspaper announcements and church files. In the event the ceremony was performed by a justice of the peace, he or she will have a record of it. Check with a clerk at the county or municipal hall of records to discover where records of civil ceremonies are maintained if these are held separately from the actual marriage license/certificate.

An adoptive mother helping her son to search recalled she'd been told the birthmother was to marry after she left the hospital. Although the marriage was not to the birthfather, knowing the married name could make it possible to contact the mother. The son knew his own birth name. He went to the hall of records and searched marriage records, starting with those for the day his birthmother was released from the hospital. After searching through only fifteen days, he found her name and that of her new husband. He went to the local library and found a report of the marriage in the area newspaper's vital statistics section. From that he learned his birthmother's age, her hometown, and the names of attendants at the wedding ceremony.

Birthparents on the trail of a relinquished child can make use of records relating to marriage as much as would a searching adoptee. The primary prerequisite is having a name to work with, together with some sense of the dates to check. For example, if you were told at the time of relinquishment that your child was going to a young Catholic couple who married two years before, you might at one point find it possible to check marriage records as an aid to tracking down the present identity and location of your child. You will usually need a name, but remember that other facts combined may give you an opportunity to locate the names. Using the example above, list what information you have. You already know the couple has been married two years and that they are members of the Catholic Church. In addition, the agency has given you a physical description of both adoptive parents and told you the husband was a pharmacist in his father's drugstore. With a little luck and some time spent researching newspapers in outlying areas to your agency, you may locate the missing couple. You know the persons' ages. Will your agency tell you if they live in a rural or city area? Use your imagination and piece your puzzle together. Ask a search group for advice. You have valuable information; now you must learn to use it.

Divorce Records

The failure of a marriage, leading to separation and divorce, also occasions official record keeping. Divorce records will list names of the couple involved, date and place of marriage, date and place of divorce, names of children (including adopted, but not relinquished children), residence, and a description of property held by the couple. Most states have an index to divorce records, and they will generally be kept with the other vital statistics records. There may or may not be a charge to view them or have them searched. Consult the appendix at the back of this book for individual state information on divorce records.

Divorces filed will be listed in local newspapers. Check this source as well to obtain information. You may also find that church records include data on divorce of any member of the congregation or parish.

Death Records

Adoptees and birthparents can find that records of death in a birth or adoptive family prove useful as a source of leads to the person sought. The official document recording a person's death is the death certificate. A death certificate can be a gold mine of information. It will indicate the name of the deceased, last place of residence, date of death, age at time of death, and cause and place of death. It may further indicate surviving family members, military service history, occupation of the deceased, or other data. Each state differs somewhat from others on what is included; some states release a lengthy certificate, while others issue certificates listing only a few necessary particulars.

If you know the approximate date of death and the state in which the death occurred—or if you suspect a certain state has the records—you can write to obtain a copy of the death certificate. If you're not sure of the actual date of death, request a search of the records over a period of time during which you think the person died. You will have to indicate your relationship to the deceased as it is known to you. In citing a reason for the records search, you can note medical need to know or judicial need relating to questions of inheritance, or you can indicate that this is a genealogical inquiry. To write for the death certificate, use the same address as you would for obtaining birth certificates. I've provided a sample form letter you can adapt for this purpose (see Sample 11).

At a search and support group meeting I attended, a birthmother told of receiving information that her relinquished child had gone to a lovely family (a common reassurance). In asking lots of questions, including questions about other members of the adoptive family, she learned that the maternal grandfather had died just prior to the adoption. She had already determined the area where the family was located, and a lengthy search of the death records for that area produced several possible leads. By following through systematically, she was able to discover the family she sought.

There are other death records you can turn to as well. You can check an area newspaper for an obituary notice. (Keep in mind it will run a day or two *after* the date of death.) The obituary customarily lists surviving children and provides other leads you may wish or need to pursue at some point—church membership, lodge membership, birth date, hospital or other location where the person died, the funeral date, and the name of the funeral home involved. The names of surviving children and/or other relatives are customarily accompanied by a note of each person's town of residence. Married names are given for women in the family. Adopted children are routinely treated as integral members of the surviving family.

Just exactly what you learn that benefits you depends on your or your child's relationship to the deceased. If the record is of your birthmother, say, those surviving could include siblings as well as a surviving partner, possibly your birthfather. If the record is of a member of an adoptive family, the survivors could include the adoptive parents as children of the deceased or, if one of the adoptive parents died, your relinquished child as a child of the deceased.

You may be able to pursue an aspect of your search via mortuary or cemetery records. Of course you need to have a reasonable idea of which mortuary or cemetery to direct yourself to. Once you have that, you may upon request be able to obtain a copy of the obituary notice, a copy of any printed matter given out at the funeral service, indication of the type of service and the date, information on whether the deceased was buried in a family plot, names of other family members buried there and when, and whether there is perpetual care on the grave site—and if so, who is keeping up the payments.

Mortuaries and cemeteries routinely deal with genealogists and will not be surprised or disturbed by your inquiries. You will not need to prove relationship nor send your inquiry via certified mail. Ask for all information in their files. For their convenience, include a self-addressed, stamped envelope to facilitate reply. If you decide to call instead of write, the best time to contact a funeral home is early in the morning or on Sundays, when services are usually not held. You might call to ask what the most convenient time is to visit the mortuary or cemetery if you decide to go in person to request and review records on file there.

If there's no indication the person you're searching for has died, why would you want to go through mortuary or cemetery or other death records? Suppose no one has even mentioned death, much less the name of a specific funeral home. You don't even have a full name to search. Let me illustrate with a set of circumstances how bits and pieces of information, including death records, can be fitted together to help locate someone who's living. I'll use the example of an adoptee searcher.

These are the particulars you've learned:

- You have a change-of-name record from the court handling your adoption. Your indicated birth surname is Roncelli.
- Your agency has informed you that your grandparents played no role in your adoption. In fact, your grandfather had recently died. (Your mother was unmarried at the time she relinquished you, so this is your maternal grandfather.)
- Agency records indicate your birthmother was born in Hancock County, Illinois.
- A call to the agency which handled your adoption has elicited your grandparents' first names, George and Lois. The surname was refused you as identifying information—but you obtained that through another source.
- You have discovered through hospital records that your mother was twenty years old at your birth.

With these facts, this is what you can do: Send a letter to the Illinois Vital Statistics Department requesting a copy of the death certificate for George Roncelli. The estimated date of death is in the months or year prior to your adoption. Using your mother's age as a rough guideline, you estimate your grandfather's date of birth. If you were adopted as an infant in 1957, he was probably from forty to fifty years of age, which would give a birth date somewhere about 1917 to 1927. So, in your letter you ask for a search of the records for a death certificate for George Roncelli, who died in 1956 or 1957, probably in Hancock County. You note his birth date as falling in or about the decade between 1917 and 1927.

Provided all your previous discoveries are accurate, you stand a good chance of obtaining a death certificate listing the full name of your grandfather and particulars as to last residence. Also given will be the name of the mortuary handling disposition of the remains. Now you can write a letter to the mortuary requesting a copy of the obituary, which should provide the names of all surviving children. One of these will be your birthparent. The town of residence will likely be given for each surviving child.

One adoptee, in working to locate her birthmother, was able to make some use of mortuary and cemetery records. All she knew at the time was the date of death for her maternal grandmother, the approximate date of death for her maternal grandfather, and the town they lived in. A check in the telephone directory for that town gave her the name of local funeral homes. She wrote a brief letter to the indicated addresses, asking for information and citing a legal need to know. The result was that the mortuary handling funeral arrangements sent back a copy of the obituary for her grandmother and copies of the interment order to the cemetery for both her and the grandfather. In the cover letter sent with these was a note that one son was in charge of payments for care of the grave, and his current address was indicated. That son, of course, was a brother to her birthmother.

What do you need to know before you can take advantage of these death records? That depends. Different pieces of information can fit together in various combinations to provide you a sense of direction to pursue. It can also depend on whether you are writing for information or are able to check files in person. If you go in person, you may be able to search the records even though you have only a date of death and no name, or a name and not a date of death. You will have to have a good or reasonable idea of locality. If you are writing for information, you will need to provide more specifics. Of course, it also depends on where you're writing. It's easier to check records in a small town than in a major city. Has a private, religious, or governmental agency worker mentioned a death in the adoptive or relinquishing family at or about the time of adoption or relinquishment—or at any other fairly identifiable period of time? You may be able to uncover the corresponding record relying simply on the date and a relative certainty about where the deceased lived or died.

If you have a name, you can also turn to probate records, which relate the disposition of any estate a deceased person may have left behind. These indicate all people receiving money or property from a person's estate, with addresses of the property involved and addresses for all persons named.

Probate records are open to the public. You can walk into any county courthouse or hall of records and look through the index to these records. When you see a name you want—even if you choose one at random—you fill out a card with the name and case number, hand that to the clerk, and you will be brought that probate file to review. You can go through as many of these files as you want.

Older records are frequently stored separately from those that are more recent. My county's index of records immediately available covers the most recent fifteen years. If your situation is such that you are researching a death that occurred previous to a cutoff date for recent records, you will have to inquire about arranging access to the older files.

Adoptees who have learned their birth surname can check probate records in that name. To check the records in person, that surname would be enough, but if you are writing, you need to specify, in most cases, a first name as well. Birthparents would need a knowledge of the adoptive family's surname, which is often difficult to come by.

I've provided sample form letters that you can adapt for requesting various death records (see Samples 11–13).

School Records

If you have reason to believe the person you seek attended an institution of higher learning, write to colleges and universities in the area of your search. The state archives can provide you a list of schools operating within the state during the years you want to review. Patterson's *American Education,* a book that can be found in the reference section of your library, will list the addresses of all colleges, universities, junior colleges, high schools, grammar schools, and private schools in the United States. These are given by state and city.

Colleges generally keep a library copy of the student yearbook for each year. If you know the college the person you seek attended, then you should certainly ask for a photocopy of the yearbook pages listing him or her. A letter to the school's library requesting a photocopy of pages listing the surname you are seeking can supply you with important leads. The yearbook will list clubs, associations, major area of studies, and achievements. Fraternity or sorority affiliations will be noted, and maybe religious association. These provide further avenues for potential clues. The yearbook will most likely also have a photograph of the person you seek, especially if he or she was in the graduating class for that year.

Sometimes yearbook information points in the direction of a subsequent career. Say the person you're on the trail of majored in metallurgical engineering. That's a fairly directed major, suggesting he or she had a specific career goal in mind. Chances are good that the person established some professional association once out of school. In this case you'd check *The Encyclopedia of*

SAMPLE 11

LETTER REQUESTING A
DEATH CERTIFICATE

Date

Department of Vital Statistics
Address
City, State

Dear Registrar:

Would you please search for and provide a full transcript of the Certificate of Death for:

(name of person on certificate)
Sex and race:
Date of death: (approximate if unknown)
Born: (give approximate dates if exact date is unknown)
Name of spouse:
Residence at time of death:

Please advise who received the ashes of the deceased if cremation occurred.

My relationship to the above is (list as it actually is), and my reason for this request is judicial need.

Enclosed is a certified check in the amount required for a search and a copy of the record.

Sincerely,

(your signature)
Address
City, State

Note: You may need to request this information on a form provided by the Department of Vital Statistics. If so, write to request the form and ask to receive forms needed to obtain birth, marriage, and divorce records.

SAMPLE 12

LETTER REQUESTING
MORTUARY RECORDS

Date

Name of Mortuary
Address
City, State

Dear Sir:

I am an active genealogist and have been tracing my family background and relationships for many years.

A service was held at your mortuary on (date) for (name of the deceased). I would appreciate any help you can provide with respect to the following:

1. A copy of the obituary. If this is not available, do you know what newspaper it was printed in?
2. Any surnames involved.
3. Relatives' names and addresses.
4. The deceased person's religious affiliation.
5. Any printed material distributed at the funeral. If there was such material, can you send me a copy?
6. Is the burial plot kept on a perpetual basis? Who is maintaining it?
7. Is there a family plot? What other members of this family are buried in the same area?
8. Any newspaper clippings or other information kept in your files.

Thank you very much for your time and consideration. I am enclosing a stamped, self-addressed envelope for your convenience in replying and a check for ____ to cover any photocopying expenses.

Sincerely,

(your signature)
Address
City, State

Note: You should include at least 50 cents per page to be copied. It can be difficult to estimate how much material may be available. Be assured you will be notified if the amount you remit is not enough.

This same basic letter could be used for cemetery information.

SAMPLE 13

LETTER REQUESTING
PROBATE RECORDS

Date

Probate Department
Hall of Records, (name of county)
Address
City, State

Dear Records Clerk:

Please send me photocopies of information held by your office on (name of person). (His/Her) death took place on (give date) in the county of (name of county).

I have a judicial need for these records. (1) My relationship to the above is (state as in fact it is).

Please include *all* information held in the probate packet.

I am enclosing a check for _____ to cover any photocopying expenses.

Sincerely,

(your signature)
Address
City, State

Other Possible Inclusion:

1. *Substitute:* I need these records for genealogical purposes.

Note: See the preceding sample letter for requesting mortuary records for a suggestion about determining photocopying costs.

You may need to have this letter notarized and to prove relationship.

Associations in your library's reference section to see if you can identify a professional or trade association of metallurgical engineers. Just as the American Medical Association includes the vast majority of medical doctors, so many other professionals and trade specialists have their own special-interest group or association. You can direct inquiries to whichever of these is appropriate for a list of active members.

Unfortunately, you can't always count on this line of approach working out. Many college and university graduates, particularly those obtaining a liberal arts degree, go on to careers that have no direct bearing on the major area of study. A student who graduated as an English major and served as editor of the college literary review may now be working in publishing, but he

SAMPLE 14

LETTER REQUESTING YEARBOOK INFORMATION
FROM A COLLEGE LIBRARY

Date

Library
College
Address
City, State

Dear Librarian:
   Would you please send me a photocopy of all students in attendance with the last name of _____ from your yearbook for the years of _____? (1, 2, 3)
   I am enclosing a check in the amount of _____ to cover photocopying expenses. The stamped, self-addressed envelope is for your convenience in replying.

Sincerely,

(your signature)
Address
City, State

Other Possible Inclusions:
   1. I am currently putting together a surprise album for a friend's birthday and would like to include several photocopied pages from (his/her) college annual.
   2. I have so few pictures of my (mother/father) from (her/his) early years that I would appreciate copies of any photos taken from (her/his) college annual.
   3. Since the death of my (mother/father), I realize we have no pictures from (her/his) college days. Please send me a photocopy of any pictures from (her/his) college yearbook.

or she could just as easily be anything from a schoolteacher to a travel agent to a homemaker.

I've provided a sample letter of request to a college library for yearbook information (see Sample 14). Let me caution you against using adoption search as the reason for your request. The information you're requesting is not private information, but a librarian disapproving of adoption search could refuse your request if he or she so chooses.

A letter to the college's alumni association, to the Past Student Records Office, or to the Admissions Office may also prove worthwhile. I've provided sample letters for your adaptation (see Samples 15 and 16). You might also ask who the president of the graduating class was for the year(s) your relative might have been in attendance. When will the next class reunion be? Who's the class coordinator for reunion or alumni affairs?

It's possible you will be put in touch with the president or class reunion

SAMPLE 15

LETTER REQUESTING INFORMATION
FROM A COLLEGE ALUMNI AFFAIRS OFFICE

Date

Alumni Affairs Office
College or University
Address
City, State

Student Activities Director:

I am trying to contact a friend from the class of _____. The last known address I have is _____.

Will you please check your alumni files for a past student named _____ and send me a current address reference? (1)

Your time and help is much appreciated. I am enclosing a stamped, self-addressed envelope for your convenience in replying.

Sincerely,

(your signature)
Address
City, State

Other Possible Inclusion:
  1. *Add:* Please let me know the name and address of the Reunion Coordinator for the year(s) I've indicated.

SAMPLE 16

LETTER FOR REQUESTING
PAST STUDENT RECORDS

Date

Registrar
Past Student Records
College
Address
City, State

Dear Registrar:

Please review your student records and forward to me information on a past student by the name of _____. (He/She) was in attendance at your school about (list several years if unsure of dates).

I understand some information cannot be released, but I have been advised the following will be made available to me:

Full name of student
Dates of attendance
Birth date and age at entrance
Major field of study
Degrees earned
Social Security number
Last school attended
Address upon entrance
Next of kin
Fraternal organizations

Thank you for your consideration and help. If you have any additional information, please supply me with that also. If your records do not list all of the above information, please send me what you have. (1)

I am enclosing a check in the amount of _____ to cover any photocopying expenses. Also enclosed is a stamped, self-addressed envelope for your convenience.

Sincerely,

(your signature)
Address
City, State

Other Possible Inclusion:
    1. *Add:* If you will not release the information, but have a current address, will your policy allow you to forward a letter written by me?

Note: This is a *very* formal letter and one that will be considered with care. A more personal letter can sometimes win cooperation from a small school.

coordinator for your birthparent's or child's class. He or she may know the person you seek and release a current address, or at least prove ready to forward a letter from you. Sometimes it's possible to purchase a copy of a class reunion pamphlet. This may include photos and current address information for class members.

I wrote a letter to a university in the South during my search, asking for details from my birthmother's records there. I had good reason to believe she might have attended this school. I wrote that my mother was dead. I knew so little about her educational background—would they please send me what information they had? The letter I received in response gave me her dates of attendance, noted her activities and interests, and also mentioned that she had attended another university in years previous to graduation from their school.

A few colleges occasionally issue alumni directories. These are compilations of the names and addresses of all alumni—usually organized by class—that the college has been able to maintain contact with. The directories rely on data the alumni themselves provide, which generally include career information. However, directories may not be issued regularly; there may be intervals of ten years or more between those that do appear.

You need at least a surname, approximate dates of attendance, and, of course, some idea of what school to address yourself to before you can make use of school records. You will probably have to piece this information together from two or more other sources of detail. Obviously you should get as much information as possible from private, religious, or governmental agency records. Press for as much detail on educational background as you can get —most of it is unquestionably nonidentifying. The agency may give you useful school information that could provide leads. A statement such as "Your birthmother was vice-president of her college graduating class, and your father was active on his college basketball team" might bring about the following. You can estimate the year of graduation from the age given you by the agency. You've learned there are three colleges that cover the area your birthparents lived in at that time. Old yearbooks provide you the names of class officers, thus giving you a list to work from. If you have your birth name, this list may provide a clue. You may have the surname of one of the basketball team members or one of the class vice-presidents. Even a first name may provide you with a lead.

If you can't get a clear fix on where the person you seek is now through school records, perhaps you can contact a classmate. Classmates, especially in more rural areas, can often prove helpful in tracing the movement of fellow alumni. Think of yourself. If an old friend of one of your classmates asked for your aid in locating that person, wouldn't you be inclined to help?

Don't despair if indications are that your birthparent or child never attended a college or university. You can take much the same approach in searching through high school records. High schools conventionally issue yearbooks, too. Many high school classes hold reunions at five- or ten-year intervals. Some school districts have conducted follow-up surveys on former students. Contact the Superintendent of Schools in the city or county where your search indicates the person you seek attended high school to find out if these and other records were kept, for what years they were kept, and where they are now housed.

Local newspapers commonly print the names of graduating high school seniors. Check with the newspaper or write the state archives in the appropriate state to see if you can get a photocopy of the list of graduating students in the town you've pinpointed as—or think probably is—where the individual you're tracking went to high school. You may need to check the lists for several years if you don't know the exact graduation year. Learning a particular class year for your relative makes it easier to request other school records.

When writing high school officials, married women will probably do best to sign letters with their married name. This eliminates the chance that school officials might doublecheck to find if the letter of inquiry originated with someone who attended the school or not. Married men might consider writing in their wife's name, if the impression you wish to convey is that you're writing for information on a school chum.

Church Records

It's possible to discover vital information through church records.

If you have information on your birthparents' religious affiliation and have some idea if and when you were baptized or christened, you may be able to pursue these leads. Birthparents who learn that the adoptive family has had their child baptized or christened can follow much the same route of inquiry.

You should keep in mind that churches also have general membership records, as well as confirmation records, Sunday School records, marriage records, and death records on members. Sometimes a church will also have a record of a marriage performed there that was not of active church members.

Church records may exist on a central or regional (diocese, synod, and so on) level or be maintained locally. If you know the denomination with which your birthparent or child was or is associated, call a local church of that denomination to find out what is kept locally and what is kept in the denomination's regional or central archives. I've provided a sample letter you can adapt when writing for church records (see Sample 17).

SAMPLE 17

LETTER FOR
REQUESTING INFORMATION FROM CHURCH RECORDS

Date

Church Archives
Address
City, State

Dear Records Department:

I am trying to locate the church records on a family member, (give full name if possible).

Please send me the following information from your archives and any additional information you may have that will enable me to document fully (his/her) church activities, with the dates indicated for those. (1)

1. Date of membership
2. Church marriage records
3. Branch church attended

If your records are not centralized, please send me the name of the local church/parish functioning in the city of (name of city) during the years from (give estimated date of relative's birth) to (present/estimated date of relative's death).

I've enclosed a stamped, self-addressed envelope for your convenience. Also enclosed is a check for _____ to cover any photocopying expenses.

Thank you for your time and consideration in this matter.

Sincerely,

(your signature)
Address
City, State

Other Possible Inclusion:
1. *Any of the following:* Death records, confirmation records, offices held in the church, information from letters of transfer to other branches.

Note: As set up here, this would go to a church archives. You can easily modify it for a branch (local) church. In that case, ask for *all* records kept and if they may be reviewed by you.

Again, sometimes you may have to backtrack through a grandparent's religious records to get on the trail of more current information. In that case you may well have to rely on church records that are kept in centralized archives. Here are the central records sources I've located for several denominations:

American Baptist Historical Society
Samuel Colgate Baptist Historical Library
1106 South Goodman St.
Rochester, NY 14620
(716) 473-2319

Catholic University of America
Department of Archives and Manuscripts
Mullen Library, Room 33
Washington, DC 20017
(202) 635-5065

American Congregational Association
Congregational Library
14 Beacon St.
Boston, MA 02108
(617) 523-0470

Protestant Episcopal Church in America
Church Historical Society
Library and Archives
P.O. Box 2247
Austin, TX 78767
(512) 472-6816

Friends Historical Association
Swarthmore College
Swarthmore, PA 19081

American Jewish Archives
Hebrew Union College
3101 Clifton Ave.
Cincinnati, OH 45220
(513) 221-1875

Lutheran Churches in America
Library
820 38th St.
Rock Island, IL 61201
(309) 788-5635

Mennonite Historical Library and Archives
Bethel College
North Newton, KS 97117

Presbyterian Church in the United States
341 Ponce De Leon Ave., NE
Atlanta, GA 30308
(404) 873-1531

Gardner A. Sage Library
Official Archives of the Reformed Church in America
(formerly Dutch Reformed Church)
New Brunswick Theological Seminary
New Brunswick, NJ 08901

Historical Committee of the Southern Baptist Convention
127 9th Ave., North
Nashville, TN 37234

Some church records have been published—the Works Progress Administration records taken on churches during the Depression can still prove very useful. Look in your library for a copy of *A Survey of American Church Records, Church Archives in the United States and Canada,* and the *Bibliographical Guide for American Church History.* The Daughters of the American Republic (1776 D Street, NW, Washington, DC 20006) has an excellent library of church records and will share information with nonmembers. As mentioned in a previous chapter, the Church of Jesus Christ of Latter-Day Saints has a network of libraries that are particularly good in genealogical collections.

There's no guarantee a local church will prove as cooperative as you'd like. Some will be very helpful, while others do not allow individuals to make use of their records. However, at meetings of search and support groups I've attended, numerous birthparents and adoptees have testified to the value of church records, particularly baptismal certificates. I'd say you have at least an even chance of winning access to these.

An adoptee who did not know her birth name or the names of her birthparents was told that she had been baptized four days after her birth. She knew her parents' religious affiliation and the city of her birth. She contacted the appropriate churches in her city of birth to trace all baptisms for the day indicated. There turned out to have been only one. She questioned the minister of the church where that baptism had been conducted and discovered her own birth name, her mother's name, the names of her godparents, and the circumstances of her birth.

Individuals who are searching records of Jewish congregations will find that the same considerations govern obtaining records from those. For other non-Christian congregations, such as the Bahai, refer to an area center known to you or to the national headquarters for direction on what records are kept and where. Whenever writing for religious records, keep your letter brief. Ask for the name of a clergyman or other spokesman you can refer to in your search area if the records you need are not centrally kept.

Military Records

Do you have reason to believe a missing relative served in any branch of the military? Was there a war or draft registration during this period? Then there's some chance you may be able to win information from military records on that person, although these can be difficult to obtain.

Military records from the period prior to World War I are open records. These would be of use to you if you were pursuing an aspect of your search through genealogy (see Chapter 4). Subsequent military records are subject to very strict controls, limiting access. The standard General Service Administration form "Request Pertaining to Military Records" states:

> The Military Departments have restrictions regarding the release of information from records of military personnel. A service person can obtain almost any information contained in his own record. The next of kin, if the veteran is deceased, and Federal offices for official purposes, are authorized to receive most types of information from a military service or medical record. *Other requesters must have the Release Authorization in item 6 of the request signed by the veteran, or, if deceased, by the next of kin.* Employers and others needing proof of military service should accept, as authentic, the information shown on documents issued by the Armed Forces at the time service persons are separated.

You are actual next of kin to the service person you seek, but you do have to be able to prove that. If he or she is deceased, you may be able to get information through this channel. Write for the request form to the National Personnel Records Center (Military Personnel Records), 9700 Page Boulevard, St. Louis, MO 63132. There is a fee, plus a service charge for the records search, which can vary, depending on the effort the search requires.

The request form asks a range of questions of a quite specific nature—full name, Social Security number, date and place of birth, branch of service, dates of active duty, and service number. You will probably not be able to answer most of them, as they include information that you as a searcher are not likely to know. Unfortunately, the odds are probably against your being able to use this information source to your advantage. However, if you have some combination of the requested details, it's worth a try.

If you know the branch of service in which your relative served, you can try writing the records center for that service branch. You may get nothing more than the standard GSA request form, as this is used by all the services. But you may get a response that includes the name of a records administrator you could contact for a clearer sense of what other types of military records might be made available to you. You might find that a partially completed request form wins more response from the service branch than from the National Personnel Records Center. You might also want to try addressing the Military Archives Division of the General Services Administration in Washington.

Here are the addresses for the various military records centers.

United States Air Force Military Personnel Center
Military Personnel Records Division
Randolph Air Force Base, TX 78148

Air Reserve Personnel Center
7300 East 1st Ave.
Denver, CO 80280

Commandant
United States Coast Guard
Washington, DC 20590

Commandant of the Marine Corps
Headquarters, United States Marine Corps
Washington, DC 20380

Marine Corps Reserve Forces
Administration Center
1500 East Bannister Rd.
Kansas City, MO 64131

Military Archives Division
National Archives & Records Service
General Services Administration
Washington, DC 20408

Commander
United States Army Reserve Components
Personnel & Administration Center
9700 Page Blvd.
St. Louis, MO 63132

Commander
United States Army Enlisted Records and Evaluation Center
Fort Benjamin Harrison, IN 46249

Chief of Naval Personnel
Department of the Navy
Washington, DC 20370

Naval Reserve
Personnel Center
New Orleans, LA 70146

Army National Guard Personnel Center
Columbia Pike Office Building
5600 Columbia Pike Blvd.
Falls Church, VA 22041

Although the service records for the individual's term in whichever branch of the military he or she served are hard to come by, there are two other sources of military data to which you have somewhat freer access. Selective Service (draft registration) records are open to the public. For registration information, write to Atlanta Federal Records Center, 1557 St. Joseph Ave., East Point, GA 30344. To make any headway here, however, you will almost certainly need a full name, an indication of the local Selective Service Board where the person registered, and probably a birth date.

The Veterans Administration's Freedom of Information Act, Section 1.503, specifies information that must be released to persons about veterans:

> The monthly rate of pension, compensation, dependency and indemnity compensation, retirement pay, subsistence allowance, or educational allowance to any beneficiary shall be made known to any person who applies for such information.

Of course, in this case you have to be able to provide the name reference and enough service data so that the Veterans Administration can locate the records for the person you're tracing. And you'll note that the information you get won't include anything that amounts to identifying information—you're supposed to provide that.

The Veterans Administration provides extensive medical services through its network of VA hospitals. If you know or think the person you're seeking received medical treatment from the VA, you may get some information via that route. The person's name will be entered in the VA computer as having received medical treatment benefits.

I learned that the VA will release information that is not detrimental on any deceased officer. In working to trace my birthfather, I called the VA three times, and each time I received different answers on what information I might be able to get. I never had enough information identifying my birthfather to be able to pull further information out of the VA computer, but I was at least able to induce an officer to run what I had through the computer. Name and service number would have produced the desired results, but what searcher will ever have a service number? I always told VA spokesmen my father was ill and wanted to get in touch with an old navy friend. (The "old navy friend," in this case, would have been my birthfather.) I know the branch of the service, have a partial name, have a battalion number, and know where he fought and with what company, but these are not sufficient for a computer check. A Social Security number and a full name, or a full name and date of birth, would be more valuable. Besides that, the person would have to have received medical treatment from the Veterans Administration to be listed, and I did not know that he had received treatment—I was just trying.

Your local Veterans Administration, Benefits and Assistance, address will be listed in your telephone directory under United States Government. The VA will not release a current address for any veteran their records show still to be alive. However, I've found the VA will help you by forwarding a letter to a relative or "buddy." Write or ask your local VA office for details and the forms needed.

There are lesser-known sources of information on military personnel, but these are not that easy to use. For example, each branch of the service has a book listing the officers serving in that branch. The book gives a lineal number (which indicates seniority), name, date of achieving the indicated rank, sex, and year of birth. The actual name of the book is different for each branch of the service, but a reference to the Lineal List or the Blue Book will be enough to make clear what you are after. For example, the Navy calls its book *Registry of Commissioned and Warrant Officers of the U.S. Navy and Reserve Officers on Duty.*

Some time ago I met a birthparent who had learned that her child had gone to a family with a military background—the adoptive father was a career officer. She knew the date of the adoption and also where the family had originally come from (another state). She also knew that the family had adopted two other children. Through a long and arduous process that is too complicated to relate here, she was able to use a service Blue Book to locate the name corresponding to this information and a few other particulars she knew. She went through three years of Blue Books—each with more than 52,000 names—before she was able to match a name and the particulars given for that person with information she knew about her child's adoptive father.

Often a searcher will not even know for sure whether or not the missing relative ever served in the military. How would you know whether it could prove worthwhile checking out the possibility that he or she did? Here you'd work on the basis of probabilities. Was draft registration required about the time the person came of age? Were these war years? Was enlistment high during the years you're concerned with? The answers to these questions can give you a sense of whether a stint in the military might reasonably have been expected. Naturally, all these remarks have greater pertinence for men than for women.

If you've learned that your birthfather or your son fought in World War II or another conflict, there's an outside chance his name appeared in a report filed by a war correspondent. Ernie Pyle, probably the most famous of war correspondents during World War II, eventually compiled and edited his reports in book form. At the end of his books are listings of the servicemen's names given in the book text. There are a fair number of books with this type of listing—*Guadalcanal Diary* by Richard Tregaskis, *Battle Report* by Walter Karig, and *Bloody Buna* by Lida Mayo are just three examples. Ask your reference librarian if she knows or has record of other books with this type of information. Check *Books in Print* (the subject index) and/or the library card catalog under headings for a conflict in which your birthfather or son might have served.

Property Records and City Directories

If you learn or guess that the person you seek owns or has owned either his or her own home or other real estate, you may want to review property records maintained in and for your area of search. Property records are public records accessible to everyone. They are kept at the county court house or hall of records, where title searches on the part of individuals and businesses are a routine occurrence.

To use property records for a home owner, you would need to know both a name and a county of residence. If you have this information, you can refer to a general index of property records that will direct you to the specific document detailing acquisition or transfer of any property held in the name you have. Here, for example, is how the entry for my family's home reads in the Orange County (California) General Index of Grantors.

Title*	Grantors & Defendants**	Grantees & Plaintiffs***	Number of Document	Date of Filing	Book	Page
TR DD	Askin, Charles R. & Ida J.	Home S&L Assn. BFC	13238	4/18/69	8932	44

*Nature of Instrument. The key explains this to mean Trust Deed.
**The full and exact title: Grantors & Defendants—also mortgagors, lessors, vendors, assignors, appointors, parties releasing, judgment debtors, wills bonds, parties against whom liens are claimed or attachments issued, mining locator, name of mine, proof of labor, and so on.
***The full and exact title: Grantees & Plaintiffs—also mortgagees, lessees, vendees, assignees, appointees, parties whose mortgages are released, and so on.

This reference pinpoints location of the actual title or deed to the property, which you can then have photocopied.

If the person you're tracking down continues to reside at the address given, from this point on it's a simple matter of making contact there. However, often it will turn out that the property has been transferred to new ownership. In that event, the new owners will be indicated, together with a record of the date of transfer. Your next step in this case would be to get in touch with the new owners. They may have some indication of where the previous owners moved to.

For example, you've traced your birthfather to a county in a neighboring state. You have his name, but you can't find a current telephone listing. A check of the property records for the county shows he sold his home, and through the records you find out who purchased the home. You contact the current owners and ask if they have any information on where the previous owners are now living. They respond, "His company transferred him to San Diego." You can now follow the same process to establish an address reference in San Diego if there's no telephone listing given for him there.

The limitation here is that property records list only property owners. Those who rent or lease property will not be indicated. However, there is an alternate reference source that can be used as a supplement or in place of property records to locate persons living in a given locality, whether or not they own property there. This reference source is the city directory.

Not all cities have directories, and individuals who have unlisted telephone numbers may not be listed in a city directory. On the other hand, it is at times possible to locate an address reference for someone who isn't listed in a local telephone directory. City directories are published by companies—or sometimes by a Chamber of Commerce—primarily as a service to area businessmen. They generally include lots of advertising in addition to address information. They are similar to telephone directories in many respects, but commonly provide more personal information than does a telephone directory. Of course this varies, depending on the directory referred to.

You will find city directories kept in state archives, in the office of the local Chamber of Commerce (but for that locality only, as a rule), or in public libraries. To discover what directories, if any, were kept for your area of search, ask your reference librarian for assistance. You may also find it helpful to refer to a search and support group in that area for information on available directories.

The two most widely used directories in past years have been the *Haines Criss-Cross Directory* (published by Haines & Co., 8050 Freedom Ave., NW, North Canton, OH 44720, telephone 216-494-9111) and the *Polk Directory* (published for many years by R. L. Polk & Company, 431 Howard, Detroit, MI 48231, telephone 313-961-9470).

Haines leases its directories to businesses, libraries, professional agencies, and certain individuals. (Write to the address indicated above if interested to see if you qualify for a lease.) Subscribers to the Haines service can request any information contained in previously issued directories, which will be provided at no extra charge. If your library leases a present directory, you may find this a valuable service to take advantage of.

The Haines directories have three types of listing—one by telephone number, one by address, and one by ZIP code. From this directory you can determine not only who resides at a given address, but you can ascertain neighbors' names as well. That may be of benefit if the person sought has moved since publication of the particular directory referred to. A subsequent directory, if there is one, should also provide an indication of who currently lives at an address previously given for that person.

When writing for information—most likely you will be doing so through a library—ask for a photocopy of pages listing the surname you are searching in a given city. You will probably be estimating a date of residence, so list several years before and after that date. That will assure the best chance of locating the record you want.

The *Polk Directory* is also divided into three sections. There are listings by surname, by address, and by telephone number. This directory often indicates the name of a spouse, place of employment, occupation, and whether the individual listed owned or rented property at the address given. Your state archives or a large public library should have past Polk directories. When referring to these, again use a range of years when requesting photocopies for listings of a given surname or for a street address.

Suppose you found a 1955 listing in a Polk directory—how would you use the information there? If the person listed owned his or her house, you know there have to be property records—deeds and transfer-of-title papers when the person sold the residence. The indicated occupation could provide a useful clue in correlation with other information. What company did the person work for? Maybe this person was transferred by the company. Maybe employment records that exist indicate other address references for family members or show that the person left to work for another company. Possibly neighbors still in the area know where he or she moved to. Maybe one or another of them is still in touch on a regular or occasional basis.

There are a number of other directory publishers established in and serving different parts of the country. The Association of North American Directory Publishers (P.O. Box 317, Bellows Falls, VT 05101) includes the following publishers, listed here with an indication of the area covered. (Note that this list includes only members of ANADP. Be alert to the possibility of a nonaffiliated directory publisher serving your area of search.) Write the publishers who serve your area of search and ask what cities they print directories for, where their archives are located, and how you can receive a photocopy of any listings from years past. Ask the cost of providing photocopies. Enclose a self-addressed, stamped envelope for the publishers' convenience in replying to your inquiry.

Publisher	Cities Located in
B & B Publishing, Inc. P.O. Box 417 Kailua, HA 96734 (808) 261-6798	(request this information from the publisher)
BID Publishing Company 111 Center Park Dr. Knoxville, TN 37922 (615) 690-4257	Georgia, Kentucky, Tennessee
Combined Area Telephone Directory, Inc. 6161 North May, Suite 263 Oklahoma City, OK 73112 (405) 842-4075	Kansas, Oklahoma, Texas
Dellcor Publishing Company P.O. Box 12574 Ft. Worth, TX 76116 (817) 429-5172	Oklahoma, Texas
Directories Publishing Co., Inc. P.O. Box 9156 Metaire, LA 70005 (504) 837-9800	Louisiana
Feist Publications, Inc. 106 Stafford P.O. Box 98 Spearville, KS 67876 (316) 385-2603	Kansas
Greater Channel Area Telephone Directory, Inc. P.O. Box 90785 Houston, TX 77090 (713) 353-8545	Texas
Guide Publications, Inc. 56 Linden St. Hackensack, NJ 07601 (201) 489-4882	New Jersey

Publisher	Cities Located in
Home Owners Guide of Florida, Inc., Local Blue Book 231 Southwest 21 Terrace Ft. Lauderdale, FL 33312 (305) 581-2200	Florida
Hudco Publishing Co., Inc. 200 Century Park South Suite 206 Birmingham, AL 35226 (205) 979-1525	Alabama, Mississippi
Information Publisher, Inc. 6601 West 78th St. Edina, MN 55435 (612) 941-4800	Minnesota
Johnson Publishing Company P.O. Box 455 Loveland, CO 80537 (303) 667-0652	Arkansas, California, Colorado, Georgia, Kentucky, Illinois, Louisiana, Montana, Nebraska, Oklahoma, Oregon, Pennsylvania, Tennessee, Texas, Wisconsin, Wyoming
Kaiser Handi-Book Publishers, Inc. 375 Irving Ave. Port Chester, NY 10573 (914) 939-2610	Connecticut, New York
The Little Yellow Book, Inc. 318 Cleveland Ave. P.O. Box D Highland Park, NJ 08904 (201) 247-7207	New Jersey
Lomar, Inc. (*see* Johnson Publishing Company)	California, Colorado, Idaho, Kentucky, Minnesota, Montana, Nebraska, Nevada, New Mexico, New York, Oregon, Pennsylvania, South Dakota, Wyoming
Luskey Brothers & Co., Inc. 608 East Broadway Anaheim, CA 92805 (714) 774-5683	California
H. A. Manning Company P.O. Box 317 Bellows Falls, VT 05101 (802) 463-3913	Maine, Massachusetts, New Hampshire, New York, Vermont

Publisher	Cities Located in
Metro Publishing Company 400 Production Court Blue Grass Corporate Center Louisville, KY 40299 (502) 491-8506	Kentucky, Mississippi, Ohio, Tennessee
National Suburban Directories, Inc. 1236 Sherman Ave. Evanston, IL 60202 (312) 475-7002	Illinois
Oklahoma Telephone Directories, Inc. 5549 East Skelly Dr. Tulsa, OK 74135 (918) 664-6580	Arkansas, Oklahoma
Old Heritage Advertising & Publishers 2271 Administration Dr. St. Louis, MO 63141 (314) 432-5543	Missouri
Phone Directories Company P.O. Box 887 Provo, UT 84601 (801) 377-8330	Arizona, Colorado, Idaho, Nevada, New Mexico, Oregon, South Dakota, Utah, Wisconsin, Wyoming
The Price & Lee Company 564 Whalley Ave. New Haven, CT 06509 (203) 389-5308	Connecticut, Massachusetts
Tele-Pages, Inc. 1259 Route 46 Parsippany, NJ 07054 (201) 335-0106	New Jersey
VIP Guide Corporation 6 South Moger Ave. Mount Kisco, NY 10549 (914) 241-0264	Connecticut, New York
Western Publishing Company (*see* Johnson Publishing Company)	(request this information from the publisher)
White Directory Publishers, Inc. 605 Grover Cleveland Highway Buffalo, NY 14226	Florida, New York
Yellow Book Corporation 440 Merrick Rd. Oceanside, NY 11572 (516) 766-1900	New York

Voter Registration Records

If you have a name and a probable or certain county of residence for the person you're searching for, you may be able to use voter registration records to your advantage. These can supply you with an address reference, indication of political party affiliation, and month and day of birth. (The year of birth is commonly not given, but this can be estimated with no great difficulty, as a social services department will almost always release the age of your birthparents at the time of your birth.)

Current voter records are kept at the county level. These can generally be viewed without charge or proof of relationship. They may be called precinct books, rosters, or voter registrations. Older records may be kept at local libraries or possibly in the state archives. State law governs disposition of these records. Ask the appropriate county registrar of voters whether old records have been preserved and where they are kept.

One adoptee used voter registration records in this way: She was searching in the state of her birth, although she now lived hundreds of miles away in another state. She had learned the first names of her birthparents from the social services department that had administered her adoption. Her adoptive parents had been told the birthfather was from a small farming community in the state and had learned his last name from a social services clerk. She figured the community must lie close to the city where she was adopted, or her birthparents would have dealt with another large city's social services department. (This is the sort of deduction that can lead to valuable information or to a complete dead end. You sometimes have to take a chance.) She obtained a map of her home state and drew circles around areas with large cities and those with the largest social services departments. That left the primarily rural areas. Now she observed which of those lay closest to her city of adoption. She then wrote letters to the voter registration offices in the several counties included, asking for a record listing the first and last name of her birthfather as she knew it. Most did not respond, but one sent back a letter stating the information could not be released before payment of an indicated fee. The searcher quickly sent off a certified check, assuming this response would not have come without good reason. The information that was returned gave the name, month and day of birth, party affiliation, voting precinct number, and home address.

Another adoptee I know of traced her birthmother to a city in the South. But when she searched through the telephone directories for that area, she could not find the name she had listed. However, a visit to the voter registration office turned up the needed address. It turned out her birthmother had an unlisted telephone number. (A hint: If you suspect that someone you're searching for has an unlisted telephone number, call directory assistance and ask for the listing. Although the operator will not give you an unlisted number, the reply given will generally confirm whether there is an unlisted number for the party, which means at least you're searching in the right area. Otherwise, you will be advised that the records show no listing whatsoever.)

As you can see, reliance on voter registration records may require only a full name and a reasonable idea of the area of residence. But while in these cases the searchers were rewarded with success, they might almost as easily have met with failure, since there is no compulsory voter registration in the United States.

Motor Vehicles Department Records

The vast majority of adult Americans have a driver's license, and drivers' licenses have become one of the primary documents of identification for people in this country. Businesses routinely rely on them to verify addresses. Individuals also can use driver's license records to trace people, although you will need a good reason for doing so. Many searchers have found the most acceptable reason to be that they are trying to locate someone who passed a bad check. In most states there are statutory limits on who may apply for and receive personal address information through the Motor Vehicles Department, but these limitations are rarely stringently enforced. To find out what the rules and procedures are for your state, refer to your local Motor Vehicles Department office or write to the state address given in the appendix of this book. If there is a fee, the informational material you receive will indicate that. In California the charge for a Motor Vehicles check on any individual with a current license was still just 75 cents in 1980.

In order to make use of these records, you will already need to know a full name and birth date, or a full name and address. (As a rule, searchers are working to obtain a current address.) You will have to fill out a request form that is forwarded to the state Motor Vehicles Department office, then wait for a reply. The information that is returned to you, assuming the person holds a currently valid driver's license from that state, will be all that is listed on the driver's license itself. You may even receive an exact photocopy of the license. In any event, you will be given a current address reference.

This avenue of search can be especially helpful for locating individuals who maintain unlisted telephone numbers.

Social Security Administration

The Social Security Administration (SSA) has a policy authorizing it to forward mail from one individual to another for "humanitarian purposes." Obviously this is in cases where the first individual has no clear address reference for the person he seeks to contact. Since most adults have a Social Security number and file, chances are good that the SSA has at least a relatively recent employer's address reference—it may very well have a current home address, particularly if Social Security benefits are being paid.

I have not personally heard of any instances of search efforts pursued through this channel, but Hal Aigner, author of *Faint Trails,* does relate one experience.

Mr. Aigner used the SSA to locate his half brother. He had his half brother's name, the approximate year of his birth, the approximate years he served in the military, and his birthmother's name. It would have been very helpful to have a Social Security number, too, but that was out of the question. Mr. Aigner forwarded what information he had and gave the reasons he had for wanting the SSA to forward a letter he'd written to his half brother indicating a desire for contact.

The SSA, on receipt of this request, carefully worked to locate the half brother through its extensive record files. Once identification was made, the SSA wrote a letter to the half brother, setting out Mr. Aigner's desire for contact and giving the reasons for that pretty much as Mr. Aigner had expressed them in his correspondence with the SSA. The SSA letter added that, even though the message was being forwarded by a government agency, there was no legal obligation to reply. A second letter went to Mr. Aigner, indicating that the SSA had identified his half brother and that an agency correspondence had been mailed, including the letter to be forwarded. To him the SSA added that there was no way to provide assurance that the letter would be received or that any response would follow; in any event, the SSA would send no follow-up letters.

Essentially the same procedure applies for anyone hoping to make contact through the Social Security Administration. You should recognize that the desire to establish contact with a birthparent or a relinquished child may not be sufficient "humanitarian" reason of itself to prompt the SSA to work for you in search efforts. I suspect health problems, a legal need to know, or inheritance would be the most acceptable reasons for contact. I would not give genealogical inquiry as a reason.

If you want to try the SSA, write a letter to the Social Security Administration, Location Services, 6401 Security Blvd., Baltimore, MD 21235, saying you want to contact an individual. The best information to give is a complete name and Social Security number, but, as already observed, it's unlikely you'll have the latter. If you can provide a place and date of birth, however, that will usually suffice. Enclose in your envelope a letter to the person you want to contact, but *do not seal that letter.* The SSA must verify that it qualifies under the "humanitarian purposes" rule. Only after that verification will they forward it. It gets sent to the person's last known employer, if the records do not show the person is currently drawing benefits that are sent directly to him or her. The employer then hands the letter to the person or, if he or she has since moved on, may forward it to a subsequent employer.

Newspaper and Magazine Ads

Local newspapers can prove a valuable source of information, especially if your search is concentrated in an area served by a newspaper that routinely reports births, weddings, and deaths among local residents. Your reference librarian can help you determine what newspapers exist or have existed in your area of search.

Earlier in this chapter I made note of how newspaper reports of births, marriages, deaths, graduations, and so on can provide leads to the person being sought. In addition to that, you may find it proves worthwhile running a personal ad in a newspaper in your area of search to generate information or enable contact.

Should you wish to pursue this possible route to information, there are one or two points particularly to keep in mind. First of all, there are laws that protect a person's rights of privacy. Your ad should not be so worded as to amount to an invasion of privacy. Remember, too, that when you run an ad naming someone, you can put the person named in the position of having to explain to people in the community. Identifying someone by name as the mother or father of a relinquished child would be ill-advised for reasons related both to rights of privacy and to a potential for embarrassment. Discretion is always the basic rule to follow.

How you word your ad should be decided by the information you have and the information you need. I'm providing you here with several examples of good ads that have been run—ads designed to win information without focusing unwelcome, curious attention on the personal affairs of the party sought.

> Genealogist needs information on the ___(name)___ family in the (specify area of search) area. Any information will be appreciated. (your name and address)

> (Your married name) looking for old school friend (name of the person you are seeking). Anyone with knowledge of present address write (your name and address).

> Looking for lost relative (person you are seeking). Anyone with information please contact (your name and address).

If you find this sort of ad produces no information, you might try another approach—assuming you remain convinced there is information to be won in this community. You could offer a cash reward. You might simply add an element of greater interest. An ad like the following would certainly pique the interest of most people.

> Inheritance information needs to be forwarded to (person you are seeking). Anyone with information about the above, or other family members, please contact me or forward my address to same. (Your name and address).

Your inheritance information may be as little as informing your relative that your rights of inheritance were waived by the courts—check your state's laws, as in some states adoptees retain inheritance rights—or as much as stating you wish to include the missing person in your will. Again, whenever placing an ad in which you name another person, keep in mind that you don't want to embarrass or expose the person you are seeking. The chances of a satisfying future meeting can be jeopardized by thoughtless advertising and careless disclosure of facts.

If you still do not have a name to work with, you may wish to try a different approach. For example:

> Information needed on babies born ___(date)___ at (name of hospital). Please contact (your name and address).

> Anyone with information regarding children adopted from (name of agency) during ___(year)___ please contact (your name and address).

Genealogical magazines, in particular *The Genealogical Helper* and *Family Finder,* also take ads for information on missing family members. Your ad in one of these would be slanted toward fellow genealogists rather than to someone who might be directly acquainted with the person you're seeking. So it would read differently:

(Your name and address) seeking information on (list full
name if possible). Born in the state of _____ on approximately (list several years). Is (he/she) in your city directory or phone book? Need address and married name.
Please help.

Naturally, the particulars would vary according to whom you're seeking and
what you already know.

What Else?

I've already mentioned genealogy in my discussion of reference resources.
You may find that a study of genealogy will help you identify and locate
information sources you had not previously recognized as available. This will
prove especially helpful if you have leads that require tracing an extended
family relationship.

I've also noted that under the Freedom of Information and Privacy Acts
you can obtain information held on you by any agency of the federal government. Some of that information might provide a lead to your relative that you
didn't previously have.

You may find an employment record you can use to good effect. Or you
may uncover a record of association with a club, professional organization, and
so on, that you can then contact for membership information.

Whatever source of information you utilize, whether one of those listed in
this book or known only to you, exercise imagination, common sense, and
consideration for others in working to achieve full advantage from it.

There's no precise recipe to follow for guaranteed search results. You have
to adjust to the unique circumstances that affect you in your search. Keep an
open ear, an open eye, and an open mind—those will prove the most useful
for assuring you move toward your search goal.

7

Search and Support Groups

Adoptee/birthparent search on a widespread scale and conducted openly is a recent phenomenon. For years individual men and women, with only their personal sense of determination and persistence to keep them going, explored previously untried sources and experimented with unproved methods in efforts to reestablish the broken connection that troubled them. In doing so they experienced the frustrations of encounters with a broad range of people who could not or would not understand their motives. Fortunately, many also came into contact with others like themselves, who expressed understanding, who were willing—eager, in most cases—to share their own search experiences with them.

It is out of this kind of sharing that search and support organizations were born. Now there are groups spread across the country to which you can turn for understanding and encouragement of the sort that only other searchers can provide you.

A word of caution, however. You may believe groups will conduct the actual search for you, expecting that they are professionals who of course have all the right answers and can direct you to a single, simple solution. You may think that after one meeting you'll be able to return home, write and send off one prescribed letter, then sit back and wait for all the desired information to come in by return mail.

If this is what you're looking for from a group, you're looking in the wrong place. Groups will help you establish a sense of direction; they will offer useful advice based on the experiences of group members. But they won't do your searching for you, and they aren't in possession of some secret formula that will guarantee your search will suddenly become as simple as sending off an order to a mail-order-catalog house. If you want someone else to do the work for you, there is generally only one way to accomplish that: Hire a professional.

You can. However, before doing so, turn to Chapter 9, "Taking It One Step Further," for advice on how to go about retaining professional search assistance.

Also, don't confuse your search and support organization with the reference section of your local library. You may hear about a publication of interest or a source of information that proved useful to one or another member of the group. But when it comes to looking up address references or locating a newspaper published in the area of your search—that is, generally learning to identify and hone in on the scattered sources of information you must often rely on in pursuit of leads, the appropriate source of aid is your reference librarian.

So, what benefit do you get from a group? You get reinforcement of your hopes. You get encouragement in pursuit of an intensely personal goal that many others around you will not understand and may not support. You get advice on possible directions to take in your search. You get a perspective on your attitudes toward yourself in your search, and toward others reacting to you during this period—perspective which comes from people who have been or are where you are now.

Your attitude, how you define your needs, and how the local chapter of the search and support group to which you turn is run all determine what you can and will receive from the group. The potential is considerable.

Understanding Friends

To begin with, groups provide you a source of new friends who understand what you are doing. Here is a place you can come to and not have to explain why you are searching. You won't be put into a defensive position on a controversial social problem; you won't continually find yourself having to restate your right to know. And these people understand the problems you are or will be facing during your search.

If you've decided to search, conducting the search will assume a very important part of your life. For those who find few members of their family willing or able to understand and few friends who give genuine support, groups offer a place to keep your sanity. Don't we all feel the need to talk about our accomplishments in life? Our hopes? Our fears? When we set out to do a difficult task and find we had more strength and courage than we thought, isn't it pleasant to have friends who recognize and acknowledge that difficult task well done? When your search hits a snag or dead end and you have no other leads to follow, nowhere else to turn, supportive friends may be the impetus that enables you to dig deeper inside yourself, to start anew in another direction.

The friends you meet will have much in common with you and each other. At the same time, they will come from varied backgrounds, so that each has his or her personal line of experience and viewpoints to share. You will fit in both for the goals and motivations you share with other group members, *and* for the individual differences that exist between you and each of the others.

The Arizona-based organization Search recently conducted a survey among ninety-six adult adoptee members (past and present). Note the similarities and differences existing in just this one group.

Present age: average, 35; oldest, 74; youngest, 18

Sex: female, 80%; male, 20%

Adoption agency: public, 57%; private, 43%

Age at adoption: between birth and one year, 74%

Adoptive siblings: other adopted children, 49%; born into family, 25%

Birthmother's age at child's birth: average, 25; oldest, 40; youngest, 14

Birth order: only child, 14%; first child, 44%; second child, 24%

Adoptive home atmosphere: happy, 63%; unhappy, 20%; mixed, 17%

Problems existing in adoptive homes (including some "happy" ones): alcoholism; compulsive gambling by one parent; divorce; mental problems and abuse; child shuffled around from home to home

Child told of adoption: at "early age," 63%; age 6–8, 14%; age 12–18, 18%; as adult (including "by accident"), 4 members

Told adoptive parents of search: 67%

Adoptive parents deceased: 18%

Adoptive parents (of those living) who gave information: 78%

The point is that every variety of adoptive situation is likely to be reflected among group members. Here, more likely than anywhere else, will be people you can talk to about your own situation and find an open, listening ear with an understanding, sympathetic mind responding directly to what is common or uncommon in your circumstances. No other group of friends will be able to be supportive in quite that fashion.

That is not to say that your search and support group will or ought to replace friendships you've developed over the course of the years. In a great many instances the opposite will happen. Because you have available to you the interest and encouragement of members of the group, you may well find it easier to forgive and tolerate what you see as the failings of personal friends who don't understand your need to know. In my own experience of group meetings, I've repeatedly found group members counseling each other on the value of patience and understanding for the difficulties search presents for family members and friends. The organization is set up to be an *added* support resource for you, not to supplant previous relationships to which you had looked for support.

Like individuals seeking guidance, groups also need to find support, encouragement, and a place to share new ideas and information.

The American Adoption Congress offers many groups this type of help. In the "President's Message" of the fall issue of *Open A.R.M.S Quarterly,* Penny Partridge (the 1981–82 president) described the AAC as follows:

> What is the AAC?—The AAC is a coalition—"coalesce" means "grow together" —of individuals and groups across North America who care about making adoption more open. The AAC is an acknowledgement of the many people who, on their own or in groups, are working toward this goal in a great variety of ways. The AAC is a means of educating ourselves about this and a channel through which we can educate the rest of the adoption community and the general public. The AAC allows groups, large and small, to learn from each other, and for individuals, whether in a group or not, to connect up with the larger network.

The conception of the AAC began in May of 1979 and final bylaws, election of officers, and membership information was established in Kansas City in 1981. The AAC concerns itself with all those involved in adoption: adoptees, birthparents, adoptive parents, social workers, judges, lawyers, and the general public.

Highlighted groups that offer a referral service (that is, Adoption Search Institute and Triadoption Library) will have current information on hand for those individuals who wish to learn more about the American Adoption Congress.

Search Workshops

Many search and support groups conduct search workshops on a regular basis. These are special meetings, featuring no speakers or films, to which members bring all documentation of their search efforts to date. The entire session is given over to reviewing work in progress and discussing new directions to follow.

How the workshop specifically operates depends on the group's membership and organization. In a small, rural area, your group workshop may consist of only three or four members, each possibly at a different stage of search or involved in a different type of search. In a large urban area, your group may be set up so that certain members are designated to act as search assistants. An occasional group will have trained specialists as search assistants. You may work with a single member or a search assistant. In large groups, you may join together in a small subgroup with others searching in the same area of the country you're concentrating on.

Regardless of the group's size or organization, you can substantially benefit from a search workshop. You get the opportunity to present your search work to others who have had search experience. Their questions and suggestions can provide you with new alternatives to explore or give you the courage to carry on a difficult line of approach. Someone may have had a similar experience in an area of search that's proved troublesome for you. Someone whose search focus is quite different from yours may nevertheless have an insight into your situation that can throw things into clearer perspective for you.

Don't underestimate your value to the other group members during these workshops. You may have tapped a source of information others have over-looked. You may simply have organized your search effort in a fashion that makes search manageable for you; another group member without that capacity for self-organization can benefit through your sharing of your experience in that area. That sharing also benefits you. Your suggestion may prove the key to another member's further progress in searching. Your contribution may be just a simple statement of understanding and shared frustration that helps someone else through a difficult moment. To know you can make that kind of contribution provides you a source of strength in an endeavor that can make heavy demands on your emotional strength.

There is no exact formula for solving search problems. Any insight, information, or advice on new methods to consider can prove of use to you and those in the workshop with you. As a beginning searcher you may feel you have nothing but questions to raise, when in fact you may be voicing questions others need to consider. There is no demand that you contribute any minimum benefit to the others in the group. All you need bring to the group is a record of your own experiences for review and a willingness to share your interest in and thoughts on the search work of fellow members.

Newsletters

Virtually every group publishes a newsletter for its members. It will be printed monthly, bimonthly, or simply as funds allow. The usual listings include announcements of meetings, with dates, times, and speakers indicated. Other upcoming events of interest will be noted as well. In addition, each newsletter will make an effort to keep you abreast of changes in state law with effect on adoptee/birthparent search, progress on class action lawsuits in the courts, and new search-related information from whatever source. Reviews of books and magazine articles will provide you a useful service, directing you to discussions of adoption and search considerations you may be interested in reading.

Your group's newsletter may contain announcements of television or radio programming you will want to know of. Is there an interview scheduled with a legislator or other government spokesman on the subject of changes (or *no changes*) in current adoption laws relating to search and reunion possibilities? Look in your newsletter. Have you received advance notice of such an interview? Recognize that through the newsletter you have the opportunity to keep other members abreast of what's going on around them. Call your group's newsletter coordinator to suggest mention of it for the benefit of other members. You can receive and pass on notice of conventions or other public forums of interest to searchers in the same way.

One part of any newsletter will be reports of other searchers' successes. It is exciting to read about how a member located a birthparent, a relinquished child, or a lost sibling. News of happy reunions of course provides a welcome note of encouragement to all searchers. However, the value of these articles often goes further. A review of methods used in a highlighted successful search can be a source of new ideas for you. A word of caution on a search technique that backfired can alert you to a mistake you may unwittingly be duplicating. Reading of difficulty in a search, or of nonreceptivity on the part of an individual located through search can help keep you grounded in reality.

Search and support organizations are volunteer groups that usually do not have an established, permanent office. Meetings are held in libraries, public halls, or private homes. It can take some effort to locate the group in your most immediate area, but chances are you will be able to.

How to Find a Group

Those active in the search movement continually meet people who say, "If only I had known of your group when I did my search." It is a genuine problem for the search movement to be faced with the knowledge that there are people who want and need to be reached but don't know how to make contact. Search and support group members strongly encourage other searchers to seek out the support that is available.

By reading this book you have been alerted to the existence and work of many search and support organizations. Knowing they exist, that there may be one established in your area or nearby, is half the battle. Now, to locate a group.

Within the adoption movement, there is one independent newsletter that operates on a nationwide scale. *Open A.R.M.S Quarterly* offers subscriptions to groups, individuals, and any interested persons. One section is devoted to ads placed by persons seeking information on names, birth dates, hospitals, or other needed data. This is a new publication and a much needed source to offer help on a nationwide basis. This newsletter is covered at more length in Chapter 4.

As with so many volunteer organizations on a local level, a group's address often changes with the installation of each new president. The organization per se has no fixed address. Some groups have solved this problem by renting a post office box. Others simply direct mail to be forwarded to the new presiding officer's address. A few may drop from sight after a period of time or be replaced by a new group with a new membership.

Perhaps you've been given an address for a group and received a reply that the group has ceased to function. Don't assume that all adoptee/birthparent groups have gone out of existence. Review the listing of highlighted groups which follows this section. A nationally established organization may be able to direct you to a nearby affiliated group you aren't aware of. An organization functioning primarily in your state may be able to help you also. The Triadoption Library functions as a referral service, and one phone call or letter can produce a list of groups currently operating within your state.

Once you've located a group, allow yourself the opportunity to check out whether you'll feel comfortable in it. Most groups will permit you to attend a meeting as a guest. This makes it possible for you to learn something about the group's workings and to meet those with whom you'd be in contact as a member. Find out both what programs the group has had in the past and what activities are scheduled and projected for the future. Your questions will generally be welcomed; members will appreciate your interest in their work and organization. Call ahead to express your desire to attend a meeting as a guest-observer to learn the group's policy on visitors.

Highlighted Groups

In the state-by-state reference lists in the appendix, you will find address information on groups active in each state and on groups involved in different types of search activities. (Some groups focus primarily on helping birthparents, while others are more oriented to adoptees. Here and there are groups that aid both adoptees and birthparents but concentrate on those involved with a particular agency.) Since the number of groups functioning today is large, the list is not all-inclusive.

This chapter describes major groups. In choosing groups to highlight here,

I have considered how long a group has been functioning; whether it has been recognized by state agencies (recognition, while not a formal sanction, does indicate some degree of informal cooperation between state agencies and the search group); whether it has served as a particularly good source for specialized search information; and whether it has a strong national or state headquarters. Some of the groups included in the following section are more limited in scope of operation than others. However, these organizations seem to take the lead in offering a sense of stability and permanence to the movement, although your needs may be still better served by a local or regional group not included among those highlighted here. As a general rule, there is a commitment to cooperation among groups—they will direct you to another group that may fit your needs better if you are not wholly comfortable with the one you've chosen or do not feel its focus fits your needs. (In fact, be leery of any group that displays evident jealousy or hostility toward other search groups.)

There are several important points to remember when reading the information that follows:

1. Membership fees listed are accurate at the time of publication; membership fees may change due to increasing operating costs.
2. Always include a self-addressed stamped envelope with all your correspondence.
3. As is common among many volunteer groups, the addresses and phone numbers listed may be of the residences of the groups' current office holders and as such are subject to change. This information is being included to offer you a starting point to contact these groups. If the addresses and phone numbers prove no longer current, perhaps your letter will be forwarded, or a new phone number can be obtained.

Adoptees-in-Search (Maryland)

Adoptees-in-Search, located in the metropolitan Washington, DC area, has a nationwide membership. It is cited by the state of Maryland as a group the state works with in a cooperative effort in a number of adoption-related areas.

The purposes for which AIS was established are set forth in a brochure distributed by the group:

AIS helps adoptees, adoptive parents, birth parents and others obtain psychological support and fellowship; exchange information regarding adoption; provides for the education of persons interested in adoption procedures and problems.

AIS offers its members regularly scheduled workshops, general meetings, publications, and a birth registry. It reports that, of those members who have regularly attended meetings and followed recommended search procedures, 97 percent have received significant information.

Membership is open to anyone eighteen years of age or older. (Adoptees under eighteen are allowed membership with the written consent of the adoptive parents.) The membership fee is $17.00 for one year, but AIS accepts applications from those living outside the area for inclusion in its birth registry for $2.50. All staff workers are volunteers.

For more information, or to receive an application for membership, write: Adoptees-in-Search, Inc., P.O. Box 41016, Bethesda, MD 20014. Telephone: (301) 656-8555.

Adoptees in Search (Colorado)

Adoptees in Search was founded in the fall of 1974 as a volunteer, self-help group of adoptees. As outlined in the membership brochure, the group functions to

> . . . provide technical search assistance and emotional support to searchers. The group attempts to allay the fears of adoptive and birth parents, to enhance public awareness of the adoptive experience, and to work for the revision of present laws that withhold information from adult adoptees and birth families. . . .

AIS publishes a bimonthly newsletter containing national, state, and local adoption information, as well as search tips, book reviews, reunion stories, and miscellaneous items of interest.

Membership dues are $12.00 annually, and searchers eighteen years or older are welcomed. (AIS is supportive of underage adoptees but does not extend them actual search assistance.) This group maintains a local reunion registry and participates in the International Soundex Reunion Registry.

For additional information or an application to join, please write: Adoptees in Search, P.O. Box 27294, Denver, CO 80227.

Adoptees' Liberty Movement Association

On March 21, 1971, Florence Fisher, now president of Adoptees' Liberty Movement Association (ALMA), ran a newspaper ad that read:

> Adult who was an adopted child desires contact with other adoptees to exchange views on adoptive situation, and for mutual assistance in search for natural parents.

I'm sure Ms. Fisher had no idea this ad would generate the response it did and prove to be the seed that led to the establishment of the largest search and support group in the country, with over 150,000 names entered in its ALMA International Reunion Registry Data Bank.

ALMA is a nonprofit, tax-exempt agency based in New York. The organization has close to fifty chapters nationwide and active, working members in nearly every state of the Union. All ALMA staff members are volunteers.

The following statement from an ALMA brochure illustrates the organization's aims particularly well:

> As ALMA has grown over the years the objectives have expanded to encompass the changing needs of its members. Thousands have united to raise the consciousness of the country to the injustice of "sealed records." Mutual assistance in search still remains a priority. A network of understanding, compassion and information exists to remind members that they are not alone. The RIGHT TO KNOW is an emotional issue, but also a legal one.

In keeping with its convictions, ALMA has retained Professor Cyril C. Means, Jr., Professor of Constitutional Law at New York Law School, as its legal counsel. He prepared and presented an ALMA-coordinated class action lawsuit in defense of adoptees' right to know in the state of New York and is involved in the preparation of a second such class action suit in California. Adoptees/birthparents/adoptive parents will find the constitutional arguments raised in these suits an encouraging source of support of their civil rights. Via this kind of legal action, ALMA hopes ultimately to have sealed birth and adoption records opened to those directly affected by denial of access to them. More detailed information on the current class action suit may be found in Chapter 1.

ALMA offers many services to its members. One such service is a national network of "search buddies," individuals working through ALMA to offer advice and mutual assistance to any other member. In addition, each ALMA chapter offers search workshops which are presided over by an ALMA Search Committee. This committee is comprised of members who have completed their search and are now willing to volunteer time, advice, and moral support to any active group member.

Searchlight is ALMA's national newsletter. Local newsletters are distributed to members in each chapter. These provide information about meetings and other events on the local level, indicating meeting places, times, and speakers. Both *Searchlight* and the local newsletters offer articles about progress in legal actions, reviews of publications of interest, stories about those who have found the one they are seeking, and new search techniques.

A unique feature offered to ALMA members is a reunion workshop. This workshop offers support and constructive aid to searchers who have completed their search but still require advice and direction in subsequent difficulties they may experience.

ALMA membership is $30.00 annually, which includes registry in their International Reunion Registry Data Bank (see the appropriate entry in Chapter 8). No additional fees are ever charged. ALMA welcomes any interested person into its groups but will not actively engage in search activities for those under eighteen years of age. In addition to New York, ALMA is recognized by social service departments in the states of California, Colorado, Connecticut, Florida, Illinois, Indiana, Iowa, Michigan, Minnesota, Missouri, Nevada, New Jersey, and Tennessee.

Check your local telephone directory white pages for mention of a possible nearby chapter, or write to ALMA, National Headquarters, P.O. Box 154, Washington Bridge Station, New York, NY 10033. Telephone: (212) 581-1568.

Adoptees Search for Knowledge

Adoptees Search for Knowledge (ASK) is a small group active in, and recognized by, the state of Michigan. Its founder, Joyce Fensom, has been active in the adoption movement since the mid-1970s. Ms. Fensom and Sue Houghteling are the two core working members, devoting many long hours to helping adoptees, birthparents, and adoptive parents with their searches. Those who work with ASK soon realize size does not impose limitations on the results you can obtain.

A special feature of this group is that it will act as intermediary in search cases into which it is drawn by making contact, on your behalf, with the person you seek.

Membership dues are $15.00 a year, and membership is open to all those over eighteen years of age. Search assistance is offered on a volunteer basis, with only out-of-pocket expenses to be reimbursed.

Anyone wishing more information should direct inquiries to: ASK, 4227 S. Belsay Rd., Burton, MI 48519; or ASK, 2322 N. Eugene St., Burton, MI 48519; or ASK, 1921 Marsac, Bay City, MI 48706; or ASK, P.O. Box 762, East Lansing, MI 48823.

Adoption Forum of Philadelphia

Adoption Forum of Philadelphia was founded in 1973 and describes its aims as follows:

In light of all [the] changes taking place in adoption, the Adoption Forum of Philadelphia hopes to make some contribution toward enlightening the public and lending an experienced hand to those facing the thorny problems encountered in their journey to their roots.

Serving all members of the adoption triangle (adoptees, birthparents, adoptive parents), the group offers monthly meetings (followed by search workshops), search assistance, newsletters, book reviews, a speakers' bureau, and cooperative activities with and direction to other groups throughout the country. A special feature of this group is its annual spring conference, started in 1977. This conference provides a series of workshops, classes, and panel discussions of interest to all members of the adoption triangle.

Membership dues are currently $15.00 a year, which includes receipt of the group's newsletter and registration in the International Soundex Reunion Registry. You can obtain additional information or applications for membership by writing: Adoption Forum of Philadelphia, P.O. Box 7482, Philadelphia, PA 19101. Telephone: (215) 487-1311.

Adoption Search Institute

Adoption Search Institute (formerly ISC Institute) was established in early 1980 by Pat Sanders. Volunteers offer help both in person or by mail. There is no membership fee or charge to persons seeking help, with the exception of optional search classes.

The most unique feature of ASI is the instruction the group offers to beginning searchers. When Ms. Sanders founded Independent Search Consultants (see Chapter 9), she saw a need for professional training in search techniques. Many individuals wished to have their search done by a professional rather than proceed themselves.

As Independent Search Consultants grew, Pat Sanders found another large group of people—those who wished to conduct their own searches but lacked the skills needed. With this in mind, ASI was founded, and one of its important contributions is a series of classes offered that enable those attending to have a clear picture of what records are available, how to conduct a search, and where help can be found. Search classes are offered at a minimal fee, and comprise several sessions.

ASI is an excellent source for referral information, as it maintains close ties with groups across the country. The group works closely with the International Soundex Reunion Registry and is a member of the American Adoption Congress. I found the members of this group to be extremely well trained, since most volunteers have received certification by ISC.

For more information you may write or phone: Adoption Search Institute, P.O. Box 11749, Costa Mesa, CA. 92627.

Concerned United Birthparents

Concerned United Birthparents (CUB) was incorporated as a nonprofit organization in October 1976. It has its roots in a meeting held by four women to exchange views and discuss problems they'd experienced as parents of relinquished children. One of those women, Lee Campbell, became the group's president.

CUB offers support and problem-solving advice to its members. While not a search group, it does work closely with other organizations that provide aid in that area. CUB has published a pamphlet entitled "The Birthparent's Perspective," from which the following description of the organization's purpose and aims is taken:

> [CUB] is an autonomous national non-profit support and advocacy group for parents who have surrendered children for adoption. We also have a strong interest and concern with teen pregnancy prevention, and with informed-choice availability in all untimely pregnancies. In addition to being a resource group for studies being conducted on the aftermath of adoption, we also constitute the only nationally organized group available for those who research the dynamics of teen pregnancies and untimely pregnancies in adults. CUB is not a search organization; any searches conducted by our members are personal ventures.

CUB has branches across the United States. In the four-year period between July 1976 and June 1980, the organization provided services to more than 14,500 persons. CUB works with state family service agencies in Colorado, Connecticut, Florida, Maryland, Massachusetts, Minnesota, New Hampshire, and New Jersey.

CUB welcomes adoptees, adoptive parents, birthparents, and members of the community who have an interest in the work of the organization. Current annual membership dues are $15.00. The group publishes a monthly newsletter, conducts monthly meetings, and offers a "pen pal" and referral service to all members.

If you wish to join or receive more information, write to Concerned United Birthparents, National Administration Headquarters, P.O. Box 573, Milford, MA 01757.

Kammandale Library

The Kammandale Library identifies the public it serves as follows:

> Those interested in using this library would be: persons in need of information on family, inheritance, background, genealogical foundation, relationships with vari-

ous kinships, nationality, personality and emotional foundation, knowledge of self-identification, social contacts.

Jeanette G. Kamman is the founder and current director of this resource center. Ms. Kamman is associated with Orphan Voyage (see below), but calls her reference center the Kammandale Library to avoid confusion because of various other reference materials she houses there. Although mainly a resource center of adoption-related materials, the Kammandale Library also offers search and support help.

The library is an acknowledged resource center mentioned by the state of Minnesota and listed as such in the James J. Hill Reference Book #254. Between 125 and 150 adoption-related books are available at the Kammandale Library. In addition, a current orphan reunion clipping file is maintained and available to visitors for their reference use.

If you are interested in referring to the library, please write: Kammandale Library, 57 North Dale St., St. Paul, MN 55102. Telephone: (612) 224-5160. Library hours are by appointment only.

Kansas City Adult Adoptees Organization

This organization, incorporated in the state of Missouri in 1979, explains its purpose in the following terms:

Conducting training programs and seminars to teach (a) the research techniques required to discover family history, genealogy and adoptive facts; (b) the methods required to systematically record the pertinent information found; and (c) the techniques of discreetly handling sensitive information.

KCAAO maintains a reunion registry with over 600 members listed. To date it has been instrumental in over 200 reunions. Cooperation between this group and the International Soundex Reunion Registry and referrals to the ALMA International Reunion Registry Data Bank offer further benefits to members. This group is mentioned by the state of Missouri.

KCAAO holds monthly meetings—primarily panel discussions and workshops, occasionally featuring outside speakers. When feasible, a newsletter is published for distribution to members.

Training and assistance is limited to persons searching for an adult, unless an urgent health problem exists. Applications for membership from those who are of minority age will be filed and brought forward when the person reaches legal age of majority.

There is a one-time membership fee of $10.00, but the group will request contributions on an annual basis as the need develops.

For more information or an application to join, send your inquiry to Kansas City Adult Adoptees Organization, P.O. Box 15225, Kansas City, MO 64106. Telephone: (913) 262-0836, (816) 356-5213, or (816) 761-3671 (between 9:00 AM and 3:00 PM, please).

Liberal Education for Adoptive Families

When Liberal Education for Adoptive Families (LEAF) was formed in April of 1975, it was structured as a membership organization. Recently the group has redirected its focus to concentrate on adoption reform. LEAF no longer holds group meetings or offers membership. It now functions as a dedicated group of individuals lobbying at the state level, helping to write new laws, consulting on policy decisions on the part of public and private agencies, and compiling information to be presented in textbooks for schools.

LEAF is based in Minnesota and works closely with ALMA, CUB, Link, the Kammandale Library, the International Soundex Reunion Registry, and the Minnesota Reunion Registry.

If you are interested in more information on the workings of this group, write to: LEAF, 23247 Lofton Ct. North, Scandia, MN 55073. Telephone: (612) 636-7031.

Link

A nonprofit corporation, Link strives to aid both adult adoptees and birthparents by providing search assistance, undertaking actual search work, making referrals in conjunction with search needs, and providing details on particulars of Minnesota state law relating to adoption. This local group was organized in 1974 by Kathy Demers and Maxine Prokop. Link is based in Minnesota and works with individuals who were adopted, relinquished, or born there. It is used as a referral by the Minnesota Department of Human Services and other state agencies located in Minnesota.

There are no membership dues, but those requesting actual search efforts to be made (letters, telephone calls, research, or other work) are asked to pay a basic fee of $30.00. A letter from Link indicates, "This is negotiable with each situation, with a minimum requirement of expenses covered."

For more information or inquiries on search assistance, write: Link, c/o Nancy Corey, 1700 West 76th St., Apt. #1-C, Minneapolis, MN 55423. Telephone: (612) 861-4213 (on weekends and evenings only).

Operation Identity

This group describes itself as "a non-profit organization embracing all facets of the adoption triad, adult adoptees, adoptive parents, and birth parents." It is currently involved in search and support activities, offers speakers to local groups, and is working to motivate change in state laws on sealed adoption/relinquishment records. The organization operates within the state of New Mexico and is recognized by the New Mexico Human Services Department.

Membership is open to searchers twenty-one years of age or older, and the group requires that the person(s) who is the object of search also be at least twenty-one. Membership dues are $15.00, which include registry in the International Soundex Reunion Registry; an application for ISRR will be sent you when you receive the Operation Identity membership brochure.

Operation Identity has a search coordinator who is certified through Independent Search Consultants (see Chapter 9), and members are provided search advice and taught procedural techniques at no additional fee. Group meetings are held monthly.

For additional information, or to receive a membership application, write: Operation Identity, 13101 Black Stone Road, NE, Albuquerque, NM 87111. Telephone: (505) 293-3144 or (505) 898-5770.

Orphan Voyage

This is the oldest search and support group in the United States that I am aware of. It was founded as the Life History Study Center in Philadelphia on September 19, 1953. It has survived several changes of name and address and is now located in Colorado. Founder Jean Paton has amassed literature, newspaper accounts, and papers on adoption from around the world; this collection is probably the largest of its kind in the world. This material is kept, along with Jean Paton's Orphan Exhibit and Reunion File, in a retreat named Orphan Port.

Orphan Voyage has a great many worker-participants scattered across the country. There are branch groups located in various states, but the organization prefers working with individuals who are willing to help, rather than in groups.

Birthparents and adoptive parents of adoptees under the age of eighteen are eligible for membership. Adoptees under the age of eighteen may make use of the group's reunion registry, provided they have the consent of their adoptive parents. This group is mentioned by the state of Colorado.

Membership in Orphan Voyage entitles you to registration in its reunion registry, the use of reference materials located at Orphan Port, and the benefit of referral service to groups or individuals located near you, or in or near your area of search. In addition, you may request advisory assistance during the course of your search.

Dues are as follows: individuals—$20.00 to join, with renewal at $10.00 a year; agencies and professionals—$10.00 a year.

You can address correspondence or direct telephone inquiries to any one of the individual affiliates mentioned in the state lists in the appendix, or you can write to Orphan Voyage, National Headquarters, 2141 Rd. 2300, Cedaredge, CO 81413. Telephone: (303) 856-3937.

Post Adoption Center for Education and Research

The Post Adoption Center for Education and Research (PACER) was founded by and remains under the direction of Dr. Dirck W. Brown. This is not a group established to promote search efforts. Rather, it concentrates its energies on improving the adoption experience for all those involved in it.

PACER offers a referral service to other support groups, genetic counseling, legal assistance on adoption, medical assistance relating to adoption, counseling for those considering adoption, classroom curricula on adoption, research studies, audiovisual materials, books, periodicals, bibliographies, workshops and seminars, consultations for professional and lay groups, and programs for and interaction with the community. The programs of discussions and surveys on problems relating to adoption have given this group a special place among active search and support organizations.

This unique, information-resource group welcomes the participation of any person or group interested in its activities. There are no membership fees or regularly published newsletters. For more information, write: Post Adoption Center for Education and Research, Palo Alto Medical Center, 860 Bryant St., Palo Alto, CA 94301. Telephone: (415) 326-8120, ext. 20.

Search

Search, founded in the spring of 1976 by Ginger Gibson Rogers, describes itself as "an independent organization offering a free service of idea exchange, volunteer support and educational guidelines in the adoption triangle." Search is located in the state of Arizona and is recognized by the state Social Services Department and by private adoption agencies; it has grown to be an extremely active state search and support group. Its present membership is in excess of 130 adults. During the first five years of its existence, the group has seen more than 100 reunions.

Search offers its members monthly meetings, a monthly newsletter, and use of its reference library. Its meetings are open to adults in search, although they do not advocate birthparents searching for minors or minors searching for birthparents. Counseling is also available. Membership dues of $5.00 per year include registration in the International Soundex Reunion Registry.

Those interested in this group should write: Search, P.O. Box 1432, Litch-field Park, AZ 85340. Telephone: (602) 935-9702.

Triadoption Library

This organization offers adoptees and birthparents a place they can contact to discover a group working in their area, an individual working in their area, or advice on what group is probably best suited to their particular needs. In addition, the Triadoption Library's referral service includes record searchers, psychologists, lawyers, and search consultants.

Mary Jo Rillera searched for and found her birthparents and her relin-quished child. As a participant in the adoption movement, she was witness to the lack of communication between search and support groups and saw the need for a centralized clearinghouse providing information and adoption-related materials to all groups and individual searchers. With this in mind, she sent out fifty-three letters to various groups asking what particular problems they faced in their work and what kind of information services they felt they needed. Groups responding indicated especially the following needs: (1) a referral service open to all adoptees and birthparents; (2) a centrally main-tained file where groups and individuals could register and list their services; (3) a permanent home for information and reference materials relating to adoption; (4) a bookstore offering self-published and other adoption materials that were difficult to locate. On the basis of these responses, Ms. Rillera established the Triadoption Library in November 1978.

The library houses a large collection of materials and will share its informa-tion with anyone who contacts it. Its files include updated state laws, a collec-tion of city directories, books and articles published on the subjects of adoption and relinquishment, genealogical research materials, and many other reference guides. In addition, the Triadoption Library offers many books and gift items for sale, and it maintains a small lending library from which individuals may check out adoption-related books for a nominal daily charge. The library is open to the public at no charge. At present the library is open a limited number of weekday hours, but an expansion of hours is anticipated. On Saturdays the library is used to hold search workshops or other meetings. The library staff is comprised completely of volunteers.

At present over 250 groups (including branches) participate in and support the activities of the library. New groups wishing to participate should write to the library, indicating their name, address, membership charges, aims and purposes, and any other information that should be noted in the library's reference file. There are no charges either to groups or to individuals using and becoming part of the referral service.

You do not need to be a member to utilize the library's services. Your individual questions will be answered by mail or on the telephone at no charge. Triadoption Library's financial support comes from the Friends of Triadoption Library, who also work as volunteers to staff the library, participate on speakers' panels, and engage in fund-raising activities. Membership fees range from $10.00 for a Contributor to $1,000 for a Benefactor.

The library is located at the Westminster Community Service Center, 7571 Westminster Ave., Westminster, CA 92683. To receive more information, write: The Triadoption Library, P.O. Box 5218, Huntington Beach, CA 92646. Telephone: (714) 892-4098.

Truth Seekers in Adoption

This group was founded in 1973 by LaVerne McCurdy and works within the state of Illinois. It is concerned with all members of the adoption triangle: adoptees, birthparents, and adoptive parents.

Volunteer search assistants are an important part of this organization. Truth Seekers in Adoption describes its services as follows:

YOU ARE THE SEARCHER. We provide the search guide, but you do as much as possible on your own. In the event that you do not feel that you can take a certain step in your search, your guide should be consulted. The greater the individual effort you extend, the greater reward in the event that you reach your goal.

Any out-of-pocket expenses incurred by a search assistant is expected to be reimbursed, and the method of payment should be worked out in advance with any assistant.

TSIA offers regularly scheduled meetings, encourages discussion groups, and provides training for new assistants. It publishes a newsletter, *The Seeker*, to keep all members informed on new happenings, activities, and search information.

The group has completed more than 500 searches, involving more than 3,000 individuals.

The initial membership fee is $25.00. Interested persons should write: Truth Seekers in Adoption, P.O. Box 286, Roscoe, IL 61073. Telephone: (815) 765-2730 or (312) 625-4475.

Washington Adoptees' Rights Movement

The state of Washington, through its judicial system, has introduced a policy of using court-appointed intermediaries to aid adoptees and birthparents with their searches. These court-appointed intermediaries are members of the nonprofit Washington Adoptees' Rights Movement (WARM). This arrangement has its origins in a proposal made to the King County Superior Court and adoption agencies to use this group of volunteer workers to aid adoptees and birthparents in their efforts to contact each other. Not all counties participate in this intermediary system.

Many search and support groups strongly oppose the use of intermediaries and thus the role played by WARM. These opponents are in principle against the interposition of any agent or person between the individual adoptee/birthparent and his records. Others feel WARM provides a useful means of doing what needs to be done in order to aid searchers. In any event, most agree that this is a sincerely dedicated group of volunteers who have approached the idea of helping from a different angle.

To initiate action under this system, you must first petition the court in the jurisdiction where your adoption or relinquishment took place to open its records. At that point the court contacts an intermediary from WARM, who is instructed to meet with you. The intermediary has access to the court's sealed documents and works with the information contained there, although he or she is sworn to secrecy by the court and faces a contempt-of-court violation if subsequent procedures are not carried out in accord with secrecy requirements.

Once all information has been gathered, the WARM confidential intermediary sets to tracing the individual you seek. If that person is located, the intermediary makes contact in an effort to obtain a release statement to present to the court. The court will generally set a time limit of six months on WARM's efforts to locate a person. This may be extended on approval of the court. If a direct contact is desired and the appropriate release statements have been obtained, the information is brought before the court for consideration. Where it is discovered that the birthparent sought is deceased, the court will grant a request for opening the heretofore sealed records.

WARM speaks of a 98 percent success rate, with only 2 percent of those contacted refusing their consent to a meeting. The group's membership brochure states, "Our outstanding success rate, one of the best in the nation, is due to the discreet third party approach taken by our intermediaries and the never-ending dedication of our members, especially the Confidential Intermediaries (C.I.) and Search Advisors."

The state of Washington does not encourage independent search, but there are no state laws that prohibit such search.

WARM publishes a monthly newsletter, *Mediator,* conducts group discussion sessions, and participates in the International Soundex Reunion Registry.

Membership is open to adoptees, birthparents, and adoptive parents over the age of eighteen. Searches are not conducted for children under the age of eighteen unless ordered by the court.

The fee to join WARM is $150. Time spent by WARM volunteers in search for you is donated, but you must reimburse any expense incurred by the intermediary in connection with your search. Since out-of-pocket expenses can mount substantially, you should discuss all financial arrangements and method of payment before the intermediary proceeds with the search.

For more information or an application to join this group, write: Washington Adoptees' Rights Movement, Good Neighbor Center, Hillaire School #12, 15749 NE 4th St., Bellevue, WA 98008. Telephone: (206) 747-5045. Office hours are 9:30 AM to 4:00 PM Monday through Friday. Chapters are located in Seattle, Everett, Tacoma, and Spokane.

8

Reunion Registries

Reunion registries are designed to provide a means by which relatives separated by relinquishment and adoption can locate each other. They are files maintained by private groups or public agencies holding on record the names, addresses, and other identifying information of searchers, like yourself, who are hoping to locate a relinquished child, a birthparent, or a sibling from whom they've been separated. It is not unusual for adoptees, birthparents, or siblings to discover each other through a listing in one or another reunion registry. It is, in all likelihood, the easiest route to a successful search. That does not mean it is one you should wholly count on.

The first reunion registry was established in 1952 by Jean Paton, founder of Orphan Voyage. Since that time other registries have been established, most within the past decade. New ones are appearing more and more frequently. Many small search and support groups now maintain their own registry, usually with listings from the specific area in which they operate. They generally supplement one of the larger registries, to which they will have an established link.

There are two basic categories of reunion registries: group (private) registries and state registries.

Group (private) registries have for the most part been set up and are maintained by private search and support groups. The process of application to these registries is relatively informal. Your sending in a completed application form is taken as implicit consent to release of information by the registry at any time that a link is established to you via a contact made with the registry.

State registries have been set up and are maintained by the respective states in which they've been established. (Unfortunately, they exist in only a few states, but the people in the adoption movement are hopeful that they will increase in number in the future.) State registries function on a more formal level than private group registries. As a general rule, you must apply via a notarized letter, and an affidavit of consent is required before information is released to any third party. In some cases state registries provide adoptees and birthparents with the explicit option to request that they *not* be listed. In one case, Minnesota, a request for registration by an adoptee actually initiates a search for the birthparent.

In the case of both highlighted group (private) registries and the state registries, the information given here reflects that provided me in response to my requests for details; in several cases the information received was only partial or not readily forthcoming. As a result, I have been able to provide only general information. This does not mean that in the case of any particular registry you would not be well-served as an individual on file. What it does mean is that you should consider the use of a registry with your own situation in mind, asking initially for information to supplement that given here so that you can determine how the registry will work in your case.

How Do Reunion Registries Work?

Reunion registries work on the simple principle of matching up information on file.

In each case—whether you're an adoptee, birthparent, or separated sibling —you send away for an application form, complete as much information as you have, then return the form, with whatever fee is required, to the address indicated.

Certain information that can contribute to an identification will be needed to make a match possible, and that information will be requested on the application. You may feel you don't have enough information—you may not know your birth name, for example, if you're a searching adoptee—but you generally have more useful information on hand than you think. You can at least indicate sex, and you probably know your date of birth. Well, that's a beginning. Do you know the state of relinquishment? The court in which it was handled? The hospital where you were born? What was the name of the adoption agency involved, and what information did it give you? Parents' religion? Occupations? Do you have a change of name filed with the court overseeing your adoption? What is the docket or case number indicated on any court proceedings?

If you are a birthparent, what did the agency tell you about the home your child was going to? The adoptive parents' occupations? Other children in the family and their ages? Birth dates, hospital names, court case numbers, and the like are other items you can probably provide without too much difficulty. From either side of the adoption situation, you can probably provide more facts to list for eventual match-up than you may at first think.

Once your application is received by the reunion registry, your responses on the application form are coded. Any previous or subsequent referral to the registry that lists substantially similar or identical particulars in a number of areas will automatically be checked against yours. When the match is close enough to assure the two searching parties are actually searching for each other, the reunion registry moves to make contact possible.

As awareness of the services of the reunion registries grows, it can be expected that more and more birth families will be reunited this way. In fact, search and support groups report more and more reunions effected through both parties locating each other by means of these registries. There is, however, no guarantee that you will benefit from joining a registry. In order for a match-up to occur, two persons have to be searching for each other. Increasing state involvement, particularly where the state mandates an immediate records search by the administering agency, may improve chances when only one person registers. But keep another fact in mind: Joining a registry puts you on permanent file. Your search is put on record, so that two years from now, five years from now, even ten years from now another party initiating a search for you will be able to locate that record and thereby eventually locate you. Even if your search comes to a halt on all other fronts, joining a reunion registry keeps it alive at least to some degree. No, there's no guarantee of benefit, but you will certainly want to consider the possibility for benefit that exists.

Which reunion registries should you look to? Below is information about the four largest group registries and all the state registries established to date. Don't overlook the possibility of benefit from the many other, small reunion registries that exist. As mentioned, these frequently function within a limited geographical area. Contact a search and support group in your area of search —particularly where your adoption or relinquishment took place—and ask if the group maintains a reunion registry.

Highlighted Private Registries

The ALMA International Reunion Registry Data Bank

The Adoptees' Liberty Movement Association, the largest of the search and support groups, also maintains the largest reunion registry, which has been set up for the benefit of its members. The total number of participants at last count was more than 150,000 people. Such a large number provides many opportunities for potential searcher match-up.

ALMA describes its registry as "a multi-level cross reference file system located at the national headquarters, utilizing data to match birthdates, names, etc. to facilitate a reunion. . . . It is by far the largest, most successful registry in existence."

You must be an ALMA member to register with the ALMA Reunion Registry. The annual membership fee is $30.00. You can apply for membership at any local branch of ALMA (see the state reference list in the appendix to locate the branch nearest you), or you can write: ALMA, National Headquarters, P.O. Box 154, Washington Bridge Station, New York, NY 10033.

Concerned United Birthparents (CUB) Reunion Registry

This registry was formed and is operated by the largest birthparent support group in the world. Since its formation in 1976, over 13,000 individuals have registered.

Applicants are placed in the registry under the birth date of the offspring. If two applicants submit the same birth dates, a check is made into sex, state of birth, and additional facts known. If all information matches, the applicants are contacted.

Services are offered to any individual who has been separated from a family member, through adoption, relinquishment, family feud, kidnapping, divorce, or any other circumstances.

There is an initial registration fee of $5.00. Membership in the registry is separate from membership in CUB. There are no restrictions for applying; all those searching for lost family members are welcome.

Those interested in this registry should write for more information, or request an application to join, from Concerned United Birthparents, National Administration Headquarters, P.O. Box 573, Milford, MA 01757.

International Soundex Reunion Registry

The International Soundex Reunion Registry was conceived by and is managed and supported by one dedicated woman, Emma May Vilardi. She established it in the mid-1970s with the intention of providing a centralized registry open to all adoptees/birthparents and to any search and support groups.

ISRR uses the Soundex Coding System (see Chapter 4). When registration forms are received, the information is translated into a single code line. "This code line," according to ISRR, "is capable of seven points of match and enables the registrar to check over 1000 entries in about five minutes. In its present form, it is computer ready."

Since its inception, ISRR has grown to include more than 10,000 individual registrants and 176 participating groups. Registration is open to anyone eighteen years of age or older. Those under eighteen who apply have their applications placed in a "hold file" until their eighteenth birthday, at which time they are brought over into the active files. There are currently more than 1,000 applications awaiting maturity.

ISRR has recently begun services for two groups with special needs: those searchers with a pressing medical need and those individuals who used, or were products of, artificial insemination.

In an effort to help searchers with medical problems, or possible medical problems, ISRR has established a MEDICAL-ALERT file. Whether you belong to a group or not, if you have a medical need, you should obtain a registration form from the address listed below. Mark your form, in bold letters across the top, MEDICAL-ALERT. Include a brief letter of explanation with your registration. Regardless of the number of applications received on that day, your letter will receive priority processing. ISRR files will be checked to learn if the person you seek is registered; if so, you will be contacted immediately. If the Soundex system does not produce a match, then ISRR will alert all affiliate groups and enlist their help. The affiliates will then search their files, call on any sources of information they may have, and inform their members of your need. Groups, as well as individuals—adoptees or birthparents—should keep this valuable service in mind.

The second service offered provides for those searchers who have discovered they are a product of artificial insemination and for birthparents who used artificial insemination. After obtaining an ISRR registration form, mark in bold letters across the top, AID (Artificial Insemination Donor).

ISRR, and many of those involved in the adoption movement, are aware of the special problems of AID searchers. Few states have *any* laws controlling doctors or clinics who use AID and offer this type of service. Paid donors are usually sought by advertising in a newspaper or by personal contact through a doctor.

How long a clinic keeps its records is up to the administrator. Donors are required to fill out a medical form, which is usually used as a means of selecting the donor by the birthmother.

ISRR places AID records together in hope of providing a match or a means of furnishing further information to searchers.

Although the registration ratio is currently two to one in favor of adoptees, it is interesting to note the tremendous increase in birthparents registering with ISRR. During 1979 the number of new birthparent registrations was actually greater than that of new adoptee registrations.

The state of Minnesota makes use of ISRR as a complement to its own reunion registry. Numerous search and support groups mention that they do the same.

Groups wishing to become affiliated with this unique registry need only submit information about their group and request a master copy of the Soundex registration form to be used for listing present and future members with ISRR. Individuals need only request and fill out an application. Application forms or further information are obtainable from Emma May Vilardi, ISRR, P.O. Box 2312, Carson City, NV 89701. Membership is free to all participants, but letters of inquiry must include a self-addressed, stamped envelope for reply.

Orphan Voyage Reunion Registry

The oldest of all the registries, Orphan Voyage has approximately 2,000 registered applicants in its files. Jean Paton, who first conceived of the idea of a reunion registry in 1949 and then put it into effect in 1952, describes the objectives of the registry in a pamphlet entitled *Orphan Voyage, A Program:*

> The Reunion File is intended to assist those who do not have any other resource in the search, who have followed all clues to no avail, those who wish to register in the face of the uncertainties of life, so that even if something happens to them, at least the person who seeks them later will have something in the way of fruit for his trouble.

Registration is open to applicants of all ages. You must be an Orphan Voyage member to be listed, however. (For membership fees and other particulars, please see the description of Orphan Voyage and its work in Chapter 7.) For a registration form or further information, write to: Orphan Voyage, 2141 Rd. 2300, Cedaredge, CO 81413. Telephone: (303) 856-3937.

State Reunion Registries

The following reunion registries are maintained and administered according to guidelines established by state law. Write to the appropriate agency in the state where your search centers to receive exact information and instructions for registering.

At the present there are only five states with working reunion registries. However, several states are actively considering the implementation of this kind of service, and others are at least starting to study the registry program in the states listed here. Several other states have some form of a registry, but this usually takes the form of allowing notations in adoption files. This type of registry is mentioned in the state-by-state listings.

If your state is not among those listed here, write to the state social services (or equivalent) department or to a search and support group in your state to discover if a new registry has just been set up, is being set up, or is under consideration.

Maine

On September 21, 1979, the state legislature passed a law allowing the State Registrar of Vital Statistics to assist adoptees and birthparents when both wish to make contact. This is the statutory foundation for the state's reunion registry.

The state does not help applicants search for missing relatives. The only service provided is for registry and for notification of a match when such occurs.

Applicants must be eighteen years of age or older. The application form becomes a permanent record, so any changes of address or name should be submitted in order that all information on file remains current.

For more information, or to request an application, write: State of Maine, Office of Vital Statistics, Department of Human Services, 221 State St., Station 11, Augusta, ME 04333. Telephone: (207) 289-3181. There is a fee payable when you return your application.

Michigan

On September 10, 1980, Public Act No. 116 went into effect to allow adoptees and birthparents somewhat easier access to records. The subsequently established registry is less concerned with effecting reunions than it is with maintaining a file of statements that either consent to or deny release of information in public or private agency records that could serve to identify a relinquishing parent or relinquished child. Different procedures are established according to whether relinquishment was before or after the date Public Act No. 116 went into effect.

If your records are held in the state of Michigan and you wish to submit a form consenting to the release of information, write to: Michigan Department of Social Services, Adoption Central Registry, P.O. Box 30037, 300 S. Capitol Ave., Lansing, MI 48909. If you wish to facilitate a reunion, include your current name and address as information that may be released.

Ask about fees for joining the registry when you first write for a consent form or information.

Minnesota

The Minnesota Reunion Registry was established by an act of the Minnesota legislature on June 1, 1977.

This state registry is unique for the close ties that it maintains with volunteer search and support groups. Minnesota lists five sponsors that offer services to searchers: Adoptees' Liberty Movement Association (ALMA), Concerned United Birthparents (CUB), Kammandale Library, Liberal Education for Adoptive Families (LEAF), and Link. The state will refer searchers to these groups for mutual search assistance, research and referral information, support groups, and public and private education relating to adoption and adoption laws. The cooperating sponsors hold their own monthly meetings and combined quarterly meetings, and issue newsletters to their membership. In addition to cooperating with these sponsors, Minnesota supplements its reunion registry through affiliation with the International Soundex Reunion Registry; applicants to the state's reunion registry are automatically listed with ISRR.

The law establishing the Minnesota Reunion Registry distinguishes between adoptions/relinquishments occurring before June 1, 1977, and those taking place after that date. Birthparents relinquishing a child on or after June 1, 1977, are informed by the court at the time of relinquishment of their right to file an affidavit to consent to or refuse release of birth information when their child turns twenty-one. A different procedure is established in the cases of those whose adoption was carried out before August 1, 1977.

Adoptees twenty-one years of age or older may request information on their birth certificate from the State Registrar of Vital Statistics, 717 Delaware, SE, Minneapolis, MN 55440. This request starts a search for the birthparents listed on the certificate. The agency must make "responsible efforts" to locate the birthparents of adoptees requesting information or a reunion. Once the birthparents have been located, they are confidentially notified of the adoptee's desire to contact them. They then have four months in which to file with the state registrar an affidavit of consent or refusal to be identified. If a statement of consent is filed, the identifying information is released to the adoptee. If not, the certificate remains sealed. In that event the only recourse for those seeking the information is to file a request for a court order to open the records.

There is no fee to join the Minnesota Reunion Registry. However, there is a quarterly newsletter entitled *Midwestern Regional Report* for those interested in adoption-related developments in this area of the Midwest, for a $10.00 subscription fee.

For additional information or an application for registration, direct inquiries to: State Registrar, Section of Vital Statistics, Minnesota Department of Health, 717 Delaware SW, Minneapolis, MN 55440. Telephone (612) 296-5316.

Nevada

Nevada Law No. 127.007, passed in 1979, established a state reunion registry, with files maintained by the Welfare Division of the Nevada Department of Human Resources.

Applicants will need to send a notarized letter stating their desire to be listed in the registry and their openness to having identifying information in their records released to a searching relinquished child or birthparent. For registration or other information, write to: Nevada State Reunion Registry, Welfare Division—Department of Human Resources, 251 Jeanell Dr., Capitol Mall Complex, Carson City, NV 89710.

One interesting fact to emerge from my research was that, while Minnesota works in cooperation with the International Soundex Reunion Registry—a private registry based in Nevada—the state of Nevada does not. This is a prime illustration of the kind of inconsistencies that plague the adoption movement on a national level.

New Jersey

New Jersey has been a leader among states on the development of flexible policies regarding release of information. In 1977 it established an Authorization for Release of Adoption Information Registry.

To apply to this registry simply send a notarized letter stating your wish to be listed. When all parties involved have filed such a letter, the information in the records is released.

Send your letter of application by certified mail, return receipt requested, to: The Bureau of Resource Development, Division of Youth and Family Services, Box 510, Trenton, NJ 08625.

9

Taking It One Step Further

You've read through the information presented so far in this book and you may find yourself thinking that search seems too complicated a process for you to manage. Perhaps you've been searching already, but no leads seem to be developing. Maybe you feel you simply haven't the inner resources to undertake the weeks or months of looking, hoping, and waiting that search appears likely to entail. Isn't there another way to go about it?

Alternatives to undertaking search efforts on your own do exist. You can follow any one of these three approaches: (1) line up someone who can and will help you with difficult aspects of your search; (2) find someone who will actually conduct the search for you; (3) initiate court action in an effort to unseal the adoption/relinquishment records that hold the identifying information you want to know.

Enlisting Assistance

No one has to undertake a search alone, without any kind of assistance. As already noted, search and support groups exist in every state, and these provide the most readily available source of practical advice and ideas on how to manage a search. But even then you still have to do most of the actual work yourself. Reunion registries can simplify things considerably, but only if the person you seek is on file with the registry you refer to; if not, you still have to go on searching. However, there are other sources of assistance available to you.

Legal Consultants

There may be times you feel the need for legal counsel during your search. You may not feel entirely at ease adapting the sample forms given here to assign a limited power of attorney or to draw up a waiver of confidentiality. You may feel it desirable to have any correspondence with state agencies, hospital administrations, and so on, in which you assert your rights to information held on you, issued under an attorney's letterhead—or at least reviewed by an attorney.

If you have your own attorney, then it's a simple matter of consulting with him or her when questions arise that involve legality or legal form. If you do not have your own attorney, look in your telephone directory for your county's bar association and ask for assistance in obtaining the legal counsel you require. Of course, you should discuss fees for whatever services are to be performed. These can be substantial, and you want to know in advance what kind of financial burden you will incur as the result of any work your attorney does for you. Your county bar association may provide a relatively inexpensive legal clinic for county residents. (In my county you can obtain legal advice for a fee of $30.00 an hour.) Find out if your county bar association sponsors any kind of legal clinic. You can also refer to a local branch of the Legal Aid Society, which provides free or inexpensive legal advice to eligible persons. Contact your local society to find out what the rules are that determine eligibility for legal assistance.

Intermediaries

An intermediary is someone who acts for you in contacts with other parties. To many searchers *intermediary* is a dirty word. That is because adoption agencies act as intermediaries, too often without regard for searchers' needs or feelings. Courts too act as intermediaries—or appoint them—also frequently with results that are not satisfactory to a searcher. In these situations, the intermediary makes decisions for you that do not depend on any instruction from you or that do not take your search goals into sympathetic consideration.

However, you can make arrangements on your own, whereby you designate someone to act on your behalf. If you feel that someone else can speak for you better than you can speak for yourself or if your emotions and sense of involvement are too overwhelming or conflicting to allow you to deal with a situation as thoughtfully as is necessary, it makes sense to consider using an intermediary.

Who will act as your intermediary? The possibilities are numerous. You may ask your spouse or someone you trust to act for you. You may ask a fellow searcher to act for you. Another alternative is to hire a professional consultant or private investigator (see below) to serve as intermediary.

Weigh the advantages of employing an intermediary against the possible pitfalls in relying on someone else to speak for you. Will that person represent you and your interests capably? There may be times when you have only one opportunity to win the cooperation of someone who has access to or holds information valuable to you. In the sensitive situation of establishing actual first contact with the person you're seeking, will a subsequent meeting between you and your relative be easier or harder if you use an intermediary? Here, it's advisable to rely on an intermediary only if you're convinced it's absolutely necessary—because you know right now you can't handle it well yourself.

If you've decided to use an intermediary in your search, you will have to provide him or her with a waiver of confidentiality. Individuals will not be allowed access to personal records kept on you without explicit authorization from you. Your waiver may be specifically directed to one record or file or it may be broadly stated to include all records and files. The scope of your waiver depends both on what you're looking for and on the intermediary involved. A private investigator or other professional consultant may ask that you sign a waiver of confidentiality prepared as a standard form. Exercise caution, be aware of what you're signing. If there's a chance any of your private records come to be held by an intermediary, make sure you'll get them back when the search work done for you is concluded. See Sample 18 for a waiver of confidentiality that you can adapt for use with an intermediary.

Some consultants may ask you formally to assign them a limited power of attorney so that they can obtain personal documents in your name. Be extremely careful here. State clearly and specifically what *limited* powers you are delegating, whom you're delegating them to, and what time limit is set on exercise of them. Be sure you don't foolishly grant unlimited power of attorney. An unlimited power of attorney would enable your intermediary to take control of all your affairs, including disposition of property you own and committing you to contractual obligations without first consulting with you. You may want to get legal advice if you're faced with a request for a grant of power of attorney to an intermediary.

Contacts

The word *contact* conjures up images of espionage activity, with illegal information surreptitiously passing from hand to hand. It's a fact that in adoption search there are contacts who are paid for their services of obtaining information. I have heard of adoptees paying as much as $1,000 for their birth name, obtained through an "agent" with access to sealed files. And then I

SAMPLE 18

WAIVER OF CONFIDENTIALITY FOR USE
BY AN INTERMEDIARY

To Whom It May Concern

I, (give present name), also known as (give name by adoption/at time of relinquishment if different, or give name at birth if known), residing at (give current street, city, county, and state address), do state the following:

Permission is given to (name of agent or consultant) to maintain private records on me and to keep certain files on me as listed below. This permission is granted starting (month, day, year) and shall extend to (month, day, year).

Those records covered by this affidavit waiving confidentiality in respect of the person herein named are: hospital records, court records from (list court of jurisdiction), agency records (list agency or private adoption intermediary), birth records, and any other documents or information pertaining to (adoption or relinquishment). (1)

It is clearly understood that all records and information obtained under this waiver of confidentiality shall be forwarded intact to the undersigned upon the final date herein indicated.

Signed _____ Dated _____

Have a notary public certify your signature.

Other Possible Inclusion:

1. *Add:* The person herein named shall not undertake any personal or written contact with individuals named in the documents indicated, other than officials or records administrators whose cooperation is necessary to assure obtaining of the documents themselves.

Note: This letter should be very clear on what records and rights you wish to grant. You may wish an attorney to draw up the waiver for you.

know another adoptee who paid only $25.00 for the name of her birthmother. In either case, it's doubtful the name was obtained by legal means.

You're the kind of person who, on finding a lost wallet, calls the police and turns it in, all money and credit cards accounted for. At the supermarket you always tell the cashiers when they return you too much change. You vote in every election, believe in motherhood, and think apple pie is the ultimate in good food. Are you the kind of person who would use a contact to obtain information illegally?

Only you know the answer to that question. Some searchers make this distinction: *no*—to obtain information on others that might be used against them; *yes*—to obtain information on oneself or one's family that is freely available to the average person who is not part of the adoption triangle. It is a fact that laws exist about the passing of certain types of information. You should be aware that you expose yourself to risk whenever you participate in illegal activity, whatever your motives.

If you use a contact, be very wary when paying cash to a source unknown to you. If your source is reliable, payment is often made after you're satisfied the information received is correct—with only a partial payment made before then.

Many contacts are not the person actually obtaining the information. Contacts often are the individuals who know a sympathetic source whose identity they protect. They are, in effect, another form of intermediary. You may not be able to ascertain whether the source is a legal one or not—it may simply be someone in your area of search who has genealogical/search resources and experience that go far beyond that which you have. You only know information is being promised you that you very much want to have.

Before dealing with contacts, make every effort to ascertain their reliability. Can other searchers attest to their reliability? Ask yourself what you stand to gain for the price you must pay. Recognize that there are risks to be faced— risk of possible involvement in illegal activity, even the risk that you are being victimized in a cruel confidence hoax.

Records Searchers

A records searcher does what the name says—concentrates on searching census, birth, death, or any of a number of records pertaining to an individual or family. Ideally, a records searcher is a person who is aware of what information is available at municipal, county, and state offices or archives, and who knows how to use these records and other documentary sources to your best advantage. A records searcher can check through more record sources with greater understanding and speed than you can. While you might find yourself spending hours poring over a given record file, the records searcher would know if there was an index to those records and be able to check through the file with greater efficiency. Don't engage a records searcher just because you see one advertised as such; ascertain what experience and references he can offer and determine if he has been involved in your kind of search and is familiar with your area of search.

Under a program established by Independent Search Consultants (see below), there are now certified records searchers. The program has been in operation a few years only, so certification has not yet become general practice.

You can find individuals whose background is sufficiently extensive so that the question of certification is beside the point. However, if you want the security of competence that certification indicates, you can write to ISC for referral to a certified records searcher.

Records searchers may be part-time enthusiasts or full-time professionals, who will most likely charge for their services. Fees will probably be charged according to the needs in your case and depending on difficulty of access to the records you want searched for you. Be certain you know what the charges will be before you allow any records searcher to search for you. Make sure to ask if the fee quoted is all-inclusive or whether expenses will constitute an additional charge. Keep the question of expenses in mind. Many states charge a fee to view certain records; in California, for example, there is a $2.00 per hour charge to view marriage records. If expenses will be charged you in addition to a basic service rate, be sure you know all the expenses that may be involved. For example, will there be travel expenses you're expected to reimburse the records searcher for? How will these expenses be computed? When working with someone who charges an hourly rate, you may also want to agree on a maximum fee, so that the charges don't exceed your budget. If making a flat fee arrangement, determine specifically what the records searcher will be doing for that fee.

Search Assistants

A records searcher is obviously a form of search assistant in the sense that he meaningfully assists in your search. However, among searchers there is a distinction drawn between records searchers and search assistants. A records searcher commonly limits work to records search only. A search assistant works on a broader level than a records searcher, counseling on search techniques and helping you apply them to your individual needs.

Many search and support groups are associated with volunteer or professional search assistants trained to aid you in your search. Charges can range from nothing for someone who volunteers his or her time to as much as $50.00 per hour for a professional. Obviously, you need to know what any charge would be before you have a search assistant work with you. Contact a local group for the name of a recommended search assistant if you want this kind of help. Once you are in contact with such an individual, be careful to outline the type of help you hope to have provided and any fee arrangement. Any professional arrangement you make should be in writing and spell out the type of help you are seeking and the charge for this help.

Independent Search Consultants

Independent Search Consultants is an organization founded in the fall of 1979 by Pat Sanders to establish a reliable training and certification program for adoptee/birthparent search consultants. Mary Jo Rillera of the Triadoption Library (see Chapter 7) and Emma May Vilardi of the International Soundex Reunion Registry (see Chapter 8) introduced this organization to search and support groups across the country. Because of these endorsements from the adoption search movement, ISC has been able to establish itself solidly in a relatively short period of time.

ISC has a standardized program of education and training leading to certification. All applicants for certification must present personal recommendations, document their training hours, and take a qualifying examination. The organization offers special classes, and credit is given toward training hours for those attending these classes. After completing the necessary hours and the examination, the applicant submits all information to be reviewed to the ISC Certification Board.

Four types of certification are offered:

1. State certification—acknowledged expertise in one particular state.
2. National certification—acknowledged expertise in three or more states.
3. Specialized certification—acknowledged expertise in a foreign country, specialized knowledge of adoption laws, or specialized knowledge in research areas.
4. Records search certification—acknowledged expertise in availability of records and records review, but no direct search consultation.

The period of certification is five years in each case. The cost to become certified ranges from $50 for a records searcher to $100 for a national consultant.

In the past, working with search consultants was a hit-or-miss process for searchers. Usually consulting services were available only through a few search and support groups, and matching the consultant's experience with your particular needs was difficult. This might have been a typical case: Your consultant's experience was with search in Wyoming, but your search was centered in New Jersey; your consultant was a birthmother, you an adoptee; her relinquishment had been privately managed, while yours was a public agency adoption. Your consultant's line of experience in a different state and from a different perspective in the adoption triangle meant that she had to work with problems and state laws that she was not familiar with. ISC's goal is to eliminate this kind of mismatch by providing training and expertise in all types and areas of search, and then to serve as a clearinghouse to match certified consultants with searchers requiring their particular expertise.

Once you register with Independent Search Consultants, your name is placed in the ISC referral files. You will be given the names of three search consultants familiar with the type of search you require and the state(s) involved. All consultants set their own fees and make a personal decision if they will search for a minor child or help a minor child search for a birthparent. ISC does not have a group policy regarding age limitations on those searching or being sought. Charges range from nothing for those consultants willing to donate time to $25.00 an hour. You should discuss all charges at the time you contact one of the consultants you are referred to.

To receive more information or to request the services of a consultant, send a self-addressed, stamped envelope with your inquiry to Independent Search Consultants, P.O. Box 10192, Costa Mesa, CA 92627.

Independent Search Consultants has drawn up a code of ethics to be followed by all consultants. It is included here, not only as an indication of the professionalism that has come to characterize this aspect of search activity, but also to show you what *any* reputable consultant or other intermediary should offer you.

ISC CODE OF ETHICS

A search consultant realizes that he has moral obligations to the client, to the profession, and to society as well. His honesty must be above suspicion, his skill and reasoning ability well developed, and his competency of the highest degree. Understanding all of this, I make the following commitments:

TO THE CLIENT:

I will use all resources available to me to acquire information beneficial to the client.

I will obtain from the client all information so far assembled, so as to avoid duplication.

I will keep accurate and complete records of the client's search.

I will not promise success on any level, but will enter into and carry on the search with every expectation of success.

I will communicate directly and clearly with my client and will keep him fully informed on the progress of the search.

I will consider each client's case confidential.

I will not make any personal contacts other than at the client's specific request and with his permission.

I will be discreet and will advise the client to use discretion in his search.

I will remember that the search is the client's.

TO THE PROFESSION:

I will not knowingly act in a manner detrimental to the best interests of the profession.

I will not undertake or advise any illegal acts.

I will unhesitatingly refer my client to another consultant or other professionals when I can no longer be of help to him.

I will not injure the professional reputation, prospects, or practice of another consultant.

I will not use my position or influence within an organized adoption search and support group to recruit clients.

TO THE PUBLIC:

I will maintain professional integrity at all times.

I will be aware that search consultation as a profession is relatively new and must earn a reputable name for itself.

I will remember that the area of adoption search is often a delicate one and must be handled with care and thoughtfulness.

Genealogical Consultants

You may find that your search necessarily leads you into genealogy, because sometimes only through tracing extended family lines across several generations does it seem possible to locate a missing relative. You can, if need be, call on the services of professional genealogists who will do genealogical research for a fee. Such consultants are trained and experienced in searching records, using indexes, and applying techniques for tracing relatives. The usual distinction between genealogical consultants and consultants more specifically concentrating in the adoption search area is that the former deal mostly with records on persons now dead, while the latter concentrate on those living, or at least presumed to be living.

Your local genealogy group can usually direct you to a qualified consultant or provide you with a list of such consultants. A local historical society may be able to do so as well. Your reference librarian may be able to provide direction here; state libraries and state historical societies will send you a listing of recommended consultants. The Church of Jesus Christ of Latter-Day Saints (the Mormon Church) will send you a list of genealogists accredited by them; these individuals will be highly trained and skilled in genealogical techniques. The church list will carry names from all over the United States and from various foreign countries.

Note that genealogical magazines commonly carry ads for specialized assistance or information sources (see Chapter 4). An individual genealogist may have searched through census records from a particular area and compiled an index for that area. For a nominal charge, sometimes as low as $1.00, he or she will provide you a one-line family listing from those census records. Or perhaps he or she is offering information from area birth or probate records. It is possible that such a person could in a limited sense be considered a consultant. More to the point, that person might have information helpful to you.

Hiring Someone to Search for You

You may hire a private investigator to search for you. A good private investigator can frequently find whatever information you need. I've found professional investigators as a group to be highly professional and particularly adept at locating missing persons. And, of course, this is essentially what you're working to accomplish in your search.

Private investigators work in mysterious ways, at least from a layman's perspective. They seem to have superior access to records and reliable, established contacts to provide needed information in any of a number of areas. They have the means to get hold of information you would find difficult to obtain on your own.

The greatest value I see in hiring private investigators is the relative speed with which they get results. Most often, you submit all your information to them, and before long you have the additional information you want. No, it doesn't always work out that way, but it does happen regularly. You'd spend months collecting and sorting through material that a good private investigator gets hold of and evaluates quickly. One private investigator who has undertaken a number of search assignments told me that in one case his search took only fifteen minutes. The longest took several weeks.

How do you go about hiring a private investigator to work for you? You can obtain addresses from listings in area Yellow Pages of the telephone directory. You can check with an attorney you know for a possible recommendation. Many search and support groups will provide you the name of a private investigator used by other members. A check with the local Better Business Bureau would turn up any complaints lodged against a particular private investigator or private investigative agency. Start by contacting at least three who work in your area of search. That will give you a good idea of the rates charged and the services offered. Find out how much information you are likely to obtain for the amount you have to spend. Ask what types of missing person searches they specialize in and whether they're familiar with your type of search. Ask how long they have been in business.

In making a determination to hire, you should exercise the same good judgment you'd exercise in hiring anyone. Stress what you want done and what limitations you're setting. If you use a private investigator in a supplementary fashion, be sure you both understand and agree on what the range and cost of service will be. Do you want the private investigator to have any contact with the person sought? State that clearly. Do you want the private investigator to undertake the entire search for you, or do you wish that he handle a particular aspect of your search only? In either event, be sure he meets your needs.

Most private investigators like to work on a retainer, if not on payment of a full fee in advance. It works something like a checking account—you deposit a given sum of money with the private investigator, and he draws on that until the balance reaches zero. If you decide there's more you want done, you can deposit money into "the account."

It's customary for the private investigator to alert you whenever your "balance" approaches zero. Suppose you've provided a $100 retainer for a private investigator charging $25 an hour plus expenses. He will probably contact you after three hours of searching. If you choose not to continue once the retainer account reaches zero, he will send you all the information obtained to that point. If you want to continue, you send an additional $100 check or whatever the amount is. It will depend on your budget, on your satisfaction with what the private investigator has been able to discover, and on your feeling whether this is the best way to proceed with your search. Time can also be an important consideration. Included here is a sample retainer agreement (Sample 19) that you can adapt for your purposes.

You may turn to a private investigator in order to ensure privacy. You may not be able to receive letters or make calls freely. You may not be able to withstand the emotional conflicts raised by pushing and probing for information related to your adoption or relinquishment. By turning your search over to a professional, you are removed from these problems. But remember, you run a risk of your confidentiality being compromised or your search goal being endangered if you take on a private investigator who is not familiar with adoptee/birthparent search. You run even greater risk if you do not communicate a clear understanding of how you want your search conducted. Hiring a private investigator is a step that should be taken only after careful consideration of your needs and resources *and* a thorough discussion of these with the professional involved.

SAMPLE 19

RETAINER AGREEMENT

The undersigned, (your name), of (your home address), hereinafter called "the client," does hereby retain and employ (list name, business, or assigned agent) as (agent, attorney, consultant) in connection with (state nature of business to be undertaken).

Payment for services rendered shall be on the basis of:

A. A total fee (including expenses) $_____
     or retainer received $_____

B. An estimated fee which shall be
     no less than $_____
     and no more than $_____

C. Fees plus expenses. It is understood and agreed that the agent herein indicated shall be due monies for the following expenses: (list as specifically as possible)

No additional expenses shall be incurred and charged the client without express written consent from the client. The fee shall be computed on a(n) (hourly/flat) rate of $_____. The total charge to the client of fees *and* expenses shall not exceed a total sum of $_____.

Likely expenses are estimated at $_____. The agent hereby agrees to advise the client at such time as it is evident that this estimated figure will be exceeded, and will not incur further expenses on the client's account without the client's express consent.

Client: <u>(your signature)</u>   Dated: _____
Assigned agent: <u>(signature)</u>   Dated: _____

Note: Many agents, private investigators, and consultants have their own retainer forms. Read through them carefully. Insist that everything you wish to have spelled out be included.

Going to Court

As an alternative to searching, you can try initiating a court action to unseal adoption/relinquishment records. You should recognize, however, that this can be as time-consuming and emotionally draining an experience as the most difficult search. While it's evident that public attitudes are slowly changing and that the law in some states is beginning to reflect this change, existing laws, on the whole, are still weighted against you.

Each state has its own set of procedures to follow. In some states it's possible to file a request to unseal your records without an attorney having to be present. An appearance before a judge in the appropriate court of jurisdiction is all that is required. This informal hearing may result in release of all the sealed information upon your presenting a valid—to the court, not just to you—need to know. In other states a more formal procedure must be followed, with an attorney pleading your case. Restrictions on release of information may be so stringently worded and observed that not even the best-pleaded case could get any records released to you.

If you're contemplating a court action, the first thing to do is to find out what the process is for petitioning to have records unsealed in the state in which your adoption or relinquishment took place. Call or write the appropriate court of jurisdiction for the necessary details. You'll need the answers to many questions before proceeding. Do you need an attorney to plead your case? If so, do you need to be present as well? What papers or forms must you present to start the action? How long will the case take? If you now live in another state, is it possible to have the proceedings conducted there? (Some states will allow the hearing to be held in your state of residence.) What court costs will there be?

Costs will be a major consideration. Chances are you will need or want legal counsel representing you. Perhaps you can locate legal clinic services or are eligible for Legal Aid Society assistance, but you'll probably have to retain your own attorney. If you employ an attorney, how many hours of legal work are likely to be required? You have to decide how much money you're both willing and able to spend to start an action. There are other cost factors to take into account also. Is your court in another state? Does this action involve travel expenses and/or time off from work? Remember, regardless of the outcome of your case, you will have to pay the burden of the expenses involved.

What will you use as reason for insisting that your records should be opened to you? You need to prove good cause—that is, a substantial, *legally sufficient* reason that will prompt the court to do as you ask. Consider carefully what reasons the judge will recognize as valid. Study past cases fought in your state. If you discover that four cases have recently been won on grounds of a medical need to know, while three have been lost that cited a psychological need to know, take this into account. For a sense of what other compelling arguments you may be able to raise, look back to Chapter 1 of this book. Unless your state has provision for an informal hearing without counsel before a judge, I urge you to consult with an attorney before taking any action.

While court action may be an alternative to search, it is rarely an easy alternative. It often proves more difficult and more costly. If the case is decided against you, as it very well may, then you're back where you started. The decision again is whether or not to search. At present, search affords a greater likelihood of success than court action.

10

Ending Your Search

You've come so far, and finally it's your red-letter day. This should be the easiest part of your search, you'd think, but many find it the most difficult. You have the name of your birthparent or child and the telephone number in hand, yet you can't seem to make the call. Friends and family find it impossible to understand why you have reached this point and at the last step seem to falter.

This is an intensely personal moment. The decision to establish the contact you've worked so hard to make possible is strictly yours. I do not believe anyone else is qualified to make the decision for you. If you were my good friend, however, I would provide you moral support, help you in whatever way I could, and acknowledge your decision, whatever it is, as the right one for you.

When you make the decision to contact, take some time to review how you will go about it. You may decide that putting your thoughts into a letter first is preferable to a telephone call immediately. Think what you will say. Recognize that you may be faced with any of a number of reactions—surprise almost certainly, but perhaps expressed as shock. You probably hope for joyful acceptance, but you instinctively realize you face possible rejection. You may get a mixed response, one that is neither clearly acceptance nor rejection.

You want to establish contact in a frame of mind that has you as prepared as you can be for whatever you may discover. You want to be firm in your resolve and in your sense of self-esteem. You must recognize that the moment of contact almost certainly will be a difficult one for your relative too. Fantasies, guilts, and fears exist on both sides. Because of your search you may have already started to confront many of these, but your relative may not. He or she may need time to adjust to your sudden appearance on the scene. A first reaction of bewilderment and confusion is not so unlikely. Give your relative, *and yourself,* time to make the adjustment. It may not be until a subsequent occasion that either of you is fully able to take in the other person as he or she is, without the interference of old feelings of resentment or guilt, or with the illusions that have existed for years all dispelled.

Although the tie between you is biologically the closest that exists, as individuals you will at first be strangers to each other. Even under the best of circumstances, it will take time for your relationship to take shape. Contact is the end of your search, but in terms of building a relationship with your child or birthparent, whatever that comes to be, it's only a beginning.

It's possible you may decide or be forced to accept that a close relationship with your newly located child or birthparent is impossible. Perhaps you dreamed of something that now evidently will not come to pass. You may be inclined to feel you've failed. *Don't.* Your search has always been an activity with a double focus: discovering the identity of someone who is genetically linked and also exploring in depth your own sense of who you are. Regardless of the outcome as far as discovering another's identity goes, you cannot help but have achieved a clearer perspective of yourself. How can that be a failure? Don't let disappointment blind you to the discoveries you've made about yourself—about the courage you've displayed in accepting the challenge facing you, about the determination and imagination you were able to bring to bear in seeing a difficult project through.

If you're reading through this book with the idea of undertaking a search of your own, you'll have your own secret thoughts and fears about what you might learn. Facing those through the process of search will always assure you a worthwhile return on efforts expended. To me there is no such thing as complete failure in a search.

Appendix

STATE-BY-STATE LISTING

This section contains state-by-state information for your search. In gathering this information I asked the appropriate state agency or department how adoption and relinquishment were handled. It is a difficult, if not impossible, task to present the information simply by listing the appropriate names and addresses, since state laws in these matters are complex and varied. A report from the Child Services Association, "Information Paper on Issues and Recommendations Regarding Sealed Adoption Records," shows how confusing the subject of state laws is:

> It should be a simple matter to determine which states have open records and which do not. But, it is not. Laws are seldom clear in terms of which records are sealed, who may have access to the records, what information is contained therein and what specific information is considered sealed. In addition, the effect of a law is felt less in its actual wording than in its interpretation and administration which vary not only from state to state but within a state over time. A final problem is that it is difficult to keep up with new legislation in this area across 50 states. For instance, most articles cite Connecticut and Florida as having open records, but both states rescinded those statutes in 1973 (although a recent court order in Florida may have reinstated their open records).

This explains occasional vagueness and some omissions for various states in this appendix. Here are notes about the categories found under each state. The importance and use of each category has been explained in the text. This listing is to help you carry out your search in an efficient, informed, and economical manner. It will save you many hours of looking for addresses and sources, and it will define the many options open to you under law.

State Information Department: This department is concerned with answering your questions or directing you to the proper source to find the information sought. Do not hesitate to use it to save you many hours of searching for the right person or agency to answer your specific question.

State Agency: If you know the agency that handled your adoption/relinquishment, contact it directly. If you do not know where your adoption/relinquishment took place (a county agency, a private adoption/relinquishment, or an agency that is no longer functioning), write to the state address given. To locate the address of a private agency still functioning, call the information operator or check the telephone directory in the city where it is located.

Court of Jurisdiction: This is the court that is empowered to act on your adoption/relinquishment. Some states have several courts that are so empowered, depending on circumstances in the case. Please note this is the court that holds trials but also the court that in some states allows an adoptee/birthparent a private meeting with a judge to determine access.

Birth, Death, Marriage, and Divorce Records: These are the vital-statistics or record-holding departments to write or visit in order to obtain any of the documents indicated. If you know in what city or county these records are held, use the listing applicable.

Archives/Record Holdings: These are libraries with large collections of genealogical holdings. The information you need may be housed here, in a large public library, a local historical library, or a small newspaper archive. If the information you seek is not available through the address given, this library will be able to direct you to the proper source.

Department of Motor Vehicles: These are state agencies to contact to discover the codes, costs and accessibility of automobile records in your state.

Search and Support Groups: All the groups functioning today are not listed here. I have attempted to represent most states and each type of search and support group available. Some groups focus on helping adoptees, while others primarily aid birthparents; occasionally you may discover a group helping both adoptees and birthparents. The three largest groups (ALMA, CUB, and Orphan Voyage) are listed with their National Headquarters address only. Check your local telephone directory or information operator, or write the headquarters to receive a current local address.

The groups with two asterisks following their names are mentioned by the state social service departments as active groups in their states.

State Reunion Registry: Reunion registries are files maintained by private or public agencies, containing names and addresses of searchers hoping to locate a relative from whom they've been separated. Those states that have established a registry are noted here. Explanations on how to join, costs, and additional necessary information are given in Chapter 8. In this section you will find changes in policies; pending legislation, or laws that have been considered; and possible trends that may review and update restrictions now placed on searchers.

Age of Majority: Several states will have two, three, or four ages of majority in their adoption laws. The age of majority for obtaining nonidentifying information may be eighteen, while the age of majority for participation in the reunion registry is twenty-one. Many states have policies rather than laws covering the release of information. Searchers should keep this in mind and recognize the age of majority listed may not prevent their obtaining some information, the release of which is governed by state law. If there is any doubt, contact the state agency listed.

Laws Governing Opening Records: These laws govern the procedures to open and unseal your records.

Laws Governing Inheritance: A birthparent always has the option of leaving an inheritance to a birth child, and a birth child to a birthparent, whether recognized by law or not. The laws governing inheritance listed in this appendix are those that refer to the legal rights of adoptees/birthparents/adoptive parents under each state's laws.

Policies: This section explains state policies to the extent that I have been able to determine, as well as pending legislation, existing laws, or laws that died in committee. The latter are presented to show interest in changing laws or to give a feel of a state's thinking.

Author's Observations: There were several laws, procedures, or statements that I found particularly interesting. The author's observations are just that, my own.

ALABAMA

State Information Department:	State Capitol Montgomery, AL 36130 (205) 832-6011
State Agency:	Bureau of Family and Children's Services State Department of Pensions and Security Administrative Building 64 North Union St. Montgomery, AL 36130
Court of Jurisdiction:	Probate Court
Birth and Death Records:	Bureau of Vital Statistics State Department of Public Health Montgomery, AL 36130

State office has records since January 1, 1908. A search fee is charged.

Marriage Records:	Bureau of Vital Statistics *see address listed above* Probate Judge in county where the license was issued

Fee includes search and copy of record if found.

Divorce Records:	Bureau of Vital Statistics *see address listed above* Clerk or Registrar of Court of Equity County where divorce was granted

Fee includes search and copy of record if found.

Archives/Record Holdings:	Department of Archives and History Archives and History Building 624 Washington Ave. Montgomery, AL 36104
Department of Motor Vehicles:	Motor Vehicle and License Tax Division Department of Revenue 3030 Eastern By-Pass P.O. Box 104 (36101) Montgomery, AL 36111 (205) 832-6740

Search and Support Groups: Adoption Study Project
                                                  1250 Lake Forest Circle
                                                  Birmingham, AL 35244

State Reunion Registry: Alabama does not have a registry at the present. Refer to Chapter 8 for a list of group registries.

Age of Majority: 19 years or older

Laws Governing Opening Records: Code of Alabama, Section 38-7-13. "Any person who has arrived at the age of 19 and who was placed by the department or by a licensed child-placing agency shall have the right to receive from the department or from the child-placing agency information concerning his placement; except, that the name and address of a natural parent or relative shall be given by the department or the licensed child-placing agency only with the consent of said natural parent or relative."

   Code of Alabama, Section 26-10-4. "He [state registrar of statistics] shall then cause to be sealed and filed the original certificate of birth with the decree of the court and such sealed package shall be opened only upon the demand of said child when he has attained his majority or adopting parents or by the order of a court of record."

Laws Governing Inheritance: Code of Alabama, Section 26-10-5. "For the purposes of inheritance of property under the laws of descent and distribution, an adopted child, whether now or hereafter adopted under the laws of Alabama or some other jurisdiction, shall bear the same relation to his adopting parents and their natural and adopted children as if he were the natural child of such parents. . . . (C) . . . Upon such adoption, all rights of inheritance of the adopted child's natural parents and their kindred shall cease, unless otherwise specifically provided in the final order of adoption. . . ."

Policies: A letter from the Governor's Office dated June 20, 1980, states, "When an adoptee returns for information about his family, a social worker from the Department of Pensions and Security or a licensed child-placing agency gives the adoptee information about his family. The social agency makes an effort to locate the natural parent or relative and if the natural parent or relative is willing to have a contact with the adoptee, this is arranged."

ALASKA

State Information Department: State Capitol
                                                  120 4th St.
                                                  Juneau, AK 99811
                                                  (907) 465-2111

State Agency: Department of Health and Social
                                                  Services
                                                  Pouch H-05
                                                  Juneau, AK 99811

Court of Jurisdiction: Superior Court

Birth and Death Records: Bureau of Vital Statistics
                                                Department of Health and Welfare
                                                Pouch H-02G
                                                Juneau, AK 99811

      State office has records since 1913.

Marriage Records: Bureau of Vital Statistics
                                                see address listed above

      State office has records since 1913.

Divorce Records: Bureau of Vital Statistics
                                                see address listed above

      State office has records since 1950.

                                                Clerk of Superior Court
                                                Judicial District where divorce was
                                                   granted

First district—Juneau and Ketchikan. Second district—Nome. Third district—
Anchorage. Fourth District—Fairbanks

Archives/Record Holdings: State Library
                                                History and Archives
                                                State Office Building
                                                Pouch G
                                                Juneau, AK 99801

Department of Motor Vehicles: Division of Motor Vehicles
                                                Department of Public Safety
                                                4111 Aviation Dr.
                                                P.O. Box 960
                                                Anchorage, AK 99510
                                                (907) 272-1561

Search and Support Groups: ALMA Chapter, Glennallen

Consult telephone directory or information operator, or write National Headquarters, listed under New York, for current address.

                                                CUB Representative, Anchorage

Consult telephone directory or information operator, or write National Headquarters, listed under Massachusetts, for current address.

State Reunion Registry: Alaska does not have a state registry at the present. Refer to
Chapter 8 for a list of group registries.

Age of Majority: 18 years or older

Laws Governing Opening Records: Alaska Statutes, Section 20:15.150. *Confidential
nature of hearings and records in adoption proceedings.* (b) "All papers and records
pertaining to the adoption whether part of the permanent record of the court or
of a file in the department or in an agency are subject to inspection only upon
consent of the court and all interested persons; or in exceptional cases, only upon
an order of the court for good cause shown."

Laws Governing Inheritance: Alaska Statutes, Section 20:15.130. *Effect of Adoption Decree.* (a) "A final decree of adoption, whether issued by a court of this state or of any other state, has the following effect as to matters within the jurisdiction or before a court of this state: (1) except with respect to a spouse of the petitioner and relatives of the spouse, to relieve the natural parents of the adopted person of all parental rights and responsibilities, and to terminate all legal relationships between the adopted person and his relatives, including his natural parents, so that the adopted person thereafter is a stranger to his former relatives for all purposes including inheritance. . . ."

ARIZONA

State Information Department: State Capitol
1700 West Washington St.
Phoenix, AZ 85007
(602) 271-4900

State Agency: Department of Economic Security
Administration for Children, Youth and
Families
P.O. Box 6123
1400 West Washington St.
Phoenix, AZ 85005

Court of Jurisdiction: Superior Court

Birth and Death Records: Division of Vital Records
State Department of Health
P.O. Box 3887
Phoenix, AZ 85030

State office has records since July 1, 1909. Abstracts of county records before this date.

Marriage Records: Clerk of Superior Court
County where license was issued

Divorce Records: Clerk of Superior Court
County where divorce was granted

Archives/Record Holdings: State Library
Archives and Records
State Capitol
1700 West Washington St.
Phoenix, AZ 85007

Department of Motor Vehicles: Motor Vehicle Division
Department of Transportation
1801 West Jefferson St.
Phoenix, AZ 85007
(602) 261-7426

Search and Support Groups: ALMA Chapter, Tempe

Consult telephone directory or information operator, or write National Headquarters, listed under New York, for current address.

CUB Representative, Tempe

Consult telephone directory or information operator, or write National Headquarters, listed under Massachusetts, for current address.

Parents and Adoptees Uplifted
Rt. 1, Box 71
Williams, AZ 86046

Search **
P.O. Box 1432
Litchfield Park, AZ 85340

State Reunion Registry: Arizona does not have a registry at the present. State Senate Bill No. 1291 was proposed in the 1979–80 session by Alfredo Gutierrez. This bill concerned a registry but did not go past committee. Refer to Chapter 8 for a list of group registries.

Age of Majority: 18 years or older

Laws Governing Opening Records: Arizona Public Welfare Laws, 8-120. *Records; inspection; exceptions; destruction of certain records.* A. "All files, records, reports and other papers compiled in accord with this article, whether filed in or in possession of the court, an agency or any person or association, shall be withheld from public inspection." D. "All files, records, reports and other papers not filed in or in possession of the court shall be destroyed after a 21 year period."

8-121. *Confidentiality of information: exceptions.* A. "It is unlawful except for purposes for which files and records or social records or parts thereof or information therefrom have been released pursuant to § 8-120, or except for purposes permitted by order of the court, for any person to disclose, receive or make use of, or authorize, knowingly permit . . ."

Laws Governing Inheritance: Arizona Public Welfare Laws, 8-117. *Rights under adoption order.* (B) "Upon entry of the decree of adoption, the relationship of parent and child between the adopted person and the persons who were his parents just prior to the decree of adoption shall be completely severed and all legal rights, privileges, duties, obligations and other legal consequences of the relationship shall cease to exist, including the right of inheritance. . . ."

ARKANSAS

State Information Department: State Capitol
5th and Woodland
Little Rock, AR 72201
(501) 371-3000

State Agency: Department of Human Services
Division of Social Services
Adoption Services
P.O. Box 1437
Little Rock, AR 72203

Court of Jurisdiction: Probate Court

Birth and Death Records: Division of Vital Records
                                                Arkansas Department of Health
                                                4815 West Markham St.
                                                Little Rock, AR 72201

State office has records since February 1, 1914. Some Little Rock and Fort Smith records from 1881.

Marriage Records: Division of Vital Records
                                                see address listed above

State office has records since 1917. Full certified copies may be obtained from county clerks in county where license was issued.

Divorce Records: Division of Vital Records
                                                see address listed above

State office has records since 1923. Full certified copies may be obtained from circuit/chancery clerk in county where divorce was obtained.

Archives/Record Holdings: State Library
                                                Archives and Records
                                                One Capitol Mall
                                                Little Rock, AR 72201

Department of Motor Vehicles: Office of Motor Vehicle Registrations
                                                Department of Finance and
                                                    Administration
                                                100 Joel Y. Ledbetter Bldg.
                                                7th and Wolfe Sts.
                                                P.O. Box 1272
                                                Little Rock, AR 72203
                                                (501) 371-1885

Search and Support Groups: Orphan Voyage Chapter, Hot Springs

Consult telephone directory or information operator, or write National Headquarters, listed under Colorado, for current address.

State Reunion Registry: Arkansas does not have a registry at the present. Refer to Chapter 8 for a list of group registries.

Age of Majority: 18 years or older

Laws Governing Opening Records: *An Act to Adopt the Uniform Adoption Act for the State of Arkansas.* Section 17. (2). "All papers and records pertaining to the adoption whether part of the permanent record of the court or of a file in the Arkansas Social Services or in an agency are subject to inspection only upon consent of the Court and all interested persons; or in exceptional cases, only upon an order of the Court for good cause shown; and . . ."

Laws Governing Inheritance: *An Act to Adopt the Uniform Adoption Act for the State of Arkansas.* Section 15. (a). "A final decree of adoption and an interlocutory decree of adoption which has become final, whether issued by a Court of this State or of any other place, have the following effect as to matters within the jurisdiction or before a Court of this State: (1) . . . to relieve the natural parents of the adopted individual of all parental rights and responsibilities, and to terminate all legal relationships between the adopted individual and his relatives, including his natural parents, so that the adopted individual thereafter is a stranger to his former relatives for all purposes including inheritance. . . ."

Policies: The Department of Human Services, Division of Social Services, stated in a letter dated August 8, 1980. "We as a state cooperate with adoption/birth parent groups as much as our law allows us to."

CALIFORNIA

State Information Department:
State Capitol
10th and L Sts.
Sacramento, CA 95814
(916) 445-4711

State Agency:
Department of Social Services
Adoption Branch
744 P St.
Sacramento, CA 95814

Court of Jurisdiction:
Superior Court

Birth and Death Records:
Vital Statistics Section
State Department of Health
410 N St.
Sacramento, CA 95814

State office has records since July 1, 1905. For records before that date write to County Recorder in county of birth or death.

Marriage Records:
Vital Statistics Section
see address listed above

Divorce Records:
Vital Statistics Section
see address listed above

State office has records for final decrees entered since January 1, 1962, or initial complaint filed since January 1, 1966.

Archives/Record Holdings:
State Library
Archives and Records
914 Capitol Mall
P.O. Box 2037
Sacramento, CA 95814

Department of Motor Vehicles:
Department of Motor Vehicles
2415 1st Street
P.O. Box 1828 (95809)
Sacramento, CA 95818
(916) 445-5281

Search and Support Groups:
Adoptee Identity Discovery
P.O. Box 2217
Sunnyvale, CA 94087

Adoptees Movement
Rt. 2, Box 2654-z
Red Bluffs, CA 96080

Adoptees Research Association
P.O. Box 304
Montrose, CA 91020

Adoption Search and Support
LaVerne Center for Education
240 Bonita
LaVerne, CA 91750

Adoption Search Institute
P.O. Box 11749
Costa Mesa, CA 92627

Adoptsearch
P.O. Box 572
Berkeley, CA 94701

ALMA Chapter, Alameda
ALMA Chapter, Camarillo
ALMA Chapter, Fresno
ALMA Chapter, LaHabra
ALMA Chapter, Orange County
ALMA Chapter, Panama City
ALMA Chapter, Riverside/San
    Bernardino
ALMA Chapter, Sacramento
ALMA Chapter, San Diego
ALMA Chapter, Santa Ana
ALMA Chapter, Santa Rosa Redding
ALMA Chapter, Torrance

Consult telephone directory, or information operator, or write National Headquarters, listed under New York, for current address.

The ALMA Library
LaHabra, CA

ALMA Western Regional Office**
P.O. Box 9333
North Hollywood, CA 91609

Central Coast Adoption Support Group
P.O. Box 1937
Santa Maria, CA 93456

CUB Branch, San Diego
CUB Branch, Westminster
CUB Branch, Woodland Hills
CUB Representative, Rio Linda

Consult telephone directory, or information operator, or write National Headquarters, listed under Massachusetts, for current address.

Equal Rights for Fathers
P.O. Box 6387
Albany, CA 94706

Independent Search Consultants
P.O. Box 10192
Costa Mesa, CA 92627

Post Adoption Center for Education and
    Research
Palo Alto Medical Clinic
860 Bryant St.
Palo Alto, CA 94301

Reaching Out
P.O. Box 42749
Los Angeles, CA 90042

Search Finders of California
P.O. Box 2374
Santa Clara, CA 95055

Search Finders, Southern
1422 Keel Dr.
Corona Del Mar, CA 92625

Tennessee Adoptees in Search
4598 Rosewood
Montclair, CA 91763

Triadoption Library, Inc.
P.O. Box 5218
Huntington Beach, CA 92646

United Adoptees and Birthparents of
    Central California
2456 16th St.
Kingsburg, CA 93631

United Adoptees and Parents of Central
    California
9303 E. Bullard
Clovis, CA 93612

State Reunion Registry: California does not have a registry at the present. Refer to Chapter 8 for a list of group registries. State House Bill No. 1426 was introduced in 1979 and sought to create a state reunion registry in California. After much debate, the House Bill failed, but those searching in this state should contact the legislature for current bills pending. There is much interest in this state to create such a registry.

Age of Majority: 18 years or older

Laws Governing Opening Records: Health and Safety, Section 10439. *Availability of records and information, on petition and order.* "All records and information specified in this article, other than the newly issued birth certificate, shall be available only upon the order of the superior court of the county of residence of the adopted child or the superior court of the county granting the order of adoption. No such order shall be granted by the superior court unless a verified petition setting forth facts showing the necessity of such an order has been presented to the court and good and compelling cause is shown for the granting of the order."

Laws Governing Inheritance: Civil Section 229. *Effect on former relations of child.* "The parents of an adopted child are, from the time of adoption, relieved of all parental duties towards, and all responsibility for, the child so adopted, and have no right over it."

Author's Observations: Adoptees and birthparents from this state should take special notice of the ALMA Class Action Suit being fought there. Another note to those searching in this state is to be aware of the sympathetic statements and recommendations made by the California State Bar and the California Association of Adoption Agencies.

COLORADO

State Information Department:

State Capitol
200 East Colfax Ave.
Denver, CO 80203
(303) 892-9911

State Agency:

Department of Social Services
Post Adoption Services
1575 Sherman St.
Denver, CO 80203

Court of Jurisdiction:

Denver, Juvenile Court; all others,
District Court

Birth and Death Records:

Records and Statistics Section
Colorado Department of Health
4210 East 11th Ave.
Denver, CO 80220

State office has birth records since 1910 and death records since 1900. Some county records prior to these dates.

Marriage Records:

Records and Statistics Section
see address listed above

State has index of records for all years except 1940–67. Inquiries will be sent to the appropriate county office.

County Clerk
County where license was issued

Divorce Records:

Records and Statistics Section
see address listed above

State has index of records for all years except 1940–67. Inquiries will be sent to the appropriate county office.

Clerk of District Court
County where divorce was granted

Archives/Record Holdings: Colorado Historical Society
Colorado Heritage Center
1300 Broadway
Denver, CO 80203

Department of Motor Vehicles: Motor Vehicle Division
Department of Revenue
140 West 6th Ave.
Denver, CO 80203
(303) 892-3407

Search and Support Groups: Adoptees in Search
P.O. Box 27294
Denver, CO 80227

ALMA Chapter, Aurora

Consult telephone directory or information operator, or write National Headquarters, listed under New York, for current address.

CUB Representative**, Denver

Consult telephone directory or information operator, or write National Headquarters, listed under Massachusetts, for current address.

Orphan Voyage
National Headquarters
2141 Road 2300
Cedaredge, CO 81413

State Reunion Registry: Colorado does not have a registry at the present. Refer to
Chapter 8 for a list of group registries.

Age of Majority: 18/21 years or older

Laws Governing Opening Records: Colorado Statutes, 19-4-104. *Records—Separate
Dockets.* (1) "Records and papers in relinquishment and adoption proceedings from
and after the filing of a petition shall be confidential and open to inspection only
upon order of the court for good cause shown."

Laws Governing Inheritance: Article 4, 19-4-113. *Legal effects of formal decree.* (2)
"The natural parents shall be divested of all legal rights and obligations with respect
to the child, and the adopted child shall be free from all legal obligations of
obedience and maintenance with respect to the natural parents."

CONNECTICUT

State Information Department: State Capitol
210 Capitol Ave.
Hartford, CT 06115
(203) 566-2211

State Agency: Department of Children and Youth
Services
Adoption Resource Exchange
170 Sigourney Street
Hartford, CT 06105

Court of Jurisdiction: Probate Court

Birth and Death Records: Public Health Statistics Section
                                              State Department of Health
                                              79 Elm St.
                                              Hartford, CT 06115

State office has records since July 1, 1897. For records prior to that date write
to Registrar of Vital Statistics in town where birth or death occurred.

Marriage Records: Public Health Statistics Section
                                              see address listed above

State office has records since July 1, 1897.

                                              Registrar of Vital Statistics
                                              Town where license was issued

Divorce Records: Public Health Statistics Section
                                              see address listed above

State office has index since June 1, 1947. Inquiries will be forwarded to appropriate office.

                                              Clerk of Superior Court
                                              County where divorce was granted

Archives/Record Holdings: Department of Archives and Records
                                              Connecticut State Library
                                              231 Capitol Ave.
                                              Hartford, CT 06115

Department of Motor Vehicles: Department of Motor Vehicles
                                              60 State St.
                                              Wethersfield, CT 06109
                                              (203) 566-2240

Search and Support Groups: Adoptees Search Connection
                                              1203 Hill St.
                                              Suffield, CT 06078

                                              ALMA Chapter, Westport**

Consult telephone directory or information operator, or write National Headquarters, listed under New York, for current address.

                                              CUB Branch, Rocky Hill**

Consult telephone directory or information operator, or write National Headquarters, listed under Massachusetts, for current address.

                                              Search Groups
                                              4 Granbrook Park Road
                                              East Granby, CT 06026

                                              South End Community Service
                                              509 Wethersfield Ave.
                                              Hartford, CT 06114

State Reunion Registry: Connecticut does not have a registry at the present. Refer to Chapter 8 for a list of group registries.

Age of Majority: 18 years or older

Laws Governing Records: Connecticut has many laws that will help and direct searchers. This state is one that clearly outlines its procedures and laws. Interested persons should write and obtain these laws to have full knowledge of what information may be obtained and how to obtain it. Probate Courts and Procedure, Title 45, Section 45-68h. *Application for information. Appeal if information withheld.* (a) "Any adult adopted person who is a resident of this state may request the information provided in section 45-68e by applying in person to the court in which the adoption, termination or removal proceeding was determined or by applying in person to the agency in this state or the department which has such information. If, in cases in which the application is made to the court of probate or juvenile court, it appears that counseling is advisable with the release of such information, it shall refer such person to such agency or to the department, as the case may be. No such information shall be released unless the court of probate, juvenile court, agency or department, as the case may be, is satisfied as to the identity of such person." (b) "Any adult adopted person who is not a resident of this state may request the information provided in Section 45-68e by applying in person in accordance with the provisions of subsection (a) of this section or by applying in writing to the court in which the adoption, termination or removal proceeding was determined or to the agency in this state or the department which has such information. No such information shall be released unless the court of probate, juvenile court, agency or the department, as the case may be, is satisfied as to the identity of such person. . . ."

Laws Governing Inheritance: Termination of Parental Rights, Adoption, Chapter 778, Section 45-64a. *Effects of final decree of adoption. Surviving rights.* (3) "To terminate all legal relationships between the adopted person and his natural parent or parents and the relatives of such natural parent or parents for all purposes including inheritance . . ."

Policies: This state has several new laws and many interesting and informative policy changes. Those searching in this state should ask for all updated sections of the law.

Adoption, Chapter 778, Section 45-68c. *Information available to adoptive parents and adult adopted person.* "The following information, if known, concerning the genetic parents of any adopted person shall be given by the agency or department which has such information, in writing on a form provided by the department, to the adoptive parent or parents not later than the date of finalization of the adoption proceedings: (a) Age of genetic parent in years, not dates of birth, at birth of such adopted person; (b) heritage of genetic parent or parents, which shall include (1) nationality, (2) ethnic background and (3) race; (c) education, which shall be number of years of school completed by the genetic parent or parents at the time of birth of such adopted person; (d) general physical appearance of the genetic parent or parents at the time of birth of such adopted person in terms of height, weight, color of hair, eyes, skin and other information of similar nature; (e) talents, hobbies and special interests of the genetic parent or parents; (f) existence of any other child or children born to either genetic parent prior to birth of such adopted person; (g) reasons for child being placed for adoption or for genetic parental rights of custody being removed; (h) religion of genetic parent or parents; (i) field of occupation of genetic parent or parents in general terms; (j) health history of genetic parent or parents and blood relatives on a standardized form provided by the department; (k) manner in which plans for such adopted person's future were made by genetic parent or parents; and (l) relationship between the genetic parents. The information in this section, if known, shall upon request of the adult adopted person made in accordance with section 45–68h, be made available in writing to such person upon reaching age of majority. . . ."

Author's Observations: Section 7-41a. *Vital statistics records available for genealogical research.* "All records of vital statistics including births, marriages and deaths in the custody of any registrar of vital statistics or of the State Department of Health shall be open for research to any member of a legally incorporated genealogy society and such societies shall be permitted to incorporate statistics derived therefrom in their publications."

I wonder what the dates involved would be—how old must the records be to allow viewing?

DELAWARE

State Information Department:	State Capitol Dover, DE 19901 (302) 678-4000
State Agency:	Division of Social Services Department of Health and Social Services P.O. Box 309 Wilmington, DE 19899
Court of Jurisdiction:	Superior Court
Birth and Death Records:	Bureau of Vital Statistics Division of Public Health Department of Health and Social Services State Health Building Dover, DE 19901

State office has records for 1861–63 and since 1881. No records for 1864–80.

Marriage Records:	Bureau of Vital Statistics *see address listed above*
Divorce Records:	Bureau of Vital Statistics *see address listed above*

State office has records since March 1932. Inquiries will be forwarded to appropriate office. Fee includes search and essential facts of divorce verified.

	Prothonotary County where divorce was granted
Archives/Record Holdings:	Division of Historical & Cultural Affairs Department of State Hall of Records Dover, DE 19901

Department of Motor Vehicles:	Division of Motor Vehicles Department of Public Safety Highway Administration Bldg. Route 113 P.O. Box 698 Dover, DE 19901 (302) 678-4421
Search and Support Groups:	CUB Representative, Wilmington

Consult telephone directory or information operator, or write National Headquarters, listed under Massachusetts, for current address.

State Reunion Registry: Delaware does not have a registry at the present. Refer to Chapter 8 for a list of group registries.

Age of Majority: 18 years or older

Laws Governing Opening Records: Subchapter I, 925. *Inspection of court records.* "Anyone wishing to inspect any of the papers filed in connection with any adoption shall petition the Judge of the Superior Court concerning setting forth the reasons for the inspection."

Laws Governing Inheritance: Subchapter I, 920. *Effect of adoption on inheritance.* (a) "Upon the issuance of a decree of adoption, the adopted child shall lose all rights of inheritance from its natural parent or parents and from their collateral or lineal relative. The rights of the natural parent or parents or their collateral or lineal relatives to inherit from such child shall cease upon the adoption."

DISTRICT OF COLUMBIA

Information Department:	District Building 14th and E Sts., NW Washington, DC 20004 (202) 628-6000
District Agency:	Bureau of Family Services Social Rehabilitation Administration 122 C St., NW Washington, DC 20001
Court of Jurisdiction:	Domestic Relations Branch of Court of General Sessions
Birth and Death Records:	Department of Human Resources Vital Records Section 615 Pennsylvania Ave., NW Washington, DC 20004

District birth records on file beginning with 1871. District death records on file beginning with 1855. No death records were filed during the Civil War.

Marriage Records:	Marriage Bureau 515 5th St., NW Washington, DC 20001

Divorce Records: Clerk
Superior Court for the District of
  Columbia
Family Division
451 Indiana Ave.
Washington, DC 20001

District office has records since September 16, 1956.

Clerk
U.S. District Court for the District of Co-
  lumbia
Washington, DC 20001

District office has records prior to September 16, 1956.

Archives/Record Holdings: Library of Congress Annex
Washington, DC 20540

Department of Motor Vehicles: Bureau of Motor Vehicle Services
DC Department of Transportation
Municipal Center
301 C St., NW
Washington, DC 20001
(202) 629-3751

Search and Support Groups: Adoption Research Council
P.O. Box 23641
L'Enfant Plaza Station
Washington, DC 20024

CUB Branch, Washington, DC

Consult telephone directory or information operator, or write National Headquarters, listed under Massachusetts, for current address.

District Reunion Registry: The District does not have a reunion registry at present.
Refer to Chapter 8 for a list of group registries.

Age of Majority: 18 years or older

FLORIDA

State Information Department: The Capitol
Tallahassee, FL 32304
(904) 488-1234

State Agency: Department of Health and
  Rehabilitative Services
Family and Children's Services
Social and Economic Services
1317 Winewood Blvd.
Tallahassee, FL 32301

Court of Jurisdiction: Circuit Court

Birth and Death Records: Department of Health and
Rehabilitative Services
Division of Health
Bureau of Vital Statistics
P.O. Box 210
Jacksonville, FL 32231

State office has birth records since 1865 and death records since August 1877. Older records are scant and the majority of records date from January 1917. A search fee is charged.

Marriage Records: Bureau of Vital Statistics
see address listed above

State office has records since June 6, 1927. A search fee is charged.

Clerk of Circuit Court
County where license was issued

Divorce Records: Bureau of Vital Statistics
see address listed above

State office has records since June 6, 1927. A search fee is charged.

Clerk of Circuit Court
County where divorce was granted

Archives/Record Holdings: State Library of Florida
Archives and Records
R. A. Gray Bldg.
Tallahassee, FL 32301

Department of Motor Vehicles: Division of Motor Vehicles
Department of Highway Safety and
Motor Vehicles
Neil Kirkman Bldg.
Tallahassee, FL 32304
(904) 488-6084

Search and Support Groups: ALMA Chapter, Boynton Beach**
ALMA Chapter, Ft. Lauderdale**
ALMA Chapter, Leesburg
ALMA Chapter, Melbourne**
ALMA Chapter, Ruskin**

Consult telephone directory or information operator, or write National Headquarters, listed under New York, for current address.

CUB Branch, Tampa**
CUB Representative, Middleburg**

Consult telephone directory or information operator, or write National Headquarters, listed under Massachusetts, for current address.

Organized Search Information Service
P.O. Box 53-761
Miami Shores, FL 33153

> Orphan Voyage Chapter, Jacksonville
> Orphan Voyage Chapter, Miami
> Orphan Voyage Chapter, Miami Shores
> Orphan Voyage Chapter, Orlando
> Orphan Voyage Chapter, Tampa
> Orphan Voyage Chapter, West Palm Beach
> Orphan Voyage Representative, Cocoa
> Orphan Voyage Representative, Rockledge

Consult telephone directory or information operator, or write National Headquarters, listed under Colorado, for current address

State Reunion Registry: Florida does not have a registry at the present. Refer to Chapter 8 for a list of group registries.

Age of majority: 18 years or older

Laws Governing Opening Records: Adoption, Chapter 63.162. This is the 1980 revised law. Please see comments below for referral to the old laws in this state. *Hearings and records in adoption proceedings; confidential nature.* (4) "No person shall disclose from the records the name and identity of a natural parent, an adoptive parent, or an adopted child unless: (a) The natural parent authorizes in writing the release of his or her name; (b) The adopted child, if 18 or more years of age, authorizes in writing the release of his or her name; (c) The adoptive parent authorizes in writing the release of his or her name; or (d) Upon order of the court for good cause shown in exceptional cases."

Laws Governing Inheritance: Adoption, Chapter 63.172. *Effect of judgment of adoption.* (b) "It terminates all legal relationships between the adopted person and his relatives, including his natural parents, except a natural parent who is a petitioner, so that the adopted person thereafter is a stranger to his former relatives for all purposes, including inheritance. . . ."

Policies: Chapter 63.162 was revised in the 1980 legislature. The old law read as follows: (4) "Except as authorized in writing by the adoptive parent or the adopted child, if 18 or more years of age, or upon order of the court for good cause shown in exceptional cases, no person shall disclose from the records the name or identity of either an adoptive parent or adopted child."

Author's Observations: Florida is the only state that seems to be moving backward instead of forward. Before 1980, adult adoptees could request identifying information and receive such. Now Florida has established a policy of written release forms required from all parties involved.

GEORGIA

State Information Department: State Capitol
Capitol Square, SW
Atlanta, GA 30334
(404) 656-2000

State Agency:	Division of Social Services Department of Human Resources 618 Ponce de Leon Avenue, NE Atlanta, GA 30308
Court of Jurisdiction:	Superior Court
Birth and Death Records:	Vital Records Unit State Department of Human Resources Room 217-H 47 Trinity Ave., SW Atlanta, GA 30334

State office has records since January 1, 1919. For records before that date for Atlanta or Savannah, write County Health Department in place where birth or death occurred.

Marriage Records:	Vital Records Unit *see address listed above*

Centralized state records since June 9, 1952. Inquiries will be forwarded to appropriate office.

County Ordinary
County where license was issued

Divorce Records:	Vital Records Unit *see address listed above*

Centralized state records since June 9, 1952. Inquiries will be forwarded to appropriate office.

Clerk of Superior Court
County where divorce was granted

Archives/Record Holdings:	Georgia State Library 301 State Judicial Building Capitol Hill Station Atlanta, GA 30334
Department of Motor Vehicles:	Department of Motor Vehicles 270 Washington St., SW Atlanta, GA 30334 (404) 656-4015

Search and Support Groups:

CUB Representative, Doraville

Consult telephone directory or information operator, or write National Headquarters, listed under Massachusetts, for current address.

Orphan Voyage Chapter, Macon

Consult telephone directory or information operator, or write National Headquarters, listed under Colorado, for current address.

State Reunion Registry: Georgia does not have a registry at the present. Refer to Chapter 8 for a list of group registries.

Age of Majority: 18 years or older

Laws Governing Opening Records: Code 88-1110. *Certificates of Adoption.* "The copies of the original county birth record shall then be forwarded to the Division of Vital Statistics to be sealed with the original record in the files of the Division of Vital Statistics. Such sealed records may be opened by the Division of Vital Statistics only upon order of a judge of a superior court."

Laws Governing Inheritance: Code 74-414, Section 11. *Final Order of Adoption.* "When the final adoption shall have been granted, the parents of the child shall be divested of all legal rights or obligations from them to the child or from the child to them; and the child shall be free from all obligations of any sort whatsoever to the said natural parents."

Policies: Code 88-1714, 88-1713 Amended. No. 475 (State Senate Bill No. 150). (b) "When a new certificate of birth is established, the actual date of birth, when available, shall be shown, and the place of birth shall be shown as either the actual place of birth or as the residence of the adoptive parents, at the election of the adoptive parents. The Superior Court, in the final order of adoption, shall determine the place and so state in such final order of adoption."

Thus, persons adopted or relinquished in this state should be aware that their place of birth may be listed incorrectly.

Subsection 3. *Illegitimate children.* "If the child be illegitimate, the consent of the mother alone shall suffice. Such consent, however, shall not be required if the mother has surrendered all of her rights to said child to a licensed child-placing agency, or to the State Department of Family and Children Services."

HAWAII

State Information Department:

State Capitol
415 South Beretania St.
Honolulu, HI 96813
(808) 548-2211

State Agency:

Department of Social Services and
Housing
P.O. Box 339
Honolulu, HI 96809

Court of Jurisdiction:

Family Court

Birth and Death Records:

Research and Statistics Office
State Department of Health
P.O. Box 3378
Honolulu, HI 96801

State office has records since 1853.

Marriage Records:

Research and Statistics Office
see address listed above

Divorce Records: Research and Statistics Office
                                         see address listed above

State office has records since July 1, 1951.

                                         Circuit Court
                                         County where divorce was granted

Archives/Record Holdings: State Archives
                                         Iolani Palace Grounds
                                         Honolulu, HI 96813

Department of Motor Vehicles: Director of Finance
                                         City and County of Honolulu 96814
                                         (808) 546-7533

                                         Director of Finance
                                         City and County of Hawaii, Hilo
                                         (808) 935-5721

                                         Director of Finance
                                         County of Maui, Wailuku
                                         (808) 244-7844

                                         Director of Finance
                                         County of Kauai, Lihue
                                         (808) 245-3661

Search and Support Groups: Contact a National Organization for individuals working in this state.

State Reunion Registry: Hawaii does not have a registry at the present. Refer to Chapter 8 for a list of group registries.

Age of Majority: 18 years or older

Laws Governing Opening Records: Family, Section 578-15, *Secrecy of proceedings and records.* "The records in adoption proceedings, after the petition is filed and prior to the entry of the decree, shall be open to inspection only by the parties or their attorneys, the director of social services and housing or his agent, or by any proper person on a showing of good cause therefor, upon order of the court. . . ."

Laws Governing Inheritance: Please write to the Department of Social Services and Housing with your direct question regarding inheritance in this state.

IDAHO

State Information Department: Statehouse
                                         700 West Jefferson St.
                                         Boise, ID 83720
                                         (208) 384-2411

State Agency: Department of Health and Welfare
                                         Statehouse
                                         Boise, ID 83720

Court of Jurisdiction: Magistrate Court

Birth and Death Records: Bureau of Vital Statistics
                                                State Department of Health and
                                                    Welfare
                                                Statehouse
                                                Boise, ID 83720

State office has records since 1911. For records from 1907–1911, write County
Recorder in county where birth or death occurred.

Marriage Records: Bureau of Vital Statistics
                                                see address listed above

State office has records since 1947.

                                                County Recorder
                                                County where license was issued

Divorce Records: Bureau of Vital Statistics
                                                see address listed above

State office has records since 1947.

                                                County Recorder
                                                County where divorce was granted

Archives/Record Holdings: Idaho State Historical Society Libraries
                                                Library and Archives Building
                                                325 West State
                                                Boise, ID 83702

Department of Motor Vehicles: Motor Vehicle Division
                                                Department of Law Enforcement
                                                3311 West State St.
                                                P.O. Box 34
                                                Boise, ID 83731
                                                (208) 384-2586

Search and Support Groups: ALMA Chapter, Boise

Consult telephone directory or information operator, or write National Headquarters, listed under New York, for current address.

                                                CUB Representative, Boise

Consult telephone directory or information operator, or write National Headquarters, listed under Massachusetts, for current address.

State Reunion Registry: Idaho does not have a registry at the present. Refer to Chapter
8 for a list of group registries.

Age of Majority: 18 years or older

Laws Governing Opening Records: Idaho Code, Title 16, Chapter 15. 16-1511. *Sealing
Record of Proceedings.* "Upon the motion of petitioners, or upon its own motion
the probate court shall order that the record of its proceedings in any adoption
proceeding shall be sealed. When such order has been made and entered the court
shall seal such record and thereafter the seal shall not be broken, except upon the
motion of petitioners or the person adopted; provided, however, that such record
may be sealed again as in this section provided."

Laws Governing Inheritance: Idaho Code, Title 16, Chapter 15. 16–1509. *Release of Child's Parents from Obligation—Termination of Rights of Parents and Children.* "Unless the decree of adoption otherwise provides, the natural parents of an adopted child are, from the time of the adoption, relieved of all parental duties toward, and all responsibilities for, the child so adopted, and have no right over it, and all rights of such child from and through such natural parents including the right of inheritance, are hereby terminated unless specifically provided by will."

ILLINOIS

State Information Department:
State Capitol
Springfield, IL 62706
(217) 782-2000

State Agency:
Department of Children and Family Services
One North Old State Capitol Plaza
Springfield, IL 62706

Court of Jurisdiction:
County Circuit Court

Birth and Death Records:
Office of Vital Records
State Department of Public Health
535 West Jefferson St.
Springfield, IL 62761

State office has records since January 1, 1916. For records before that date and copies of state records, write the County Clerk, county where birth or death occurred. A search fee is charged.

Marriage Records:
Office of Vital Records
see address listed above

State office has records since January 1, 1962

County Clerk
County where license was issued

Divorce Records:
Office of Vital Records
see address listed above

State office has records since January 1, 1962.

Clerk of Circuit Court
County where divorce was granted

Archives/Record Holdings:
Illinois State Archives
State Archives Bldg.
Springfield, IL 62706

Department of Motor Vehicles:
Vehicle Services Department
Office of the Secretary of State
Centennial Bldg.
Springfield, IL 62706
(217) 782-7365

222 SEARCH : A Handbook for Adoptees and Birthparents

Search and Support Groups:

Adoption Research Forum
P.O. Box 2517
Chicago, IL 60690

ALMA Chapter, Bloomington
ALMA Chapter, Lebannon

Consult telephone directory or information operator, or write National Headquarters, listed under New York, for current address.

CUB Representative, Urbana

Consult telephone directory or information operator, or write National Headquarters, listed under Massachusetts, for current address.

Hidden Birthright
P.O. Box 1651
Springfield, IL 62705

Mutual Search Assistance
P.O. Box 554
Springfield, IL 62705

Search Research
P.O. Box 48
Chicago, IL 60415

Truth Seekers in Adoption
P.O. Box 286
Roscoe, IL 61073

Yesterday's Children**
P.O. Box 1554
Evanston, IL 60204

State Reunion Registry: Illinois does not have a registry at the present. Refer to Chapter 8 for a list of group registries.

Age of Majority: 18 years or older

Laws Governing Opening Records: Chapter 40, Domestic Relations, 1522, Section 18. *Records Confidential.* "Upon motion of any party to an adoption proceeding the court shall, or upon the court's own motion the court may, order that the file relating to such proceeding shall be impounded by the clerk of the court and shall be opened for examination only upon specific order of the court, which order shall name the person or persons who are to be permitted to examine such file. Certified copies of all papers and documents contained in any file so impounded shall be made only on like order."

Laws Governing Inheritance: Chapter 40, Domestic Relations, 1521, Section 17. *Effect of order terminating parental rights or order.* "After the entry either of an order terminating parental rights or the entry of an order of adoption, the natural parents of a child sought to be adopted shall be relieved of all parental responsibility for such child and shall be deprived of all legal rights as respects the child, and the child shall be free from all obligations of maintenance and obedience as respects such natural parents."

Author's Observations: In Section 1522, mentioned earlier, the following is written under the subchapter, *Records Confidential:* "The word 'illegitimate' or the words 'born out of wedlock', or words importing such meaning, shall not be used in any adoption proceeding in any respect."

What explanation is given for the relinquishment?

INDIANA

State Information Department:	State House 200 West Washington St. Indianapolis, IN 46204 (317) 633-4000
State Agency:	Social Services Division State Department of Public Welfare 141 South Meridian St. Indianapolis, IN 46225
Court of Jurisdiction:	County Court with probate jurisdiction
Birth and Death Records:	Division of Vital Records State Board of Health 1330 West Michigan St. Indianapolis, IN 46206

State office has birth records since October 1, 1907, and death records since 1900. For older records write to Health Officer in city or county where birth or death occurred.

Marriage Records:	Division of Vital Records *see address listed above*

State office has records since 1958. Inquiries will be forwarded to appropriate office.

	Clerk of Circuit Court or Clerk of Superior Court County where license was issued
Divorce Records:	County Clerk County where divorce was granted
Archives/Record Holdings:	Archives Division Indiana State Library 140 North Senate Ave. Indianapolis, IN 46204
Department of Motor Vehicles:	Bureau of Motor Vehicles 401 State Office Bldg. 100 North Senate Ave. Indianapolis, IN 46204 (317) 633-4645
Search and Support Groups:	Adoptees Identity Doorway P.O. Box 361 South Bend, IN 46624

ALMA Chapter, Chalmers

Consult telephone directory or information operator, or write national head-quarters, listed under New York, for current address.

Assoc. for Rights of Children
18135 Heatherfield Dr.
South Bend, IN 46637

Search for Tomorrow
P.O. Box 441
New Haven, IN 46774

SEEK
213 Dreamwold M.S.
Michigan City, IN 46360

State Reunion Registry: Indiana does not have a registry at the present. Refer to Chapter 8 for a list of group registries.

Age of Majority: 18 years or older

Laws Governing Opening Records: Chapter I, Section 12. "When a new certificate of birth is established following adoption, it shall replace the original registration of birth, which shall be filed with the evidence of adoption, and withheld from inspection except by order of a court of competent jurisdiction. The new certificate shall show the actual place and date of birth."

Laws Governing Inheritance: Chapter I, Section 9. "The natural parents of such adopted person, if living, shall after such adoption be relieved of all legal duties and obligations due from them to such person and shall be divested of all rights with respect to such person."

IOWA

State Information Department: Capitol Bldg.
1007 E. Grand Ave.
Des Moines, IA 50319
(515) 281-5011

State Agency: Iowa Department of Social Services
Bureau of Children's Service
Division of Community Programs
Hoover Building
Des Moines, IA 50319

Court of Jurisdiction: District Court

Birth and Death Records: Division of Records and Statistics
State Department of Health
Des Moines, IA 50319

State office has records since July 1, 1880.

Marriage Records: Division of Records and Statistics
see address listed above

Divorce Records: Division of Records and Statistics
                                            see address listed above

State office has brief statistical records since 1906. Inquiries will be forwarded
to appropriate office.

                                            County Clerk
                                            County where divorce was granted

Archives/Record Holdings: Iowa Historical and Genealogical
                                                Library
                                            Iowa Department of History and
                                                Archives
                                            Historical Building
                                            East 12th and Grand Ave.
                                            Des Moines, IA 50319

Department of Motor Vehicles: Motor Vehicle Division
                                            Department of Transportation
                                            5238 NW 2nd Ave.
                                            Des Moines, IA 50313
                                            (515) 281-3586

Search and Support Groups: Adoptees Search Heritage
                                            P.O. Box 762
                                            Council Bluffs, IA 51501

                                            Adoptees Quest
                                            1408 Buresh
                                            Iowa City, IA 52240

                                            Adoptive Experience Group
                                            1105 Fremont
                                            Des Moines, IA 50316

                                            Family Search Counseling
                                            628 First Ave.
                                            Council Bluffs, IA 51501

                                            Orphan Voyage Representative, Cedar

Consult telephone directory or information operator, or write National Headquarters, listed under Colorado, for current address.

State Reunion Registry: Iowa does not have a registry at the present. Individuals
should ask for updated laws and those in committee as there is some interest in
forming one. Refer to Chapter 8 for a list of group registries.

Age of Majority: 18 years or older

Laws Governing Opening Records: Section 144.24. *Substituting for Original.* "When
a new certificate of birth is established, the actual place and date of birth shall be
shown. The certificate shall be substituted for the original certificate of birth.
Thereafter, the original certificate and the evidence of adoption, paternity, legitimation or sex change shall not be subject to inspection except under order of a court
of competent jurisdiction or as provided by regulation for statistical or administrative purposes only."

Section 600.16. *Termination and adoption record.* 2. "Also, the clerk of the court shall, upon application to and order of the court for good cause shown, open the permanent adoption record of the court for the adopted person who is an adult and reveal the names of either or both of the natural parents."

Laws Governing Inheritance: Section 633.223. *Effect of adoption.* "A lawfully adopted person and his heirs shall inherit from and through the adoptive parents the same as a natural born child. The adoptive parents and their heirs shall inherit from and through the adopted person the same as though he were a natural born child."

Section 600.13. *Adoption decrees.* 4. "A final adoption decree terminates any parental rights, except those of a spouse of the adoption petitioner, existing at the time of its issuance and establishes the parent-child relationship between the adoption petitioner and the person petitioned to be adopted. Unless otherwise specified by law, such parent-child relationship shall be deemed to have been created at the birth of the child."

Policies: A Social Service Department, Proposed Notice of Intended Action. 700—130.16. *Information to be released.* "Requests for information from adoption records of the department shall be made in writing to the Bureau of Children's Services or to local offices. The request shall contain as much of the following information as the individual can provide: a. Names of the adopted person and adopted parents, b. Date and place of adoption, c. Birth date of the adopted person, d. Name of the adopted person prior to adoption. . . ."

Author's Observations: Surely Iowa must lead all the other states in what information should be sealed. Most states seal evidence of birthparents' identity, legitimation, and some even the hospital or place of birth; but Iowa is the only state that mentions sealing information regarding a sex change.

KANSAS

State Information Department:	State House 10th and Harrison Sts. Topeka, KS 66612 (913) 296-0111
State Agency:	Department of Social and Rehabilitative Services Division of Children and Youth 2700 West 6th St. Topeka, KS 66606
Court of Jurisdiction:	District Court
Birth and Death Records:	Bureau of Registration and Health Statistics Kansas State Department of Health and Environment 6700 South Topeka Ave. Topeka, KS 66620

State office has records since July 1, 1911. For earlier records write to County Clerk, county where birth or death occurred.

Marriage Records:	Bureau of Registration and Health Statistics *see address listed above*

State office has records since May 1913.

	Probate Judge County where license was issued
Divorce Records:	Bureau of Registration and Health Statistics *see address listed above*

State office has records since July 1951.

	Clerk of District Court County where divorce was granted
Archives/Record Holdings:	Kansas State Historical Society Library Memorial Building Topeka, KS 66603
Department of Motor Vehicles:	Division of Motor Vehicles Department of Revenue State Office Bldg. 10th and Topeka Ave. Topeka, KS 66626 (913) 296-3601
Search and Support Groups:	Wichita Adult Adoptee Group 5402 Lamsdale Wichita, KS 67208

State Reunion Registry: Kansas does not have a registry at the present. Refer to Chapter 8 for a list of group registries. Note "Policies" below.

Age of Majority: 18 years or older

Laws Governing Opening Records: K.S.A. 65–2423. *Adoption Cases.* "In cases of adoption the state registrar upon receipt of certified order of adoption shall prepare a supplementary certificate in the new name of the adopted person; and seal and file the original certificate of birth with said certified copy attached thereto. Such sealed documents may be opened by the state registrar only upon demand of the adopted person if of legal age or by an order of the court."

K.S.A. 59–2279. *Files and records of adoption.* "The files and records of the court of adoption proceedings shall not be open to inspection or copy by other persons than the parties in interest and their attorneys, and representatives of the state department of social welfare, except upon an order of the court expressly permitting the same."

Laws Governing Inheritance: K.S.A. 1972 Supp. 59–2103. *Name of adopted child, effect of adoption.* "Upon such adoption all the rights of natural parents to the adopted child, including the right to inherit from such child, shall cease, except the rights of a natural parent who is the spouse of the adopting parent."

K.S.A. 1972 Supp. 38–128. *Same: termination of rights.* ". . . all the rights of the parent or person in loco parentis shall thereupon be terminated, including the right to receive notice in a subsequent adoption proceedings involving said child."

Policies: Taken from *Adoption Picture,* prepared by the Kansas Department of Social Rehabilitation Service, October 1974. "We can and should inform the adult adoptee of the fact that they [*sic*] can, upon request to the Bureau of Vital Statistics, obtain their original birth certificate. (When Kansas adopted the Uniform Act on Vital Statistics in 1951 it became possible for an adopted adult to obtain their original birth certificate upon request. All that is required is that the adoptee provide evidence of identity such as a driver's license.)"

Author's Observations: In light of the many people who predict open records as a forerunner to ruined lives and adoptive-family breakups, Kansas has remained stable since 1951. This is a very progressive state.

KENTUCKY

State Information Department: State Capitol
Frankfort, KY 40601
(502) 564-2500

State Agency: Bureau for Social Services
Department for Human Resources
275 East Main St.
6th Floor West
Frankfort, KY 40601

Court of Jurisdiction: Circuit Court

Birth and Death Records: Office of Vital Statistics
State Department of Health
275 East Main St.
Frankfort, KY 40621

State office has records since January 1, 1911. Earlier records for Louisville and Lexington. For births and deaths occurring in Covington before 1911, write City Health Department.

Marriage Records: Office of Vital Statistics
see address listed above

State office has records since July 1, 1958.

Clerk of County Court
County where license was issued

Divorce Records: Office of Vital Statistics
see address listed above

State office has records since July 1, 1958.

Clerk of Circuit Court
County where divorce was granted

Archives/Record Holdings: Kentucky State Library Archives
State Government Reference Service
851 East Main St.
Frankfort, KY 40601

Department of Motor Vehicles: Bureau of Vehicle Regulation
                                     Department of Transportation
                                     State Office Building
                                     Frankfort, KY 40601
                                     (502) 564-7000

Search and Support Groups: Adoptees Looking in Kentucky, Inc.
                                     P.O. Box 99184
                                     Louisville, KY 40299

                                     Searching
                                     P.O. Box 7722
                                     Louisville, KY 40207

State Reunion Registry: Kentucky does not have a registry at the present. Refer to Chapter 8 for a list of group registries. Please note "Policies" below. A bill may be introduced in the 1982 session.

Age of Majority: 18 years or older

Laws Governing Opening Records: Economic Security and Public Welfare, 199.570. *Adoption records confidential; new birth certificate.* (1) "The files and records of the court during adoption proceedings shall not be open to inspection by persons other than parties to such proceedings, their attorneys, and representatives of the department except under order of the court expressly permitting inspection. Upon the entry of the final order in the case, the clerk shall place all papers and records in the case in a suitable envelope which shall be sealed and shall not be open for inspection by any person except on written order of the court."

Laws Governing Inheritance: Protective Services for Children: Adoption, 199.611. *Order of Termination.* (1) "If the court determines that . . . it shall make an order terminating all parental rights and obligations in the parent in whom they have existed, and releasing the child from all legal obligations to his parents, and transferring such parental rights to some other person or authorized agency or department as may, in the opinion of the court, be best qualified to receive them, except that the child shall retain the right to inherit from its parents under the laws of descent and distribution until the child is adopted."

Policies: When asked the question, do you have a reunion registry and, if not, are you planning one, the Bureau for Social Services replied: "An informal one in that we add information to closed records and if adoptees later request contact with their birth family, we let them know of the mutual interest of the birth family. We also, at that time, tell the adoptees of the appropriate procedure to attempt to have adoption records opened and provide affidavits about birth family interest upon request. We would like to have a more formal reunion register in addition to our present procedures; however, limited staff prevents our doing so at this time."

Author's Observations: Economic Security and Public Welfare, 199.570. *Adoption records confidential; new birth certificate.* (3) "The new certificate shall set forth the new name, if any, of the adopted child. . . . The birth certificate shall not contain any information revealing the child is adopted and shall show the adoptive parent or parents as the natural parent or parents of the child. The new birth certificate when issued shall not contain the place of birth, hospital and name of doctor or midwife. This information should be given only by an order of the court in which the child was adopted."

These laws seem very clear, yet the Bureau for Social Services said: "The Office of Counsel thinks that good cause would probably be no more than an overwhelming, prevailing curiosity. The main consideration seems to be whether both birth family and adoptee desire contact."

LOUISIANA

State Information Department:	State Capitol 900 Riverside, North Baton Rouge, LA 70804 (504) 389-6601
State Agency:	Office of Human Development Adoption Program 333 Laurel, Room 704 Baton Rouge, LA 70801
Court of Jurisdiction:	District Court
Birth and Death Records:	Division of Vital Records Office of Health Services and Environmental Quality P.O. Box 60630 New Orleans, LA 70160

State office has records since July 1, 1914. New Orleans birth records from 1790 and death records from 1803.

Marriage Records:	Orleans Parish: Division of Vital Records *see address listed above*

State office has records since 1946. Inquiries will be forwarded to the appropriate office.

Other parishes:
Clerk of Court
Parish where license was issued

Divorce Records:	Division of Public Health Statistics State Board of Health P.O. Box 60630 New Orleans, LA 70160

State office has records since 1946. Inquiries will be forwarded to the appropriate office.

Clerk of Court
Parish where divorce was granted

Archives/Record Holdings:	State Library 760 Riverside Mall P.O. Box 131 (70804) Baton Rouge, LA 70801

Department of Motor Vehicles:				Vehicle Registration Bureau
Department of Public Safety
109 South Foster Dr.
P.O. Box 66196 (70896)
Baton Rouge, LA 70806
(504) 389-7261

Search and Support Groups:				Adoptee's Birthrights Committee
P.O. Box 7213
Metairie, LA 70010

CUB Representative, LaPlace

Consult telephone directory or information operator, or write National Headquarters, listed under Massachusetts, for current address.

State Reunion Registry: Louisiana does not have a registry at the present. Refer to Chapter 8 for a list of group registries.

Age of Majority: 18 years or older

Laws Governing Opening Records: The 1980 legislative session passed two bills affecting opening records. State House Bill No. 1018 revises Louisiana Civil Code, Section 437, *Admission to hearings; inspection or publication of proceedings; indices; adoption records confidential.* This bill also revises Public Health and Safety, Section 73, *Certified copy of the new record; sealing and confidentiality of the original birth record.* The bill states: ". . . all relative to the confidentiality of adoption records, to provide for opening and inspection of such records only upon order of the court; to repeal provisions relative to curators ad hoc; to provide with respect to the application of such procedures, and otherwise to provide with respect thereto." Section 437. A. "Records of the proceedings shall not be open to inspection except on written authorization by the court, and there shall be no publication thereof."

Laws Governing Inheritance: Father and Child, Chapter 4, Of Adoption, Article 214. *Reciprocal rights and duties of adopter and adopted.* ". . . the blood parent or parents and all other blood relatives of the adopted person, except as provided by R.S. 9:572 (B), are relieved of all of their legal duties and divested of all of their legal rights with regard to the adopted person, including the right of inheritance from the adopted person and his lawful descendants; and the adopted person and his lawful descendants are relieved of all of their legal duties and divested of all of their legal rights with regard to the blood parent or parents and other blood relatives, except the right to inheritance from them."

Policies: Public Health and Safety, 40:79. *Index to Notes.* 1. *Inspection, in general:* "Adopted person's desire to determine his legal right of inheritance from his natural parents, as recognized by LSA-CC. Art. 214, is a "compelling reason", within meaning of provision of this section providing that sealed package containing original certificate of birth shall be opened only on order of competent court for compelling reason and only to extent necessary. Massey v. Parker, App. 1978, 362 SO. 2d 1195." 3. *Inheritance, Inspection:* "Right of adopted person to inherit from blood parents and other blood relatives can constitute compelling reason for opening of sealed records of adoption. Larned v. Parker, App 1978, 360 So 2d 906."

Author's Observations: Civil Code, Section 422.9. *Anonymity of parents and adoptive parents protected.* "The formal act of voluntary surrender need not name the person or persons who are to become the adoptive parent or parents of the child surrendered. An attorney at law may be named in the act of surrender as the representative of the prospective adoptive parent or parents."

MAINE

State Information Department:	State House Augusta, ME 04333 (207) 289-1110
State Agency:	Department of Human Services 221 State St. Augusta, ME 04333
Court of Jurisdiction:	County Probate Courts: Adoption
Birth and Death Records:	Office of Vital Records Human Services Building 221 State Street Augusta, ME 04333

State office has records since 1892. For older records write to the municipality where birth or death occurred.

Marriage Records:	Office of Vital Records *see address listed above* Town Clerk Town where license was issued
Divorce Records:	Office of Vital Records *see address listed above*

State office has records since January 1, 1892.

	Clerk of District Court Judicial Division where divorce was granted
Archives/Record Holdings:	State Library LMA Bldg., State House Augusta, ME 04333
Department of Motor Vehicles:	Motor Vehicle Division Department of State Lower Capitol St. Augusta, ME 04333 (207) 289-2761
Search and Support Groups:	CUB Representative, North Berwick

Consult telephone directory or information operator, or write National Headquarters, listed under Massachusetts, for current address.

Orphan Voyage Chapter, Dexter
Orphan Voyage Chapter, South Portland

Consult telephone directory or information operator, or write National Head-quarters, listed under Colorado, for current address.

State Reunion Registry: Maine has a state reunion registry.

Office of Vital Records
Department of Human Services
221 State Street
Station 11
Augusta, ME 04333

Age of Majority: 18 years or older

Laws Governing Opening Records: Chapter 1071, Section 4008. *Records; confidentiality; disclosure,* 3B. "A court on its finding that access to those records may be necessary for the determination of any issue before the court: Access shall be limited to in camera inspection, unless the court determines that public disclosure of the information is necessary for the resolution of an issue pending before it."

Laws Governing Inheritance: Chapter 1071, Subchapter VI, Section 4056. *Effects of termination order.* 1. "Parent and child divested of rights. An order terminating parental rights divests the parent and child of all legal rights, powers, privileges, immunities, duties and obligations to each other as parent and child, except the inheritance rights between the child and his parent."

Policies: State House Bill No. 1313 is now being considered. This bill deals with release of information and if passed should be reviewed by all searchers from this state. Section 2, 19MRSA, Subsection 534. "Any medical or genetic information in the court records relating to an adoption shall be made available to the adopted child or his heirs on petition of the court."

MARYLAND

State Information Department:

State House
State Circle
Annapolis, MD 21404
(301) 267-0100

State Agency:

Department of Human Resources
Social Services Administration
11 South St.
Baltimore, MD 21202

Court of Jurisdiction:

Chancery Court

Birth and Death Records:

Division of Vital Records
State Department of Health
State Office Bulding
201 West Preston St.
P.O. Box 13146
Baltimore, MD 21203

State office has records since 1898. Baltimore has city records from January 1, 1875.

Marriage Records: Division of Vital Records
                                         see address listed above

State office has records since June 1, 1951.

                                         Clerk of Circuit Court
                                         County where license was issued

For local Baltimore information write: Clerk of Court of Common Pleas of Baltimore.

Divorce Records: Division of Vital Records
                                         see address listed above

State office has records since January 1961. Inquiries will be forwarded to appropriate office.

                                         Clerk of the Circuit Court
                                         County where divorce was granted

Archives/Record Holdings: Maryland State Library
                                         Court of Appeals Building
                                         361 Rose Boulevard
                                         Annapolis, MD 21401

Department of Motor Vehicles: Motor Vehicle Administration
                                         Department of Transportation
                                         6601 Ritchie Hwy., NE
                                         Glen Burnie, MD 21061
                                         (301) 768-7000

Search and Support Groups: Adoptees in Search**
                                         P.O. Box 41016
                                         Bethesda, MD 20014

                                         Adoption Connection Exchange
                                           (ACE)**
                                         1301 Park Ave
                                         Baltimore, MD 21217

                                         CUB Representative, Bowie**

Consult telephone directory or information operator, or write National Headquarters, listed under Massachusetts, for current address.

State Reunion Registry: Maryland does not have a registry at the present. Refer to Chapter 8 for a list of group registries.

Age of Majority: 18 years or older

Laws Governing Opening Records: Letter from the Department of Human Resources, State of Maryland. "Adoption records continue to be permanently sealed by law in Maryland. Only the court has the authority to order these seals broken and then only upon proof of just cause such as a medical emergency."

Laws Governing Inheritance: Article 16, Section 78. *Legal effect of interlocutory decree of adoption.* (b) "The natural parents of the person adopted, if living, shall after the interlocutory decree be relieved of all legal duties and obligations due from them to the person adopted, and shall be divested of all rights with respect to such person. Upon the entry of a decree of adoption, all rights of inheritance between the child and the natural relatives shall be governed by the Estates Article of the Code."

Policies: A bill was introduced in 1980 and held over during the summer recess. HB 1915. *Open Records.* Preamble. "In 1947, adoption records in Maryland were sealed. Since then, there have been changes in public attitudes as well as in social work theory and practice in response to the felt need on the part of an increasing number of adoptees to know more about their biological backgrounds. Other jurisdictions have provided for full or partial access to adoption records without apparent damage to either the institution of adoption or to the parties involved. This Act is intended to facilitate the access of adoptees to information about their heritage, consistent with the rights of birthparents; now therefore, . . ."

This pending bill will most likely go through many changes before it is considered for passage. Interested parties should ask for a copy, with all new changes, when requesting this state's laws.

MASSACHUSETTS

State Information Department:　State House
Beacon St.
Boston, MA 02133
(617) 727-2121

State Agency:　Department of Social Services
150 Causeway St.
Boston, MA 02114

Court of Jurisdiction:　Probate Court

Birth and Death Records:　Registrar of Vital Statistics
Room 103 McCormack Bldg.
1 Ashburton Pl.
Boston, MA 02108

State office has records since 1841. For earlier records write the City or Town Clerk in place where birth or death occurred. Boston records for 1848 are available in the State office.

Marriage Records:　Registrar of Vital Statistics
see address listed above

State office has records since 1841. Earliest Boston records are for 1848.

Divorce Records:　Registrar of Vital Statistics
see address listed above

State office has an Index of Records from 1952. Inquirer will be directed where to forward request.

Registrar of Probate Court
County where divorce was granted

Archives/Record Holdings: State Library
                                                     341 State House
                                                     Boston, MA 02133

Department of Motor Vehicles: Registry of Motor Vehicles
                                                     Department of Public Safety
                                                     100 Nashua St.
                                                     Boston, MA 02114
                                                     (617) 727-3700

Search and Support Groups: Cape Association for Truth in Adoption
                                                     P.O. Box 606
                                                     Woods Hole, MA 02543

                                                     Concerned United Birthparents (CUB)
                                                     National Administration Headquarters
                                                     P.O. Box 573
                                                     Milford, MA 01757

                                                     CUB Branch, Cambridge**

Consult telephone directory or information operator, or write National Headquarters, listed above.

                                                     Orphan Voyage Chapter, Peabody**

Consult telephone directory or information operator, or write National Headquarters, listed under Colorado, for current address.

                                                     Resolve National Headquarters
                                                     P.O. Box 474
                                                     Belmont, MA 02178

State Reunion Registry: Massachusetts does not have a registry at the present. Refer to Chapter 8 for a list of group registries.

Age of Majority: 18 years or older

Laws Governing Opening Records: Adoption of Children and change of Names, Chapter 210, Section 5C. *Segregation and Inspection of Papers Concerning Adoption.* "All petitions for adoption, all reports submitted thereunder and all pleadings, papers or documents filed in connection therewith, docket entries in the permanent docket and record books shall not be available for inspection, unless a judge of probate of the county where such records are kept, for good cause shown, shall otherwise order."

Laws Governing Inheritance: Adoption of Children and Change of Names, Chapter 210, Section 7. *Rights of Adopted Child as to Succession to Property.* "A person shall by adoption lose his right to inherit from his natural parents or kindred, except when one of the natural parents of a minor child has died and the surviving parent has remarried subsequent to such parent's death, subsequent adoption of such child by the person with whom such remarriage is contracted shall not affect the rights of such child to inherit from or through the deceased parent or kindred thereof."

MICHIGAN

State Information Department: Capitol Bldg.
                                            Lansing, MI 48933
                                            (517) 373-1837

State Agency: Department of Social Services
                                            300 South Capitol Ave.
                                            P.O. Box 30037
                                            Lansing, MI 48909

Court of Jurisdiction: Probate Court

Birth and Death Records: Office of Vital and Health Statistics
                                            Michigan Department of Public Health
                                            3500 North Logan St.
                                            Lansing, MI 48914

State office has records since 1867. Detroit records may be obtained from City Health Department for births since 1893 and deaths since 1897.

Marriage Records: Office of Vital and Health Statistics
                                            see address listed above

State office has records since April 1867.

                                            County Clerk
                                            County where license was issued

Divorce Records: Office of Vital and Health Statistics
                                            see address listed above

State office has records since 1897.

                                            County Clerk
                                            County where divorce was granted

Archives/Record Holdings: State Library
                                            735 East Michigan Ave.
                                            Lansing, MI 48933

Department of Motor Vehicles: Bureau of Automotive Regulation
                                            Department of State
                                            3222 South Logan St.
                                            Lansing, MI 48918
                                            (517) 373-7857

Search and Support Groups: Adoptees Identity Movement**
                                            22 Frontenac SE
                                            Grand Rapids, MI 49508

                                            Adoptees Search for Knowledge**
                                            4227 South Belsay Rd.
                                            Burton, MI 48519

                                            Adoptees Search for Knowledge**
                                            1921 Marsac
                                            Bay City, MI 48706

Adoptees Search for Knowledge**
P.O. Box 762
East Lansing, MI 48823

Adoptees Search for Knowledge**
2322 North Eugene St.
Burton, MI 48519

Adoption Identity Movement**
P.O. Box 20092
Detroit, MI 48220

ALMA Chapter, Jackson

Association for the Protection of the
Adoptive Triangle
2429 Halle, SE
Grand Rapids, MI 49506

Consult telephone directory or information operator, or write National Headquarters, listed under New York, for current address.

CUB Representative, Hastings

Consult telephone directory or information operator, or write National Headquarters, listed under Massachusetts, for current address.

Roots and Reunions
P.O. Box 121
L'Anse, MI 49946

State Reunion Registry: Michigan has a state registry.

Michigan Department of Social Services
Adoption Central Registry
P.O. Box 30037
300 South Capitol Avenue
Lansing, MI 48909

Age of Majority: 18 years or older

Laws Governing Opening Records: Michigan Adoption Code, Item 1. IX. *Additional Conditions of Adoption.* E. *Records.* Section 67. (1) "All records of proceedings in adoption cases, including any notice filed pursuant to section 33 (1) and any petition filed pursuant to section 34 (1), and all papers and books relating to the proceedings shall be kept in separate locked files and shall not be open to inspection or copy except upon order of a court of record for good cause shown expressly permitting inspection of copy."

Laws Governing Inheritance: Michigan Adoption Code, Item 1. IX. *Additional Conditions of Adoption.* A. *Rights after adoption (inheritance).* Section 60. (2) "After entry of the order of adoption there shall not be any distinction between the rights and duties of natural progeny and adopted persons, and the adopted person shall become an heir at law of the adopting parent or parents, and an heir at law of the lineal and collateral kindred of the adopting parent or parents. After entry of the order of adoption, the adopted person shall no longer be an heir at law of his or her natural parents, except that a right, title, or interest vesting before entry of the final order of adoption shall not be divested by that order."

Policies: A new law went into effect May 14, 1980, clearly outlining what information is open to searchers, release forms needed, and guidelines to obtaining that information.

State House Bill No. 4164, Chapter 10, *Section 68 (3a):* "All information on both biological parents shall be released to the adult adoptee, if both biological parents have on file with the department a statement consenting to release of identifying information." *Section 68 (2):* "A biological parent or adult biological sibling shall not receive information, other than nonidentifying information described in Section 27 (1) and (2) of this chapter, from a child placing agency, court, or file of the department relative to an adoptee, unless the adoptee, as an adult, has given written consent to the release of the information." *Section 68 (5):* "Upon receipt of a written request for identifying information from an adult adoptee, a child placing agency, a court, or the department, if it maintains that adoption file, shall request information from the department file as specified in Section 27 (5) of this chapter, pursuant to the requirements of subsections (3) and (4). Upon receipt of a response from the department file, a child placing agency, a court, or the department shall notify the adoptee in writing, within 30 days after the receipt of the response, of the identifying information to which the adoptee is entitled, or that the identifying information cannot be released and the reason why the information cannot be released. The child placing agency, court, or the department also shall notify each biological parent who has consented to release of identifying information of the reason why information cannot be released."

MINNESOTA

State Information Department:	State Capitol Aurora Ave. and Park St. St. Paul, MN 55155 (612) 296-6013
State Agency:	Department of Public Welfare Centennial Office Bldg. St. Paul, MN 55155
Court of Jurisdiction:	County Family Court or Juvenile Division of District Court
Birth and Death Records:	Minnesota Department of Health Section of Vital Statistics 717 Delaware St., SE Minneapolis, MN 55440

State office has records since January 1908. Copies of earlier records may be obtained from Clerk of District Court, county where birth or death occurred. Minneapolis or St. Paul city records may be obtained from the Health Departments in those cities for dates prior to January 1908.

Marriage Records:	Minnesota Department of Health *see address listed above*

State office has index since January 1958. Inquiries will be forwarded to appropriate office.

Clerk in District Court
County where license was issued

Divorce Records:

Minnesota Department of Health
see address listed above

State office has index since January 1, 1970.

Clerk of District Court
County where divorce was granted

Archives/Record Holdings:

Minnesota Historical Society Library
690 Cedar St.
St. Paul, MN 55101

Department of Motor Vehicles:

Division of Motor Vehicles
Department of Public Safety
State Highway Bldg.
St. Paul, MN 55155
(612) 296-2001

Search and Support Groups:

ALMA Chapter, Minneapolis**

Consult telephone directory or information operator, or write National Headquarters, listed under New York, for current address.

CUB Branch, Minneapolis**
CUB Representative, Hibbing**

Consult telephone directory or information operator, or write National Headquarters, listed under Massachusetts, for current address.

Kammandale Library**
57 North Dale St.
St. Paul, MN 55102

LEAF**
23247 Lofton Court North
Scandia, MN 55073

Link**
c/o Nancy Corey
1700 West 76th St., #1-C
Minneapolis, MN 55423

State Reunion Registry: Minnesota has a state registry.

Minnesota Reunion Registry
Box 2323
North St. Paul Station
St. Paul, MN 55109

Age of Majority: 18/21 years or older

Laws Governing Opening Records: Public Welfare Licensing Act, Section 259.31. *Hearings, Confidential.* "The files and records of the court in adoption proceedings shall not be open to inspection by any person except the commissioner of public welfare or his representatives, or upon an order of the court expressly so permitting pursuant to a petition setting forth the reasons thereof."

Laws Governing Inheritance: Public Welfare Licensing Act, Section 259.29. *Effect of Adoption.* "After a decree of adoption is entered the natural parents of an adopted child shall be relieved of all parental responsibilities for the child, and they shall not exercise or have any rights over the adopted child or his property. The child shall not owe his natural parents or their relatives any legal duty nor shall he inherit from his natural parents or kindred, except as provided in subdivision 1a."

Author's Observations: A pamphlet entitled *Original Birth Certificates* is printed by the Department of Public Welfare. It is free upon request and should be obtained by persons searching in this state. One interesting note: "However, in situations where one parent files a refusal or is deceased, the birth certificate remains sealed. If the birth parent is deceased, the adopted person may petition the court for a decision to open the records."

It would seem to me that if a birth parent is deceased, the records would be opened more freely, but just the opposite is true.

MISSISSIPPI

State Information Department: New Capitol Bldg.
Jackson, MS 39205
(601) 354-7011

State Agency: Department of Public Welfare
515 East Amite St.
P.O. Box 352
Jackson, MS 39205

Court of Jurisdiction: Chancery Court

Birth and Death Records: Vital Records Registration Unit
State Board of Health
P.O. Box 1700
Jackson, MS 39205

Marriage Records: Vital Records Registration Unit
see address listed above

State office has statistical record from January 1926 to July 1, 1938, and from January 1, 1942, to the present.

Circuit Clerk
County where license was issued

Divorce Records: Vital Records Registration Unit
see address listed above

State office has records since January 1, 1926. Inquiries will be forwarded to appropriate office.

Chancery Clerk
County where divorce was granted

Archives/Record Holdings: Department of Archives and History
Archives History Building
Capitol Green
Jackson, MS 39205

Department of Motor Vehicles: Office of the Motor Vehicle Comptroller
Department of Motor Vehicles
500 Woolfolk State Office Bldg.
501 North West St.
P.O. Box 1140 (39205)
Jackson, MS 39201
(601) 354-7411

Search and Support Groups: Contact a National Organization for individuals working in this state.

State Reunion Registry: Mississippi does not have a registry at the present. Refer to Chapter 8 for a list of group registries.

Age of Majority: 18/21 years or older

Laws Governing Opening Records: Chapter 17, Section 93-17-25. *Proceedings and records confidential—use in court or administrative proceedings.* "All proceedings under this chapter shall be confidential and shall be held in closed court without admittance of any person other than the interested parties, except upon order of the court. All pleadings, reports, files and records pertaining to adopting proceedings shall be confidential and shall not be public records and shall be withheld from inspection or examination by any person, except upon order of the court in which the proceeding was had on good cause shown; provided however, officers of the court, including attorneys, shall be given access to such records upon request."

Laws Governing Inheritance: Chapter 17, Section 93-17-13. *Final decree and effect thereof.* (d) ". . . that the natural parents and natural kindred of the child shall not inherit by or through the child except as to a natural parent who is the spouse of the adopting parent, and all parental rights of the natural parent, or parents, shall be terminated, except as to a natural parent who is the spouse of the adopting parent. Nothing in this chapter shall restrict the right of any person to dispose of property under a last will and testament."

Author's Observations: Chapter 17, Section 93-17-31. *Clerks to keep separate index, docket and minute books.* "The several chancery clerks shall obtain and keep a separate, confidential index showing the true name of the child adopted, the true name of its natural parent, or parents, if known, and the true name of the persons adopting the child and the date of the decree of adoption, and the name under which the child was adopted, or the name given the child by the adoption proceedings and a cross index shall be kept showing the said true name and the name given the child in the adoption decree, and which index shall be subject to the provisions of section 93-17-25 as to same being kept in confidence. . . ."

This section feels it is an important duty to protect the child by withholding his true name. The wording is poorly choosen as a defense to the department and shows the misguided job-responsibilities assumed by agencies in the past.

MISSOURI

State Information Department:	State Capitol Jefferson City, MO 65101 (314) 751-2151
State Agency:	Division of Family Services Department of Social Services P.O. Box 88 Jefferson City, MO 65103
Court of Jurisdiction:	Circuit Court
Birth and Death Records:	Bureau of Vital Records Division of Health State Department of Public Health and Welfare Jefferson City, MO 65101

State office has records beginning with 1910. For births or deaths before 1910 in St. Louis City, St. Louis County, or Kansas City, write to the City or County Health Department.

Marriage Records:	Bureau of Vital Records *see address listed above*

Correspondence will be referred to appropriate county where license was issued.

Recorder of Deeds
County where license was issued

Divorce Records:	Bureau of Vital Records *see address listed above*

State office will refer inquiries to appropriate county in which the decree was granted. Index since 1948.

Clerk of Circuit Court
County where divorce was granted

Archives/Record Holdings:	State Library 308 East High St. P.O. Box 387 Jefferson City, MO 65101
Department of Motor Vehicles:	Division of Motor Vehicles and Licensing Department of Revenue 413 State Office Bldg. Jefferson City, MO 65101 (314) 751-4450
Search and Support Groups:	ALMA Chapter, Clayton**

Consult telephone directory or information operator, or write National Headquarters, listed under New York, for current address.

Family Finders
5019 South Emery Rd.
Independence, MO 64055

Kansas City Adult Adoptees Organization**
P.O. Box 15225
Kansas City, MO 64106

Southwest Missouri Adoptee Association**
Route 2
Oak Crest Estates
Rogersville, MO 65742

Southwest Missouri Adoptee Association**
Route 5
P.O. Box 172
Joplin, MO 65801

State Reunion Registry: Missouri does not have a registry at the present. Refer to Chapter 8 for a list of group registries.

Age of Majority: 18 years or older

Laws Governing Opening Records: Chapter 453, Adoption and Foster Care, Section 453.120. *Records of adoption proceedings not open to inspection except on order of court—penalty for violation.* 1. "The files and records of the court in adoption proceedings shall not be open to inspection, or copy, by any person or persons, except upon an order of the court expressly permitting the same and pursuant to written application."

Laws Governing Inheritance: Chapter 453, Adoption and Foster Care, Section 453.-090. *Consequences of Adoption.* 1. "When a child is adopted in accordance with the provisions of this chapter, all legal relationships and all rights and duties between such child and his natural parents (other than a natural parent who joins in the petition for adoption as provided in Section 453.010) shall cease and determine. Said child shall thereafter be deemed and held to be for every purpose the child of his parent or parents by adoption, as fully as though born to him or them in lawful wedlock."

Policies: State Senate Bill No. 177 is being considered in this state at the date of this writing. It concerns receiving records and one portion reads: 2. "After attaining the age of twenty-one, an adopted person may apply to the court to examine the court record of the adoption proceedings to determine the natural parents, and the court shall order the record open for inspection upon written application."
   This bill would be extremely valuable to searchers if passed.

Author's Observations: State House Bill No. 1371 was co-sponsored by Representatives Reisch and Benson. Forty-four other Representatives sponsored this bill but it died in committee on February 1980. It is quoted here with no comment from the Author. 453.130. "Whenever a person adopted under the provisions of this chapter shall develop venereal infection as a result of conditions existing prior to the time such person was adopted, or shall develop feeblemindedness or epilepsy, or shall prove to be a member of a race, the members of which are prohibited by the laws of this state from marriage with members of the race to which the parents by adoption belong, a petition setting forth such facts may be filed at any time within five years after such adoption with the court which decreed the adoption, and if on a hearing the facts in such petition are established, the said court may enter a decree annulling the adoption and setting aside any and all rights and obligations that may have accrued by reason of said adoption."

MONTANA

State Information Department:
Capitol Building
Helena, MT 59601
(406) 449-2511

State Agency:
Social Services Bureau
Department of Social and
 Rehabilitation Services
111 Sanders
Helena, MT 59601

Court of Jurisdiction:
District Court/Tribal Court

Birth and Death Records:
Bureau of Records and Statistics
State Department of Health and
 Environmental Sciences
Helena, MT 59601

State office has records since 1907.

Marriage Records:
Bureau of Records and Statistics
see address listed above

State office has records since 1943. Inquiries will be forwarded to appropriate office.

Clerk of District Court
County where license was issued

Divorce Records:
Bureau of Records and Statistics
see address listed above

State office has records since 1943. Inquiries will be forwarded to appropriate office.

Clerk of District Court
County where divorce was granted

Archives/Record Holdings:
State Library
930 East Lyndale Ave.
Helena, MT 59601

Department of Motor Vehicles:
Registrar's Bureau
Motor Vehicles Division
Department of Justice
Deer Lodge, MT 59722
(406) 846-1320

Search and Support Groups: Search**
                                        Box 181
                                        Big Timber, MT 59011

                                        Search Group
                                        P.O. Box 214
                                        Melville, MT 59055

State Reunion Registry: Montana does not have a registry at the present. Refer to Chapter 8 for a list of group registries. The Social Services Bureau notes some consideration towards forming one.

Age of Majority: 18 years or older

Laws Governing Opening Records: Family Law, Adoption, 40-8-126. *Confidentiality of record and proceedings.* (3) "All files and records pertaining to said adoption proceedings in the county departments of public welfare, the department of social and rehabilitation services, or any authorized agencies shall be confidential and withheld from inspection except upon order of court for good cause shown."

Laws Governing Inheritance: Family Law, Adoption, 40-8-125. *Effect of final decree.* (2) "After a final decree of adoption is entered, the natural parents and the kindred of the natural parents of the adopted child, unless they are the adoptive parents or the spouse of an adoptive parent, shall be relieved of all parental responsibilities for said child and have no rights over such adopted child or to his property by descent and distribution."

Policies: Health and Safety, 50-15-304. *Substitute birth certificate for person adopted.* (1) "The procedure for issuing a substitute birth certificate for a person born in Montana and adopted is as follows: (a) Before the 16th day of the month following the order of adoption, the clerk of the district court shall forward a certified copy of the final order of adoption to the department or the department may accept a certified copy of a final order of adoption from a court of competent jurisdiction of a foreign state of the United States or a tribal court of competent jurisdiction. (b) The department shall prepare a substitute certificate containing: (i) the new name of the adopted person; (ii) the true date and place of birth and sex of the adopted person; (iii) statistical facts concerning the adoptive parents in place of the natural parents; (iv) the words 'department of health and environmental sciences' substituted for the words 'attendant's own signature'; and (v) dates of recording as shown on original birth certificate." (2) "The procedure for recording a substitute certificate of birth for a person born in Montana and adopted is as follows: (a) The department shall send copies of the substitute certificate to the local registrar and to the county clerk and recorder. (b) The local registrar and county clerk and recorder shall immediately enter the substitute birth certificate in its files and forward copies of the original birth record to the department. (c) The department shall seal original birth records and open them only on demand of the adopted person if of legal age or on order of a court."

NEBRASKA

State Information Department: State Capitol
                                          1445 K St.
                                          Lincoln, NE 68509
                                          (402) 471-2311

State Agency:	Department of Public Welfare Division of Social Services P.O. Box 95026 Lincoln, NE 68509
Court of Jurisdiction:	County Court
Birth and Death Records:	Bureau of Vital Statistics State Department of Health 301 Centennial Mall South P.O. Box 95007 Lincoln, NE 68509

State office has records since 1904. For births before that date, write State Office of Information.

Marriage Records:	Bureau of Vital Statistics *see address listed above*

State office has records since 1909.

	County Court County where license was issued
Divorce Records:	Bureau of Vital Statistics *see address listed above*

State office has records since 1909.

	Clerk District Court where divorce was granted
Archives/Record Holdings:	State Historical Society Library 1500 and R Sts. Lincoln, NE 68503
Department of Motor Vehicles:	Department of Motor Vehicles State Office Bldg. 301 Centennial Mall South Lincoln, NE 68509 (402) 471-2281
Search and Support Groups:	Adoptees Search Heritage 5624 Pearce St. Omaha, NE 68106
	Adoption Identity Desire 1808 West F North Platt, NE 69101
	Open A.R.M.S P.O. Box 1522 North Platt, NE 69101

State Reunion Registry: Nebraska does not have a registry at the present. Refer to Chapter 8 for a list of group registries. Please note "Policies" below.

Age of Majority: 19/25 years or older. Note "Policies" below.

Laws Governing Opening Records: Legislative Bill 992, Adoption of Children, Section 43-113. "All papers pertaining to the adoption shall be kept by the county judge as a permanent record of the county court and withheld from inspection. No person shall have access to such records except on the order of the county judge of the court in which the decree of adoption was entered on good cause shown or as provided in sections 20 to 22 of this act."

Laws Governing Inheritance: Infants, Section 43-106.01. *Adoption: relinquishment to Department of Public Welfare; relief from parental duties; no impairment of right to inherit.* "When a child shall have been relinquished by written instrument, as provided by sections 43-104 and 43-106, to the Department of Public Welfare or to a licensed child placement agency and the agency has, in writing, accepted full responsibility for the child, the person so relinquishing shall be relieved of all parental duties toward and all responsibilities for such child and have no rights over such child. Nothing contained in this section shall impair the right of such child to inherit."

Policies: Infants, Section 42-130, subsection 12. "An adopted person twenty-five years of age or older born in this state who desires access to the names of relatives or access to his or her original certificate of birth shall file a written request for such information with the bureau. The bureau shall provide a form for making such a request."

Infants, Section 43-129, subsection 11. "If at any time an individual licensed to practice medicine and surgery pursuant to sections 71-1, 102 and 107.04 or certified as qualified to practice clinical psychology pursuant to sections 71-3832 to 71-3836, through his or her professional relationship with an adopted person, determines that information contained on the original birth certificate of the adopted person may be necessary for the treatment of the health of the adopted person, whether physical or mental in nature, he or she may petition a court of competent jurisdiction for the release of the information contained on the original birth certificate."

NEVADA

State Information Department:

State Capitol
Carson City, NV 89710
(702) 885-5000

State Agency:

Welfare Division
Department of Human Resources
251 Jeanell Dr.
Capitol Mall Complex
Carson City, NV 89710

Court of Jurisdiction:

District Court

Birth and Death Records:

Division of Health–Vital Statistics
Capitol Complex
Carson City, NV 89710

State office has records since July 1, 1911. For earlier records write County Recorder in county where birth or death occurred.

Marriage Records:

Division of Health–Vital Statistics
see address listed above

State office has Index since January 1, 1968. Inquiries will be forwarded to appropriate office.

County Recorder
County where license was issued

Divorce Records: Division of Health–Vital Statistics
see address listed above

State office has index since January 1, 1968. Inquiries will be forwarded to appropriate office.

County Clerk
County where divorce was granted

Archives/Record Holdings: State Library
Archives Division
401 N. Carson St.
Carson City, NV 89710

Department of Motor Vehicles: Department of Motor Vehicles
555 Wright Way
Carson City, NV 89711
(702) 885-5375

Search and Support Groups: ALMA Chapter, Boulder City**
ALMA Chapter, Reno**

Consult telephone directory or information operator, or write National Headquarters, listed under New York, for current address.

CUB Representative, Las Vegas

Consult telephone directory or information operator, or write National Headquarters, listed under Massachusetts, for current address.

Southern Nevada Adoptees Group
22 Palm, Space #44
Las Vegas, NV 89104

State Reunion Registry: Nevada does have a state reunion registry.

Nevada State Reunion Registry
Welfare Division
Department of Human Resources
251 Jeanell Drive
Capitol Mall Complex
Carson City, NV 89710

Age of Majority: 18 years or older

Laws Governing Opening Records: Chapter 127, Adoption of Children and Adults, Section 127.140. *Confidentiality of hearings, files and records.* 2. "The files and records of the court in adoption proceedings are not open to inspection by any person except upon an order of the court expressly so permitting pursuant to a petition setting forth the reasons therefor, or if a natural parent and the child are eligible to receive information from the state register of adoptions."

Laws Governing Inheritance: Chapter 127, Adoption of Children and Adults, Section 127.160. *Rights and duties of adopted child and adoptive parents.* "After a decree of adoption is entered, the natural parents of an adopted child shall be relieved of all parental responsibilities for such child, and they shall not exercise or have any rights over such adopted child or his property. The child shall not owe his natural parents or their relatives any legal duty nor shall he inherit from his natural parent or kindred."

Author's Observations: International Soundex Reunion Registry (see Chapter 8), which is recognized by the State of Minnesota, is located in Nevada. The Department of Human Resources in Nevada has a separate registry.

NEW HAMPSHIRE

State Information Department: State House
                                          107 North Main St.
                                          Concord, NH 03301
                                          (603) 271-1110

State Agency: Bureau of Child and Family Services
                                          State Department of Health and
                                              Welfare
                                          Hazen Dr.
                                          Concord, NH 03301

Court of Jurisdiction: Probate Court

Birth and Death Records: Bureau of Vital Records
                                          Health and Welfare Building
                                          Hazen Dr.
                                          Concord, NH 03301

State office has copies as well as county offices. Fee includes search of files.

Marriage Records: Bureau of Vital Records
                                          see address listed above

State office has records since 1640.

                                          Town Clerk
                                          Town where license was issued

Divorce Records: Bureau of Vital Records
                                          see address listed above

State office has records since 1880. Fee includes search.

                                          Clerk
                                          Superior County which issued decree

Archives/Record Holdings: State Library
                                          Archives
                                          20 Park St.
                                          Concord, NH 03301

Department of Motor Vehicles: Motor Vehicle Division
Department of Safety
John O. Morton Bldg.
85 Loudon Rd.
Concord, NH 03301
(603) 271-2484

Search and Support Groups: CUB Representative, Merrimack **

Consult telephone directory or information operator, or write National Head-quarters, listed under Massachusetts, for current address.

State Reunion Registry: New Hampshire does not have a registry at the present, but State House Bill No. 529 has been referred to the Judiciary Committee. This bill concerns release of information. Searchers in this state should ask for updated information on this bill. Refer to Chapter 8 for a list of group registries.

Age of Majority: 18 years and older

Laws Governing Opening Records: Chapter 170-B, Adoption, Section 19. *Confidentiality of Records.* II. "All papers and records, including birth certificates, pertaining to the adoption, whether part of the permanent record of the court or of a file in the division, in an agency or office of the town clerk or the bureau of vital statistics are subject to inspection only upon written consent of the court for good cause shown."

Laws Governing Inheritance: Chapter 170-B. Adoption, Section 20. *Effect of Petition and Decree of Adoption; Inheritance.* II. "Upon the issuance of the final decree of adoption, the adopted child shall no longer be considered the child of his natural parent or parents and shall no longer be entitled to any of the rights or privileges or subject to any of the duties or obligations of a child with respect to the natural parent or parents; but, when a child is adopted by a stepparent, his relationship to his natural parent who is married to the stepparent shall in no way be altered by reason of the adoption." III. "Upon the issuance of a final decree of adoption, the adopted child shall lose all rights of inheritance from his natural parent or parents and from their collateral or lineal relatives. The rights of the natural parent or parents of their collateral or lineal relatives to inherit from such child shall cease upon the adoption."

Author's Observations: State House Bill No. 529 concerning release of information was requested by the Division of Welfare. I think it is important for adoptees, birthparents, and adoptive parents to recognize many states that now are reviewing past policies and actively pursuing changes.

NEW JERSEY

State Information Department: State House
Trenton, NJ 08625
(609) 292-2121

State Agency: Division of Youth and Family Services
Department of Institutions and
    Agencies
P.O. Box 510
Trenton, NJ 08625

Court of Jurisdiction: Superior Court or County Court

Birth and Death Records: State Department of Health
                                               Bureau of Vital Statistics
                                               P.O. Box 1540
                                               Trenton, NJ 08625

State office has records since June 1878. Fee includes search. An additional
charge if exact date is not known.

                                               Archives and History Bureau
                                               State Library Division
                                               State Department of Education
                                               Trenton, NJ 08625

This bureau has records from May 1848 to May 1878.

Marriage Records: State Department of Health
                                               see address listed above

An additional charge if exact year is not known.

                                               Archives and History Bureau
                                               see address listed above

This bureau has records from May 1848 to May 1878.

Divorce Records: Superior Court
                                               Chancery Division
                                               State House Annex, Room 320
                                               Trenton, NJ 08625

Archives/Record Holdings: State Library
                                               Archives and History
                                               185 West State St.
                                               Trenton, NJ 08625

Department of Motor Vehicles: Division of Motor Vehicles
                                               Department of Law and Public Safety
                                               25 South Montgomery Street
                                               Trenton, NJ 08666
                                               (609) 292-4570

Search and Support Groups: Adoption Triangle Ministry
                                               Box 156
                                               Oaklyn, NJ 08107

                                               ALMA Chapter, Bergen County **
                                               ALMA Chapter, East Brunswick **
                                               ALMA Chapter, Monmouth/Ocean
                                                   County **
                                               ALMA Chapter, Morristown **
                                               ALMA Chapter, Stanhope**
                                               ALMA Chapter, Somerdale **
                                               ALMA Chapter, Trenton **
                                               ALMA Chapter, Wayne **
                                               ALMA Chapter, Weehawkin **

Consult telephone directory or information operator, or write National Head-quarters, listed under New York, for current address.

CUB Branch, Haddon Heights **

Consult telephone directory or information operator, or write National Head-quarters, listed under Massachusetts for current address.

State Reunion Registry: New Jersey does have a registry. State Assembly Bill No. 2051 is under consideration. This bill would allow more lenient access to records. Note "Policies" below.

> The Bureau of Resource Development
> Division of Youth and Family Services
> Box 510
> Trenton, NJ 08625

Age of Majority: 18 years or older

Laws Governing Opening Records: Chapter 367, Section 9:3–52. *Records of proceedings; filing under seal; inspection; change of birth record.* (a) "All records of proceedings relating to adoption, including the complaint, judgment and all petitions, affidavits, testimony, reports, briefs, orders and other relevant documents, shall be filed under seal by the clerk of the court and shall at no time be open to inspection or copying unless the court, upon good cause shown, shall otherwise order. . . ."

Laws Governing Inheritance: Chapter 367, Section 9:3–50. *Effect of adoption; relationships of parent and child; rights of inheritance.* "The entry of a judgment of adoption shall terminate all relationships between the adopted child and his parents and all rights, duties and obligations of any person that are founded upon such relationships, including rights of inheritance under the intestate laws of this State, except such rights as may have vested prior to entry of the judgment of adoption; . . . For good cause, the court may in the judgment provide that the rights of inheritance from or through a deceased parent will not be affected or terminated by the adoption."

Policies: Those searching should be aware of policies regarding release of information. In an inter-office communication dated 8/4/77, Harold P. Rosenthal (Acting Director of the Department of Human Services, Division of Youth and Family Services) stated: "After careful review and consideration the Division [of Youth and Family Services] has decided to offer as much assistance to the adult adoptees as possible, while at the same time utilizing adequate safeguards to minimize the consequences for adoptive parents and natural parents.

"In addition to implementing this policy, BRD (Bureau of Resource Development) in conjunction with the Records Management Unit has established an Authorization for Release of Adoption Information Registry. Through this Registry, members of the biological family of an adopted child can request that information about themselves be released to an adult adoptee should an inquiry be made in the future. The Registry will enable staff to keep an accurate record of those who have given written authorization. Should you have any questions or receive any requests for information, please contact Ms. Joyce Undy, Bureau of Resource Development, directly.

Author's Observations: Taken from *Policy Regarding Release of Information in Adoption Situations.* II. *Requests from Adoptive Parents to locate Siblings of their Adopted*

Children. 1. "If the sibling being sought is also adopted, the Division's contact will be with the adoptive parents, who may accept or reject any direct contact. . . ." 3. "If the sibling being sought is residing with the biological family, no attempt will be made by the division to establish contact."

This is a good example of how an informed searcher can pick up clues. If the agency refuses to attempt contact one might be aware of possible reasons.

NEW MEXICO

State Information Department:
State Capitol
Santa Fe, NM 87501
(505) 827-4011

State Agency:
Human Services Department
Social Services Division
Adoption Services
P.O. Box 2348
Santa Fe, NM 87503

Court of Jurisdiction:
District Court

Birth and Death Records:
Vital Statistics Bureau
New Mexico Health Services Division
P.O. Box 968
Santa Fe, NM 87503

State office has records since 1880. Search of the files is included in the fee.

Marriage Records:
County Clerk
County where marriage was performed

Divorce Records:
Clerk of District Court
County where divorce was granted

Archives/Record Holdings:
State Library
300 Don Gaspar
Santa Fe, NM 87501

Department of Motor Vehicles:
Department of Motor Vehicles
Manuel Lujan Sr. Bldg.
St. Francis and Luisa Sts.
Santa Fe, NM 87503
(505) 827-2494

Search and Support Groups
OPERATION IDENTITY**
13101 Blackstone, NE
Albuquerque, NM 87111

State Reunion Registry: New Mexico does not have registry at the present. Refer to Chapter 8 for a list of group registries.

Age of Majority: 18 years or older

Laws Governing Opening Records: Adoption, 40-7-16. *Inspection of adoption filed, limitations; new birth record.* A. "The files, records and entries in adoption proceedings in the custody of the court, or of the department or of the agency involved in the proceeding, shall be separately kept, locked and preserved after filing, except in case of appeal. No person other than officials of the court, or the department or any agency who may be a party to the adoption proceedings, shall be permitted to inspect such files, records and entries except by order of the court."

Laws Governing Inheritance: Domestic Affairs, 40-7-15. *Effect of judgment of adoption; appeal.* A. "A judgment of adoption, whether issued by the court of this state or any other place, has the following effect as to matters within the jurisdiction of or before the court: (1) to divest the natural parents and the child of all legal rights, privileges, duties and obligations, including rights of inheritance, with respect to each other; . . ."

NEW YORK

State Information Department:
State Capitol
Albany, NY 12224
(518) 474-2121

State Agency:
Division of Services
New York State Department of Social
   Services
40 North Pearl St.
Albany, NY 12243

Court of Jurisdiction:
Judge or surrogate of the court in
   which the order was made.
Supreme Court

Birth and Death Records:
For all areas except New York City:

Bureau of Vital Records
State Department of Health
Empire State Plaza
Tower Building
Albany, NY 12237

State office has records since 1880. For records prior to 1914 in Albany, Buffalo, and Yonkers, write to the Registrar of Vital Statistics of that city.

For all Boroughs in New York City:
Bureau of Records and Statistics
Department of Health of New York City
125 Worth St.
New York, NY 10013

State office has records since 1898.

Marriage Records:
For all areas except New York City:
Bureau of Vital Records
see address listed above

State office has records from January 1880 to December 1907 and since May 1915.

County Clerk
County where license was issued

Records from January 1908 to April 1915.

City Clerk
Albany or Buffalo

Records from January 1880 to December 1907.

Registrar of Vital Statistics
Yonkers

Records for Yonkers from January 1880 to December 1907.

New York City Addresses
Municipal Archives and Records Retention Center
New York Public Library
23 Park Row
New York, NY 10038

State office has records (except for Brooklyn) from 1847 to 1865. Brooklyn records for this period are held at County Clerk's Office, Kings County, Supreme Court Bldg., Brooklyn, NY 11201.

City Clerk's Office
Borough in which marriage was performed

City office has records from 1866 to 1907.

City Clerk's Office
Borough in which bride resided or license was obtained

City office has records from 1908 to May 12, 1943.

Office of City Clerk
1780 Grand Concourse
Bronx, NY 10457

City office has records from May 13, 1943, to the present. Records for 1908–1913 are held in the Manhattan Office.

Office of City Clerk
208 Joralemon St.
Brooklyn, NY 11201

City office has records from May 13, 1943, to the present.

Office of City Clerk
Chambers and Centre Sts.
New York, NY 10007

City office has records from May 13, 1943, to the present.

Office of City Clerk
120–55 Queens Blvd.

Borough Hall Station
Jamaica, NY 11424

City office has records from May 13, 1943, to the present.

Office of City Clerk
Borough Hall, St. George
Staten Island, NY 10301

City office has records from May 13, 1943, to the present.

Divorce Records:
Bureau of Vital Records
State Department of Health
Empire State Plaza, Tower Bldg.
Albany, NY 12237

State office has records since January 1, 1963.

County Clerk
County where divorce was granted

Archives/Record Holdings:
New York State Historical Association
Fenimore House
Lake Road
Cooperstown, NY 13326

Department of Motor Vehicles:
Department of Motor Vehicles
Swan Street Bldg.
Empire State Plaza
Albany, NY 12228
(518) 474-0841

Search and Support Groups:
Adoptee Pen Pal Club
c/o Seventeen Magazine
830 3rd Ave.
New York, NY 10022

Adoptees Identity Movement
25 Estelle Dr.
Cheektowago, NY 14225

Adoptees Information Service, Inc.
19 Marion Ave.
Mount Vernon, NY 10552

Adoptees in Search of Answers
P.O. Box 1003
Southampton, NY 11968

ALMA Society, Inc.
National Headquarters
P.O. Box 154
Washington Bridge Station
New York, NY 10033

ALMA Chapter, Bronx
ALMA Chapter, Nyack

Consult telephone directory or information operator, or write National Head-quarters, listed above, for current address.

Always in Me
187 Englewood
Buffalo, NY 14214

Always in Me
P.O. Box 454
Orchard Park, NY 14127

CUB Representative, New York

Consult telephone directory or information operator, or write National Head-quarters, listed under Massachusetts, for current address.

Far Horizons
P.O. Box 621
Cortland, NY 13045

Northeast Adoption Association
1112 Parkwood Blvd.
Schenectady, NY 12308

Right to Know
P.O. Box 52
Old Westbury, NY 11568

Search Seekers
3 Townhouse Circle
Great Neck, NY 11021

Search Seekers
P.O. Box 205
Whitestone, NY 11357

Society for the Advance of the Rights of
Adoptees
P.O. Box 229
Syracuse, NY 13208

State Reunion Registry: New York does not have a registry at the present. Refer to Chapter 8 for a list of group registries.

Age of Majority: 18 years or older

Laws Governing Opening Records: Domestic Relations, Section 114. *Order of Adoption.* "No person shall be allowed access to such sealed records and order and any index thereof except upon an order of a judge or surrogate of the court in which the order was made or of a justice of the supreme court. No order for disclosure or access and inspection shall be granted except on good cause shown and on due notice to the adoptive parents and to such additional persons as the court may direct."

Laws Governing Inheritance: Adoption, Article 7. *Blood relatives—taking from.* 43. "An adoption has the effect of excluding the natural parents and all the natural kindred and blood relatives of the adopted child from inheriting from it, but under this section (prior to 1963 amendment), the rights of the child to inherit from his natural parents was preserved and the adoption did not take away his right to inherit from his natural kindred."

Policies: There are several bills being considered by the 1981–82 legislature. I will include portions of four bills relating to open records and reunion registries. Persons from this state should check for any new laws or those still pending.

State Senate Bill No. 4889. This bill would add portions to Section 114, mentioned under "Laws Governing Opening Records." Section 114-b. *Access to birth records.* "An original birth certificate, sealed pursuant to the provisions of this section, shall at any time be opened as a matter of right to the biological parent whose rights were terminated or to the adult adoptee upon application to the department of health. The applicant shall be provided a true copy of the original certificate, without official certifications and bearing a notation indicating that the original certificate has been amended."

State Assembly Bill No. 2018, Section 373-a. *Adoption information Registry.* (1) "There shall be established in the department an adoption information registry." (2). "The registry shall accept the registration, but no sooner than twenty-one years after the birth of a child, by the adoptee or by the parents of such adoptee whose consent to the adoption would have been required at the time of adoption; provided however, that any person whose registration was accepted may withdraw such registration prior to the release of any identifying information."

State Assembly Bill No. 4348, Section 3. "Not withstanding any inconsistent or contrary law, a person who has been adopted, or the guardian of such person, may petition the family court or the supreme court for an order of inspection. Such order shall direct a review, by the court alone, of any files related to the adoption of such person. The court shall, upon completing such review, disclose to such person the names and last known residences of any natural brothers or sisters of such adoptive person. Such order may issue without the consent of any person."

State Assembly Bill No. 4294. This bill also attempts to amend Section 114 of the Domestic Relations laws. It adds the following to the already written law: "Notwithstanding the foregoing an adopted child eighteen years of age or older, upon request, shall be allowed access to such sealed records without such order."

Author's Observations: This state has many laws regarding adoption. Persons adopting/relinquishing in this state should spend much time reviewing their rights.

NORTH CAROLINA

State Information Department:	State Capitol Raleigh, NC 27611 (919) 829-1110
State Agency:	Children's Services Branch Division of Social Services Department of Human Resources 325 North Salisbury St. Raleigh, NC 27611
Court of Jurisdiction:	Superior Court—address to Clerk of the Superior Court
Birth and Death Records:	Department of Human Resources Division of Health Services Vital Records Branch

P.O. Box 2091
Raleigh, NC 27602

State office has records from October 1, 1913. Some delayed records prior to that date.

Marriage Records: Department of Human Resources
                                         see address listed above

                                         Registrar of Deeds
                                         County where marriage was performed

Divorce Records: Department of Human Resources
                                         see address listed above

                                         Clerk of Superior Court
                                         County where divorce was granted

Archives/Record Holdings: State Library
                                         Division of Archives and History
                                         Department of Cultural Resources
                                         109 East Jones St.
                                         Raleigh, NC 27611

Department of Motor Vehicles: Division of Motor Vehicles
                                         North Carolina Department of
                                             Transportation
                                         Motor Vehicles Bldg.
                                         1100 New Bern Ave.
                                         Raleigh, NC 27611
                                         (919) 829-2403

Search and Support Groups: Adoptees Together**
                                         Rt. 1, P.O. Box 30-B-5
                                         Climax, NC 27233

                                         CUB Representative, Durham

Consult telephone directory or information operator, or write National Headquarters, listed under Massachusetts, for current address.

State Reunion Registry: North Carolina does not have a registry at the present but one is being considered in the 1981 legislative session. State House Bill No. 341 is interesting and if it passes should be noted by all those searching in this state. Refer to Chapter 8 for a list of group registries.

Age of Majority: 18 years and older

Laws Governing Opening Records: Adoptions, Section 48-26. *Procedure for opening record for necessary information.* (a) "Any necessary information in the files or the record of an adoption proceeding may be disclosed, to the party requiring it, upon a written motion in the cause before the clerk of original jurisdiction who may issue an order to open the record. Such order must be reviewed by a judge of the superior court and if, in the opinion of said judge, it be to the best interest of the child, or of the public to have such information disclosed, he may approve the order to open the record."

Laws Governing Inheritance: Adoptions, Section 48-23. *Legal effect of final order.* (2)

"The natural parents of the person adopted, if living, shall, from and after the entry of the final order of adoption, be relieved of all legal duties and obligations due from them to the person adopted, and shall be divested of all rights with respect to such person. This section shall not affect the duties, obligations, and rights of a putative father who has adopted his own child."

Policies: Adoptions, Section 48-25. *Record and information not to be made public; violation a misdemeanor.* (d) "Notwithstanding the provisions of G.S. 48-26 or any other provision of law, any medical record or other information concerning the physical or mental health of the adopted child which is contained in the records of the county department of social services or a licensed child-placing agency shall be revealed upon written request of the adopted child who has reached majority, or of the adoptive parents, provided that any information which serves to identify the natural parents of the adopted child, including but not limited to any information identifying physicians or other medical personnel, medical facilities or geographical locations, shall be excised from these medical records or other information."

NORTH DAKOTA

State Information Department: State Capitol
Bismarck, ND 58505
(701) 224-2000

State Agency: Children and Family Services
Russel Bldg.
Box 7
Bismarck, ND 58505

Court of Jurisdiction: District Court

Birth and Death Records: Division of Vital Records
Office of Statistical Services
State Department of Health
Bismarck, ND 58505

State office has some records from July 1, 1893. 1894–1920 records are incomplete.

Marriage Records: Division of Vital Records
see address listed above

State office has records since July 1, 1925. Inquiries will be forwarded to appropriate office.

County Judge
County where license was issued

Divorce Records: Division of Vital Records
see address listed above

State office has index of records since July 1, 1949. Inquiries will be forwarded to appropriate office.

Clerk of District Court
County where divorce was granted

Archives/Record Holdings:

State Library
Highway 83, North
Bismarck, ND 58505

Department of Motor Vehicles:

Motor Vehicles Department
State Office Bldg.
900 East Boulevard
Bismarck, ND 58501
(701) 224-2729

Search and Support Groups: Contact a National Organization for individuals working in this state.

State Reunion Registry: North Dakota does not have a registry at the present. Refer to Chapter 8 for a list of group registries.

Age of Majority: 18/21 years or older

Laws Governing Opening Records: Domestic Relations and Persons, 14-15-16. *Hearings and Records in Adoption Proceedings—Confidential Nature—Disclosure of Identifying and Nonidentifying Information. Retroactive Operation.* 4. "An adopted person who is twenty-one years of age or over may request the social service board to secure and disclose information identifying the adopted child's genetic parents or to secure and disclose nonidentifying information not on file with the board or a child placing agency. The social service board shall, within five working days of receipt of the request, notify in writing the child placing agency having access to the information requested of the request by the adopted child." 5. "Within three months after receiving notice of the request of the adopted person, the child placing agency shall make complete and reasonable efforts to notify the genetic parents of the adopted child. The child placing agency may charge a reasonable fee to the adopted child for the cost of making a search pursuant to the subsection. . . ." 6. "If the child placing agency certifies to the social service board that it has been unable to notify the genetic parent within three months, the identifying information shall not be disclosed. . . ." 7. "If, within three months, the child placing agency certifies to the social service board that it has notified the genetic parents pursuant to subsection 5, the social service board shall receive the identifying information from the child placing agency and disclose the information sixty-one days after the date of the latest notice. . . ." 8. "If the genetic parent has died and has not filed an unrevoked affidavit with the social service board stating that identifying information shall not be disclosed, the information shall be forwarded to and released by the social service board to the adopted child. . . ."

Laws Governing Inheritance: Domestic Relations and Persons, 14-15-14. *Effect of Petition and decree of adoption.* 1a. "Except with respect to a spouse of the petitioner and relatives of the spouse, to relieve the natural parents of the adopted individual of all parental rights and responsibilities, and to terminate all legal relationships between the adopted individual and his relatives, including his natural parents, so that the adopted individual thereafter is a stranger to his former relatives for all purposes including inheritance and the interpretation or construction of documents, statutes, and instruments, whether executed before or after the adoption is decreed . . ."

Policies: Domestic Relations and Persons, 14-15-01. *Definitions.* " 'Nonidentifying adoptive information' means:

a. Age of genetic parent in years at the birth of the adopted child.
b. Heritage of genetic parent.
c. Educational attainments, including the number of years of school completed by genetic parent at the time of birth of the adopted child.
d. General physical appearance of genetic parent at the time of birth of the adopted child, including the weight, height, color of hair, eyes, skin and other information of a similar nature.
e. Talents, hobbies, and special interests of genetic parents.
f. Existence of any other children born to either genetic parent before the birth of the adopted child.
g. Reasons for child being placed for adoption or for termination of parental right.
h. Religion of genetic parent.
i. Vocation of genetic parent in general terms.
j. Health history of genetic parents and blood relatives in a manner prescribed by the social service board.
k. Such further information which, in the judgment of the agency, will not be detrimental to the adoptive parent or the adopted person requesting the information, but the additional information must not identify genetic parents by name or location."

Author's Observations: These are by far the clearest and most easily understood laws of any state. A copy of these statutes would be very valuable in discovering additional laws governing siblings and affidavits. *Note:* There is a charge to conduct the search. Find out the amount and what services are rendered.

OHIO

State Information Department:
State House
Broad and High Sts.
Columbus, OH 43215
(614) 466-2000

State Agency:
Department of Public Welfare
Division of Social Services
Bureau of Children Services
30 East Broad St.
30th Floor
Columbus, OH 43215

Court of Jurisdiction:
Probate Court

Birth and Death Records:
Division of Vital Statistics
Ohio Department of Health
G-20 Ohio Departments Bldg.
65 South Front St.
Columbus, OH 43215

State office has records since December 20, 1908. For earlier records, write to Probate Court in county where birth or death occurred.

Marriage Records:
Division of Vital Statistics
see address listed above

State office has records since September 1949. All items may be verified. Inquiries will be forwarded to appropriate office.

Probate Judge
County where license was issued

Divorce Records: Division of Vital Statistics
                                        see address listed above

State Office has records since 1948. All items may be verified. Inquiries will be forwarded to appropriate office.

Clerk of Court of Common Pleas
County where divorce was granted

Archives/Record Holdings: State Library
                                        Archives and Records
                                        65 South Front St.
                                        Columbus, OH 43215

Department of Motor Vehicles: Bureau of Motor Vehicles
                                        Department of Highway Safety
                                        4300 Kimberly Pkwy.
                                        Columbus, OH 43227
                                        (614) 466-7666

Search and Support Groups: Adoptees Search Rights
                                        P.O. Box 8713
                                        Toledo, OH 43623

                                        Adoptees Search Rights Association
                                        P.O. Box 2249
                                        Cleveland, OH 44102

                                        ALMA Chapter, Ashland
                                        ALMA Chapter, Columbus

Consult telephone directory or information operator, or write National Headquarters, listed under New York, for current address.

The Chosen Children
311 Springbrook Blvd.
Dayton, OH 45405

CUB Branch, Perrysburg
CUB Branch, Wauseon
CUB Representative, Pataskala
CUB Representative, Amherst
CUB Representative, Dayton

Consult telephone directory or information operator, or write National Headquarters, listed under Massachusetts, for current address.

Reunite
P.O. Box 694
Reynoldsburg, OH 43068

State Reunion Registry: Ohio does not have a registry at the present. One was considered last year but died in committee. Those interested in this state should check for new laws. Refer to Chapter 8 for a list of group registries.

Age of Majority: 18 years and older

Laws Governing Opening Records: Section 3107.17. *Records and Proceedings to be confidential.* (C) "The petition, the interlocutory order, the final decree of adoption, the other adoption proceedings shall be recorded in a book kept for such purposes and separately indexed. This book shall be a part of the records of the probate court, and all consents, affidavits, and other papers shall be properly filed. Such papers, records, and books shall be available for inspection only upon consent of the court." (D) "All forms that pertain to the social or medical histories of the biological parents of an adopted person and that were completed pursuant to division (D) of section 3107.12 (Investigation) of the Revised Code shall be filed only in the permanent record kept by the court. During the minority of the adopted person only the adoptive parents of the person may inspect the form and only upon request. When an adopted person reaches majority, only he may inspect the form. The court, upon an adopted person's request to inspect the form, may consult with the agency that finalized the person's adoption to determine the manner in which the information on the form may be made available to the adopted person, and may make all or part of the information available to the adopted person through the agency."

Laws Governing Inheritance: Section 3107.15. *Effect of Adoption.* (A1) "Except with respect to a spouse of the petitioner and relatives of the spouse, to relieve the biological or other legal parents of the adopted person of all parental rights and responsibilities and to terminate all legal relationships between the adopted person and his relatives, including his biological or other legal parents, so that the adopted person thereafter is a stranger to his former relatives for all purposes including inheritance...."

OKLAHOMA

State Information Department:
State Capitol
2302 Lincoln Blvd.
Oklahoma City, OK 73105
(405) 521-2011

State Agency:
Division of Child Welfare
Department of Human Services
P.O. Box 25352
Oklahoma City, OK 73125

Court of Jurisdiction:
District Court

Birth and Death Records:
Vital Records Section
State Department of Health
Northeast 10th St. and Stonewall
P.O. Box 53551
Oklahoma City, OK 73105

State office has records since October 1908.

Marriage Records:	Clerk of Court County where license was issued
Divorce Records:	Court Clerk County where divorce was granted
Archives/Record Holdings:	Oklahoma Historical Society Historical Bldg. 2100 North Lincoln Blvd. Oklahoma City, OK 73105
Department of Motor Vehicles:	Tax Commission Motor Vehicle Division Jim Thorpe Office Bldg. Oklahoma City, OK 73105 (405) 521-3229
Search and Support Groups:	Adoptees as Adults 1515 Camden Way Norman, OK 73069

Adoptees as Adults
8220 Northwest 114th
Oklahoma City, OK 73132

ALMA Chapter, Broken Arrow

Consult telephone directory or information operator, or write National Headquarters, listed under New York, for current address.

Tulsa Adoptees
4952 East 4th Pl.
Tulsa, OK 74112

Willows Graduates
RR 8, Box 324
Claremore, OK 74017

State Reunion Registry: Oklahoma does not have a registry at the present. Refer to Chapter 8 for a list of group registries. Note "Policies" below.

Age of Majority: 18 years or older

Laws Governing Opening Records: Children, Section 60.17. *Confidential character of hearings and records.* (2) "All papers and records pertaining to the adoption shall be kept as a permanent record of the court and withheld from inspection. No person shall have access to such records except on order of the judge of the court in which the decree of adoption was entered, for good cause shown."

Laws Governing Inheritance: Children, Section 60.16. *Effect of Final Decree.* (2) "After a final decree of adoption is entered, the natural parents of the adopted child, unless they are the adoptive parents or the spouse of an adoptive parent, shall be relieved of all parental responsibilities for such child and have no rights over such adopted child or to his property by descent and distribution."

Policies: Oklahoma does not maintain a formal registry but those interested in a reunion should submit a notarized letter to the Department of Human Services.

When letters are received from both parties desiring a reunion, the information will be released. All letters are left in the files for future reference.

Author's Observations: Children, Section 60.18. *Certificates.* (2) "The state registrar, upon receipt of a certified copy of an order of decree of adoption, shall prepare a supplementary certificate in the new name of the adopted person, the city and county of residence of adoptive parents, hospital of choice of adoptive parents, and the family physician of the adoptive parents if they are residents of the State of Oklahoma, provided, however, any change of name of the physician or the hospital shall first require that the written consent of such hospital and such physician is obtained. The state registrar shall then seal and file the original certificate of birth with said certified copy attached thereto. Such sealed documents may be opened by the state registrar only upon demand of the adopted person, if of legal age, or adoptive parents, by an order of the court."

My understanding of this section of the law is that adopted persons must demand from the court or receive an order of the court to learn the true identity of his/her hospital and physician at birth. How can this law be in the best interest of the child? Adoptees from this state should be aware of the altered information on their birth certificates.

OREGON

State Information Department:
State Capitol
Salem, OR 97310
(503) 378-3131

State Agency:
Adoption Services
Department of Human Resources
Children's Services Division
198 Commercial St., SE
Salem, OR 97310

Court of Jurisdiction:
Circuit Court

Birth and Death Records:
Vital Statistics Section
Oregon State Health Division
P.O. Box 116
Portland, OR 97207

State office has records since July 1903. Earlier records for the city of Portland.

Marriage Records:
Vital Statistics Section
see address listed above

State office has records since January 1907. Fee includes search.

County Clerk
County where license was issued

Divorce Records:
Vital Statistics Section
see address listed above

State office has records since May 1925. Fee includes search.

County Clerk
County where divorce was granted

Archives/Record Holdings: State Library
Summer and Court Sts.
Salem, OR 97310

Department of Motor Vehicles: Motor Vehicles Division
Department of Transportation
1905 Lana Ave., NE
Salem, OR 97314
(503) 378-6997

Search and Support Groups: Birthparents in Oregon
P.O. Box 17521
Portland, OR 97217

Oregon Adoptive Rights Association **
P.O. Box 1332
Beaverton, OR 97075

Oregon Adoptees Rights
P.O. Box 9033
Brooks, OR 97305

State Reunion Registry: Oregon does not have a registry at the present. Refer to Chapter 8 for a list of group registries.

Age of Majority: 18 years or older

Laws Governing Opening Records: Section 7.211. *Records in adoption, filiation, probate, domestic relations and juvenile proceedings. Separate records in adoption cases; accessibility of records limited.* "The clerk or court administrator of any court having jurisdiction over adoption cases shall keep a separate journal, index and fee register in all cases of adoption filed in such court. The journal, index and fee register shall not be subject to the inspection of any person, except upon order of the court. . . . Nothing contained in this section shall prevent the clerk or court administrator from certifying copies of a decree of adoption to the petitioners in such proceeding or their attorney."

Laws Governing Inheritance: Section 109.041. *Relationship between adopted child and his natural and adopted parents.* (1) "The effect of a decree of adoption heretofore or hereafter granted by a court of this state shall be that the relationship, rights and obligations between an adopted person and his descendants and (a) His adoptive parents, their descendants and kindred, and (b) His natural parents, their descendants and kindred shall be the same to all legal intents and purposes after the entry of such decree as if the adopted person had been born in lawful wedlock to his adoptive parents and had not been born to his natural parents."

PENNSYLVANIA

State Information Department: Main Capitol Bldg.
Harrisburg, PA 17120
(717) 787-2121

State Agency: Department of Public Welfare
                                           Office of Children and Youth and
                                             Families
                                           P.O. Box 2675
                                           Harrisburg, PA 17120

Court of Jurisdiction: Court of Common Pleas

Birth and Death Records: Division of Vital Statistics
                                           State Department of Health
                                           Central Building
                                           101 South Mercer St.
                                           P.O. Box 1528
                                           Newcastle, PA 16103

State office has records since January 1, 1906. Records prior to that date may be obtained from Register of Wills, Orphans Court, county seat where birth or death occurred. For Pittsburgh records from 1870 to 1905 or Allegheny records from 1882 to 1905, write to Office of Biostatistics, Pittsburgh Health Department, City–County Bldg., Pittsburgh, PA 15219. Philadelphia records from 1860 to 1915 may be obtained from Vital Statistics, Philadelphia Department of Public Health, City Hall Annex, Philadelphia, PA 19107.

Marriage Records: Division of Vital Statistics
                                           see address listed above

State office has records since January 1941. Inquiries will be forwarded to appropriate office.

                                           Marriage License Clerk
                                           County Court House
                                           County seat where license was issued

Divorce Records: Division of Vital Statistics
                                           see address listed above

State office has records since January 1946. Inquiries will be forwarded to appropriate office.

                                           Prothonotary
                                           Courthouse
                                           County seat where divorce was granted

Archives/Record Holdings: State Library
                                           Walnut St. and Commonwealth Ave.
                                           Harrisburg, PA 17120

Department of Motor Vehicles: Bureau of Motor Vehicles
                                           Department of Transportation
                                           Transportation and Safety Building
                                           Commonwealth and Forster Sts.
                                           Harrisburg, PA 17122
                                           (717) 787-8797

Search and Support Groups: Adoption Forum of Philadelphia **
                                           P.O. Box 7482
                                           Philadelphia, PA 19101

Adoption Lifeline of Altoona
414 28th Ave.
Altoona, PA 16601

CUB Representative, Altoona
CUB Representative, Pittsburgh

Consult telephone directory or information operator, or write National Headquarters, listed under Massachusetts, for current address.

Pittsburgh Adoption Lifeline
P.O. Box 613
Rostraver Branch
Belle Vernon, PA 19119

Pittsburgh Adoption Lifeline
P.O. Box 52
Gibsonia, PA 15044

State Reunion Registry: Pennsylvania does not have a registry at the present. Refer
to Chapter 8 for a list of group registries.

Age of Majority: 18 years or older

Laws Governing Opening Records: Title 23, Domestic Relations, Part III, Adoption, Section 505. *Impounding of Proceedings.* "All petitions, exhibits, reports,
notes of testimony, decrees, and other papers pertaining to any proceeding under this act or under the act of April 4, 1925, entitled 'An Act Relating to Adoption,' shall be kept in the files of the court as a permanent record thereof
and withheld from inspection except on an order of court granted upon cause
shown."

Laws Governing Inheritance: Title 23, Domestic Relations, Part III, Adoption, Section 321. *Effect of decree of termination.* "A decree terminating all rights of a parent
or a decree terminating all rights and duties of a parent entered by a court of
competent jurisdiction shall extinguish the power or the right of such parent to
receive notice of adoption proceedings."

Policies: Adoption Services Regulations, Social Services Manual dated November 8,
1978. *Records.* 21-1-50. "All the service provider's records concerning adoption
shall be treated as confidential. After 4 years, or when the child reaches his 18th
birthday, whichever is longer, records may be preserved either by microfilming or
by selective retention of information, instead of retaining the entire record. At the
option of the agency, all records may be destroyed 50 years from the date of
placement."

RHODE ISLAND

State Information Department: State House
                                        82 Smith St.
                                        Providence, RI 02903
                                        (401) 277-2000

State Agency: Department for Children and Their
                                        Families
                                        610 Mt. Pleasant Ave.
                                        Providence, RI 02908

Court of Jurisdiction:	Adoptees over 18—Probate Court Adoptees under 18—Family Court
Birth and Death Records:	Division of Vital Statistics State Department of Health Cannon Building 75 Davis Street Providence, RI 02908

State office has records since 1853. For prior records write Town Clerk, town where birth or death occurred.

Marriage Records:	Division of Vital Statistics *see address listed above*

State office has records since January 1853.

Town Clerk or City Clerk
Town or city where marriage was performed.

Divorce Records:	Division of Vital Statistics *see address listed above*

State office has records since January 1962. Inquiries will be forwarded to appropriate office.

Clerk of Family Court
County where divorce was granted

Archives/Record Holdings:	State Library Archives Division State House 82 Smith Street Providence, RI 02903
Department of Motor Vehicles:	Division of Motor Vehicles Department of Transportation State Office Bldg. 101 Smith St. Providence, RI 02903 (401) 277-3007
Search and Support Groups	CUB Branch, Cambridge

Consult telephone directory or information operator, or write National Headquarters, listed under Massachusetts, for current address.

Parents and Adoptees Liberty Movement
861 Mitchell's Lane
Middletown, RI 02840

Search Ltd.
RFD 1, Box 337
Ashaway, RI 02804

Yesterday's Children
77 Homer St.
Providence, RI 02903

State Reunion Registry: Rhode Island does not have a registry at the present. Refer to Chapter 8 for a list of group registries.

Age of Majority: 18 years or older

Laws Governing Opening Records: Courts and Civil Procedure—Courts. 8-10-21. *Records of Court.* "The records of the family court shall be public records, except that records of hearings in matters set forth in § 14-1-5 (B. Concerning adoption of Children), together with stenographic notes and transcripts of said hearings, shall not be available for public inspection unless the court shall otherwise order."

Laws Governing Inheritance: Adoption of Children. 15-7-17. *Rights of natural parents terminated—Inheritance by child from natural parents.* "The parents of such child shall be deprived, by the decree, of all legal rights respecting the child, and the child shall be freed from all obligations of maintenance and obedience respecting his natural parents except that the granting of the petition for adoption will not deprive an adopted child of the right to inherit from and through his natural parents in the same manner as all other natural children; provided, however, that the right to inherit from and through natural parents of an adopted child born out of wedlock shall be as provided in § 33-1-8; and provided, further, however, that the decree of adoption shall in no way affect all legal rights of a natural parent respecting the child and all obligations of the child of maintenance and obedience respecting a natural parent if such natural parent is legally married to the adopting parent at the time of the decree of adoption."

SOUTH CAROLINA

State Information Department: State House
Columbia, SC 29211
(803) 758-0221

State Agency: The Children's Bureau of South
Carolina
800 Dutch Square Blvd.
Bldg. D
Columbia, SC 29211

Court of Jurisdiction: Family Court

Birth and Death Records: Division of Vital Records
Bureau of Health Measurement
S.C. Department of Health and
Analysis Environmental Control
2600 Bull St.
Columbia, SC 29201

State office has records since January 1, 1915. Earlier records may be obtained from County Health Department in Charleston, Florence City, and Newberry City.

Marriage Records: Division of Vital Records
see address listed above

State office has records since July 1, 1950.

Probate Judge
County where license was issued

Divorce Records:	Division of Vital Records *see address listed above*

State office has records since January 1962.

Clerk of county
County where divorce was granted

Archives/Record Holdings:	State Library Department of Archives and History 1500 Senate St. Columbia, SC 29201
Department of Motor Vehicles:	Motor Vehicle Division Highway Department 1100 Senate St. P.O. Box 1498 Columbia, SC 29202 (803) 758-3158
Search and Support Groups:	Adoptees and Birthparents in Search ** P.O. Box 1000 West Columbia, SC 29171
	Adoptees Searching P.O. Box 1774 Anderson, SC 29622
	CUB Representative, Edgefield

Consult telephone directory or information operator, or write National Headquarters, listed under Massachusetts, for current address.

Triad **
P.O. Box 4778
Columbia, SC 29240

State Reunion Registry: South Carolina does not have a registry at the present, but has considered one for two years. See "Policies" below. Refer to Chapter 8 for a list of group registries.

Age of Majority: 18 years or older

Laws Governing Opening Records: Adoption, Section 15-45-140. *Hearings and records shall be confidential; access to records.* (c) "All files and records pertaining to the adoption proceedings in the Children's Bureau in the State of South Carolina, or in the Department of Social Services of the State of South Carolina, or in any authorized agency, shall be confidential and withheld from inspection except upon order of court for good cause shown." (d) "The provisions of this section shall not be construed to prevent any adoption agency from furnishing to adoptive parents, biological parents or adoptees nonidentifying information when in the sole discretion of the chief executive officer of the agency such information would serve the best interests of the persons concerned either during the period of placement or at a subsequent time nor shall the provisions of this chapter be construed to prevent giving nonidentifying information to any other person, party or agency who in the discretion of the chief executive officer of the agency has established a sufficient reason justifying the release of that nonidentifying information. As used in this subsection 'nonidentifying information' may include but is not limited to the following: 1. the health of the biological parents; 2. the health of the child; 3. the child's general family background without name references; 4. the length of time the child has been in the care and custody of the adoptive parents. The release of other nonidentifying information shall be made at the discretion of the chief executive officer of the adoption agency."

Laws Governing Inheritance: Adoption, Section 15-45-130. *Effect of final decree.* (a) "After the final decree of adoption is entered, the relation of parent and child and all the rights, duties and other legal consequences of the natural relation of child and parent shall thereafter exist between such adopted child and the person adopting such child and the kindred of the adoptive parents. From the date the final decree of adoption is entered, the adopted child shall be considered a natural child of the adopting parents for all inheritance purposes, both by and from such child, to the exclusion of the natural or blood parents or kin of such child."

Policies: In an article appearing in the Columbia Records, September 1980, the following statements were made regarding a reunion registry bill:
"Chances are good that thousands of South Carolinians who were adopted as infants will be able next year to get state agencies to help them find their natural parents.
"Senator Thomas Smith, D-Florence, narrowly missed getting his adoption records bill passed in the last General Assembly. This time, he thinks things will be different.
" 'I think it's the kind of issue that the longer you talk about it, the more sense it makes,' Smith said."

SOUTH DAKOTA

State Information Department: Capitol Bldg.
Pierre, SD 57501
(605) 224-3011

State Agency: Department of Social Services
Richard F. Kneip Bldg.
Pierre, SD 57501

Court of Jurisdiction: Circuit Court

Birth and Death Records: State Department of Health
Health Statistics Program
Joe Foss Office Building
Pierre, SD 57501

State office has records since July 1, 1905. Access to some earlier records.

Marriage Records: State Department of Health
see address listed above

State office has records since July 1, 1905.

County Treasurer
County where license was issued

Divorce Records: State Department of Health
                                         see address listed above

State office has records since July 1, 1905.

                                         Clerk of Court
                                         County where divorce was granted

Archives/Record Holdings: State Library
                                         Historical Resource Center
                                         Soldiers and Sailors Memorial Bldg.
                                         East Capitol Ave.
                                         Pierre, SD 57501

Motor Vehicles Department: Office of Vehicle Licensing
                                         Vehicle Licensing and Regulation
                                         Department of Public Safety
                                         Public Safety Bldg.
                                         118 West Capitol Ave.
                                         Pierre, SD 57501
                                         (605) 224-3541

Search and Support Groups: ALMA Chapter, Sioux Falls.

State Reunion Registry: South Dakota does not have a registry at the present. Refer to Chapter 8 for a list of group registries.

Age of Majority: 18 years or older

Laws Governing Opening Records: Domestic Relations, 25-6-15. *Restrictions on access to court records in adoption proceedings—Court order required for disclosure of information.* "The files and records of the court in adoption proceedings shall not be open to inspection or copy by other persons than the parents by adoption and their attorneys, representatives of the office of community services, and the child when he reaches maturity, except upon order of the court expressly permitting inspection or copy. No person having charge of any birth or adoption records shall disclose the names of any parents, or parents by adoption, or any other matter, appearing in such records, or furnish certified copies of any such records, except upon order of the circuit court for the county in which the adoption took place or other court of competent jurisdiction."

Laws Governing Inheritance: Adoption of Children, 25-6-17. *Rights and duties of natural parents terminated on adoption—Exception on adoption of stepchild.* "The natural parents of an adopted child are from the time of the adoption, relieved of all parental duties towards, and of all responsibility for the child so adopted, and have no right over it, except in cases where a natural parent consents to the adoption of his or her child by the child's stepfather or stepmother who is the present spouse of the natural parents."

Author's Observations: Two cases are cited in the Domestic Relations section of the South Dakota laws. They are as follows: (1) *Inheritance—Adopted Child from Adoptive Parent's Relatives.* "Although statute provides that after adoption, parties shall sustain towards each other legal relation of parent and child, mutual rights and duties created by adoption are limited to child and parents, so that adopted child has no right of inheritance from heirs, either lineal or collateral, of adoptive parents. In re Eddins' Estate (1938) 66 SD 109, 279 NW 244, distinguished in 136 NEB 227, 285 NW 538." (2) *Adopted Child from Natural Parents.* "A child born out of wedlock and subsequently adopted, did not, by virtue of her adoption, lose her right to inherit from her natural mother. Harrell v. McDonald (1976)—SD-242, NW, 2d 148."

Could this mean that in certain instances adoptees do not inherit from their adoptive relatives? Is there still a right of inheritance, in some cases, from the natural parents to the child?

TENNESSEE

State Information Department:

State Capitol
Nashville, TN 37219
(615) 741-3011

State Agency:

Department of Human Services
111–19 7th Ave., North
Nashville, TN 37203

Court of Jurisdiction:

Adoptions prior to 1950—Probate or
County Court. After 1950—Chancery
or Circuit Courts

Birth and Death Records:

Division of Vital Statistics
State Department of Public Health
Cordell Hull Bldg.
Nashville, TN 37219

State office has birth and death records from January 1, 1914. For earlier records write to the county where birth or death occurred.

Marriage Records:

Division of Vital Statistics
see address listed above

State office has records since July 1945.

County Court Clerk
County where license was issued

Divorce Records:

Division of Vital Statistics
see address listed above

State office has records since July 1945.

Clerk of Court
Court where divorce was granted

Archives/Record Holdings:

State Library and Archives
403 7th Ave., North
Nashville, TN 37219

Department of Motor Vehicles

Motor Vehicle Division
Department of Revenue
Andrew Jackson State Office Bldg.
500 Deaderick St.
Nashville, TN 37242
(615) 741-3381

Search and Support Groups: ALMA Chapter, Chattanooga **

Consult telephone directory or information operator, or write National Headquarters, listed under New York, for current address.

Tennessee's The Right to Know
P.O. Box 34334
Memphis, TN 38143

State Reunion Registry: Tennessee has a reunion registry in that it keeps all records of contacts, and if there is a match it advises the adoptee that he or she can initiate legal action to open the records. See "Policies" below.

Age of Majority: 18 years or older

Laws Governing Opening Records: Adoption, 36-130. *Records kept under seal—Disclosure of information—Safe keeping.* "After the final order of adoption or the final order dismissing the proceedings, all records and other papers relating to the proceedings in the office of the clerk, in the office of the department of public health, in the office of a child-placing agency and in the state and county offices of the department of human services, shall be placed and remain under seal and shall be opened only by order of the court as provided under 36-132, or as otherwise provided in this chapter."

Adoption, 36-132. *Disclosure of information upon order of judge.* "Any necessary information in the files or the record of an adoption proceeding may be disclosed, to the party requiring it, upon a written motion in the cause before the court of original jurisdiction, the judge of which may issue an order to open the record, if, in the opinion of said judge, it be to the best interest of the child or of the public to have such information disclosed."

Laws Governing Inheritance: Adoption, 36-126. *Effect of adoption on relationship.* "An adopted child shall not inherit real or personal property from a natural parent or relative thereof when the relationship between them has been terminated by adoption, nor shall such natural parent or relative thereof inherit from the adopted child."

Policies: A portion of a letter from the Department of Human Services, dated July 14, 1980: "Tennessee does maintain what we term a post adoption file to record all contacts held after finalization of the adoption. If this file contains matching requests from all interested parties (adult adoptee, adoptive parents, birth parents) the department initiates legal action to facilitate a reunion. Other reunion efforts are governed by TCA 36-140 (this law concerns reuniting siblings)."

State House Bill No. 544 was introduced, but failed, in the 1979–80 legislature. It is quoted here to indicate some interest in a State Reunion Registry: (c) "Sealed adoption records specified in Section 36-130, which could reveal or lead to the discovery of the identity of the adopted person or the natural relatives of the adopted person may be disclosed only as follows: (1) An adopted person twenty-one years of age or older may file with the department . . . stating his interest in being reunited with his preadopted siblings. . . . The Department shall maintain a file of any such request. . . . (2) An adopted person twenty-one years of age or older with the written consent of the adoptive parents, if living, may request the commissioner of the Department of Human Services to disclose to him the names and addresses of the adopted person's natural parents. . . . The reasons given by the adopted person for seeking disclosure shall be revealed to the natural parent. . . . (A) If a natural parent has died, or consents to the release of his name and address . . . shall release his name and address to the adopted person . . . (D) . . . all costs shall be assessed against the petitioner."

I did not present the bill in its entirety; anyone wishing to study it should request this most interesting bill. In order to use the above mentioned, even at the age of twenty-one, you would need your parents' written consent.

TEXAS

State Information Department:	State Capitol Austin, TX 78711 (512) 475-2323
State Agency:	Department of Human Resources 706 Bannister Ln. P.O. Box 2960 Austin, TX 78769
Court of Jurisdiction:	District Court
Birth and Death Records:	Bureau of Vital Statistics Texas Department of Health 1100 West 49th St. Austin, TX 78756

State office has records since 1903.

Marriage Records: Bureau of Vital Statistics
                                          see address listed above

State office has records since 1966.

                                          County Clerk
                                          County where license was issued

Divorce Records: Bureau of Vital Statistics
                                          see address listed above

State office has records since January 1968.

                                          Clerk of District Court
                                          County where divorce was granted

Archives/Record Holdings: State Library
                                          Archives and Library Building
                                          Archives Division
                                          1201 Brazos
                                          Austin, TX 78711

Department of Motor Vehicles: Motor Vehicle Division
                                          Department of Highways and Public
                                              Transportation
                                          40th St. and Jackson Ave.
                                          Austin, TX 78779
                                          (512) 475-7570

Search and Support Groups:

Adoptee Referral Service
P.O. Box 35609
Dallas, TX 75235

Adoptees Journey
6701 Covington Ln.
Dallas, TX 75214

Adoption Awareness Center
615 Elm Street at McCullough
San Antonio, TX 78202

ALMA Chapter, Houston

Consult telephone directory or information operator, or write National Headquarters, listed under New York, for current address.

CUB Representative, Plano
CUB Branch, Houston

Consult telephone directory or information operator, or write National Headquarters, listed under Massachusetts, for current address.

Family Tree
101 Wildwood Dr.
Texarkana, TX 75501

Hidden Heritage
8201 Richmond Ave., #34
Houston, TX 77063

Right to Know
P.O. Box 1409
Grand Prairie, TX 75050

Searchers Unlimited
P.O. Box 3613
San Angelo, TX 76901

Search Finders of Texas
150 Terrell Plaza, #49
San Antonio, TX 78208

Searchline of Texas
725 Burnwood
Irving, TX 75062

State Reunion Registry: Texas does not have a registry at the present. Refer to Chapter 8 for a list of group registries.

Age of Majority: 18 years or older

Laws Governing Opening Records: The Family Code, Title 2, Chapter 11, Section 11.17. *Central Record File.* (b) "When the department receives the complete file (pleadings, papers, studies and records) or petition and decree of adoption, it shall close the records concerning that child; and except for statistical purposes, it shall not disclose any information concerning the prior proceedings affecting the child." (d) "The records concerning a child maintained by the district clerk after entry of a decree of adoption, and all the records required to be maintained by the department are confidential, and no person is entitled access to or information from these records except as provided by this subtitle or on an order of the court which issued the decree of a district court of Travis County for good cause."

Laws Governing Inheritance: The Family Code, Title 2, Chapter 15, Section 15.07. *Effect of Decree.* "A decree terminating the parent-child relationship divests the parent and the child of all legal rights, privileges, duties, and powers, with respect to each other, except the child retains the right to inherit from and through its divested parent unless the court otherwise provides. Nothing in this chapter shall preclude or affect the rights of a natural maternal or paternal grandparent to reasonable access under Section 14.03(d) of this code."

Policies: Public Offices, Etc., Article 6252-17a. *Access by public to information in custody of governmental agencies and bodies. Declaration of policy.* Section 1. "Pursuant to the fundamental philosophy of the American constitutional form of representative government which holds to the principle that government is the servant of the people, and not the master of them, it is hereby declared to be the public policy of the State of Texas that all persons are, unless otherwise expressly provided by law, at all times entitled to full and complete information regarding the affairs of government and the official acts of those who represent them as public officials and employees. The people, in delegating authority, do not give their public servants the right to decide what is good for the people to know and what is not good for them to know. . . ."

UTAH

State Information Department: State Capitol
Salt Lake City, UT 84114
(801) 533-4000

State Agency: Division of Family Services
Department of Social Services
150 West North Temple
Salt Lake City, UT 84103

Court of Jurisdiction: District Court

Birth and Death Records: Bureau of Vital Statistics
150 West North Temple
P.O. Box 2500
Salt Lake City, UT 84103

State office has records since 1905. Requests for Ogden and Salt Lake City records from 1890 to 1904 should be addressed to City Board of Health in desired city. Records prior to 1905 in other cities should be addressed to County Clerk, county where birth or death occurred.

Marriage Records: County Clerk
County where license was issued

Divorce Records: County Clerk
County where decree was granted

Archives/Record Holdings:	Utah State Historical Society Library
	603 East South Temple
	Salt Lake City, UT 84102
Department of Motor Vehicles:	Motor Vehicle Division
	State Tax Commission
	State Fairgrounds
	1095 Motor Ave.
	Salt Lake City, UT 84116
	(801) 533-6588
Search and Support Groups:	ALMA Chapter, Salt Lake City

Consult telephone directory or information operator, or write National Headquarters, listed under New York, for current address.

State Reunion Registry: Utah does not have a registry at the present. Refer to Chapter 8 for a list of group registries.

Age of Majority: 18 years or older

Laws Governing Opening Records: Judicial Code, 78-30-15. *Petition and Report to be sealed and filed.* "The court shall order that the petition, the written report provided for in section 78-30-14, above, or any other documents filed in connection with the hearing, shall be sealed and shall not be open to inspection or copy except upon order of the court expressly permitting such inspection or copy after good cause therefor has been shown."

Laws Governing Inheritance: Judicial Code, 78-30-11. *Rights and liabilities of natural parents.* "The natural parents of an adopted child are, from the time of the adoption, relieved of all parental duties toward and all responsibility for the child so adopted, and shall have no further rights over it."

Judicial Code, 78-30-11. *Decisions under former law. Inheritance by adopted child.* "This section neither by express terms nor by necessary implication prevented an adopted child from inheriting from or through its natural parents; nor did the mere fact that the adopting parent was a blood relative prevent him from inheriting both from the adoptive parent and also from his natural parent by right of representation. In other words, the child could inherit in a dual capacity. In re Benner's Estate, 109 U. 172, 166 P. 2d 257."

Policies: State House Bill No. 193, *Release of Adoption Information,* was introduced in the 1979–80 and 1980–81 General Session. This bill is very interesting and should be requested by those searching in this state. Request a copy of this bill or an updated bill to review it in its entirety. The following is a brief excerpt:

78-30-16. "An adopted person who is 18 years of age or over may request the division of health of the department of social services to disclose the information shown on the adoptive person's original birth certificate. . . ." 78-30-17. (1) "Within six months after receiving notice of the request, the division of family services or the appropriate licensed child placing agency shall make complete and reasonable efforts to notify each parent identified on the original birth certificate of the request, and may have access to all pertinent records, including court records of the adoption and records of any agency involved in the adoption in an effort to determine the most current address of each parent. . . ." 78-30-19. Information requested by the adopted person if: (1) "An affidavit consenting to the disclosure is filed by both parents, or the survivor, within 120 days after being notified as provided in section 78-30-18." (2) "If both parents are deceased and the division of health has been so notified by the division of family services or the child placing agency who made the search for the parents pursuant to section 78-30-17."

VERMONT

State Information Department:

State House
State St.
Montpelier, VT 05602
(802) 828-1110

State Agency:

Agency of Human Services
Department of Social and
    Rehabilitation Services
103 South Main St.
Waterbury, VT 05676

Court of Jurisdiction:

District Probate Court

Birth and Death Records:

Public Health Statistics Division
Department of Health
115 Colchester Ave.
Burlington, VT 05401

Town or City Clerk
Town or city where birth or death
    occurred

Marriage Records:

Public Health Statistics Division
see address listed above

State office has records since 1857.

Town Clerk
Town where license was issued

Divorce Records:

Public Health Statistics Division
see address listed above

State office has records since 1860.

Clerk of County Court
County where divorce was granted

Archives/Record Holdings:

Vermont Historical Society Library
Pavilion Office Bldg.
109 State St.
Montpelier, VT 05602

Department of Motor Vehicles:

Department of Motor Vehicles
State Office Bldg.
120 State St.
Montpelier, VT 05602
(802) 828-2121

Search and Support Groups: ALMA Chapter, Chelsea

Consult telephone directory or information operator, or write National Headquarters, listed under New York, for current address.

CUB Branch, Cambridge

Consult telephone directory or information operator, or write National Headquarters, listed under Massachusetts, for current address.

State Reunion Registry: Vermont does not have a registry at the present, but a bill (No. 423) is currently pending in committee. Refer to Chapter 8 for a list of group registries.

Age of Majority: 18 years or older

Laws Governing Opening Records: Domestic Relations, Chapter 9, Section 451. *Placing under seal, fee, forwarding, penalty.* "The town clerk filing a new birth certificate issued by a probate court as foresaid, and each town clerk or other officer to whom is transmitted a certified copy of such new certificate or a return based thereon, shall place under seal the original certificate, copy or return filed in his office, if any, and all papers relating to the new certificate, copy or return, superscribe a suitable notation to identify the packet and forward the packet to the secretary of state who shall file and hold it in his office in a separate and locked file cabinet access to which shall be open only to the secretary of state and employees designated by him. . . . Such seal shall not be broken and such records and papers shall not be exhibited except by order of a county court, or probate court."

Laws Governing Inheritance: Domestic Relations, Chapter 9, Section 448. *Rights, duties, obligations.* "The natural parents of a minor shall be deprived, by the adoption, of all legal right to control of such minor, and such minor shall be freed from all obligations of obedience and maintenance to them. A person adopted shall have the same right of inheritance from and through his natural parents as though the adoption had not occurred, but the natural parents, predecessors in line of descent, and collateral kin of a person adopted shall be deprived of all right on inheritance from or through such person."

Policies: Domestic Relations, Chapter 9, Section 451. *Placing under seal, fee, forwarding, penalty. Annotations.* "In order to maintain the secrecy of the contents of a packet of adoption papers, the original name of the person adopted should, under no circumstances, appear on the outside of the packet. . . ."

VIRGINIA

State Information Department: State Capitol
Capitol Square
Richmond, VA 23219
(804) 786-0000

State Agency: Division of Social Services
Department of Welfare
8007 Discovery Dr.
Richmond, VA 23288

Court of Jurisdiction: Circuit Court

Birth and Death Records: Bureau of Vital Records and Health
                                                  Statistics
                                                State Department of Health
                                                James Madison Bldg.
                                                P.O. Box 1000
                                                Richmond, VA 23208

State office has records from January 1853 through December 1896 and since
June 4, 1912, to the present. For records between those dates write Health
Department, town or city where birth or death occurred.

Marriage Records: Bureau of Vital Records and Health
                                                  Statistics
                                                see address listed above

State office has records since 1853.

                                                Court Clerk
                                                County where license was issued

Divorce Records: Bureau of Vital Records and Health
                                                  Statistics
                                                see address listed above

State Office has records since January 1918.

                                                Clerk of Court
                                                County where divorce was granted

Archives/Record Holdings: State Library
                                                Archives Division
                                                State Library Bldg.
                                                12th and Capitol Sts.
                                                Richmond, VA 23219

Department of Motor Vehicles: Division of Motor Vehicles
                                                2220 West Broad St.
                                                P.O. Box 27412 (23269)
                                                Richmond, VA 23220
                                                (804) 786-3300

Search and Support Groups: Adoptees and Natural Parents
                                                  Organization **
                                                15 Caribbean Ave.
                                                Virginia Beach, VA 23451

                                                CUB Representative, Richmond

Consult telephone directory or information operator, or write National Headquarters, listed under Massachusetts, for current address.

                                                Parents and Adoptees Together **
                                                1500 Fort Hill Dr.
                                                Richmond, VA 23226

State Reunion Registry: Virginia does not have a registry at the present. Refer to
Chapter 8 for a list of group registries.

Age of Majority: 18 years or older

Laws Governing Opening Records: Chapter 11, Adoptions, Section 63.1–236. *Disposition of reports.* "No information with respect to the identity of the biological family of the adopted child shall be disclosed, opened to inspection or made available to be copied except (i) upon application of the adopted child, which child is eighteen or more years of age, (ii) upon the order of a circuit court entered upon good cause shown, and (iii) after notice to and opportunity for hearing by the applicant for such order, and the person or agency which made the investigation required by Section 63.1–223 or Section 63.1–228.

"If the identity and whereabouts of the adoptive parents and the biological parents are known to the person or agency, the court may require the person or agency to advise the adoptive parents and the biological parents of the pendency of the application for such order."

Laws Governing Inheritance: Chapter 11, Adoptions, Section 63.1–234. *Descent and distribution.* "For the purpose of descent and distribution, a legally adopted child shall inherit, according to the statutes of descent and distribution, from and through the parents by adoption from the time of entry of an interlocutory order or the final order if there is no interlocutory order and shall not inherit from the natural parents, except that a child adopted by a stepparent shall inherit from the natural parent or parents as well as from his parents by adoption."

WASHINGTON

State Information Agency:

State Capitol
Olympia, WA 98504
(206) 753-5000

State Agency:

Department of Social and Health
   Services
Bureau of Children's Services
Office Bldg. #2
Olympia, WA 98504

Court of Jurisdiction:

Superior Court

Birth and Death Records:

Vital Records LB-11
P.O. Box 9709
Olympia, WA 98504

State office has records since July 1, 1907. Copies of records from Seattle, Spokane, and Tacoma may also be obtained from City Health Department in respective city. Earlier records for the state should be addressed to the Auditor in the county where birth or death occurred.

Marriage Records:

Vital Records LB-11
see address listed above

State office has records since January 1, 1968.

County Auditor
County where license was issued

Divorce Records: Vital Records LB-11
                                              see address listed above

State office has records since January 1, 1968.

                                              County Clerk
                                              County where divorce was granted

Archives/Record Holdings: State Library
                                              Archives Division
                                              State Library Bldg.
                                              Olympia, WA 98504

Department of Motor Vehicles: Department of Motor Vehicles
                                              Highways–Licenses Bldg.
                                              Olympia, WA 98504
                                              (206) 753-6915

Search and Support Groups: Birthparent Resource Center
                                              P.O. Box 5693
                                              Seattle, WA 98105

                                              Washington Adoptees Rights
                                                Movement**
                                              Good Neighbor Center
                                              Hillaire School #12
                                              15749 Northeast 4th St.
                                              Bellevue, WA 98008

State Reunion Registry: Washington does not have a state registry at the present time but State House Bill No. 84 is being considered. Note "Policies" below. This state has an unusual policy and works closely with Washington Adoptees Rights Movement (WARM). Those searching in Washington should refer to Chapter 7 for more information regarding the workings of this search and support group. Refer to Chapter 8 for a list of group registries.

Age of Majority: 18 years or older

Laws Governing Opening Records: 22.32.150. *Records to be sealed.* "Unless otherwise requested by the adopted, all records of any proceeding hereunder shall be sealed and shall not be thereafter open to inspection by any person except upon order of the court for good cause shown, and thereafter shall be again sealed as before."

Laws Governing Inheritance: 26.32.140. *Effect of Decree of Adoption.* "By a decree of adoption the natural parents shall be divested of all legal rights and obligations in respect to the child, and the child shall be free from all legal obligations of obedience and maintenance in respect to them, and shall be, to all intents and purposes, and for all legal incidents, the child, legal heir, and lawful issue of his or her adopter or adopters. . . ."

Policies: State House Bill No. 84 is pending and concerns a registry and "confidential intermediaries". Under the definitions of this bill (6) " 'Confidential intermediary' means a suitable and qualified person appointed by the court who agrees, under oath of confidentiality, to mediate between and make contact with the natural parents and the adult adopted person to the extent allowed by the court."

WEST VIRGINIA

State Information Department: State Capitol
1800 Kanawha Blvd., East
Charleston, WV 25305
(304) 348-3456

State Agency: Department of Welfare
1900 Washington St., East
Charleston, WV 25305

Court of Jurisdiction: Circuit Court

Birth and Death Records: Division of Vital Statistics
State Department of Health
State Office Building No. 3
Charleston, WV 25305

State office has records since 1917. Prior records available from County Court in county where birth or death occurred.

Marrige Records: Division of Vital Statistics
see address listed above

State office has records since 1921.

County Clerk
County where license was issued

Divorce Records: Division of Vital Statistics
see address listed above

State office has index from 1968. Inquiries will be forwarded to appropriate office.

Clerk of Circuit Court
Chancery side
County where divorce was granted

Archives/Record Holdings: West Virginia Historical Society
Cultural Center
Capitol Complex
Charleston, WV 25305

Department of Motor Vehicles: Department of Motor Vehicles
113 State Office Bldg., No. 3
1800 Washington St., East
Charleston, WV 25305
(304) 348-2723

Search and Support Groups: Contact a National Organization for individuals working in this state.

State Reunion Registry: West Virginia does not maintain a reunion registry. However, a letter from the Governor's office, dated August 1980, states: ". . . should an adult adoptee contact us and wish to locate his or her parent or parents, our records are detailed enough to facilitate an arranged meeting, should both parties be agreeable." Refer to Chapter 8 for a list of group registries.

Age of Majority: 18 years or older

Laws Governing Opening Records: Adoption, Section 48-4-4. *Recordation of order; fees; disposition of records; names of adopting parents not to be disclosed; certificate for state registrar of vital statistics; birth certificate.* "All records of proceedings in adoption cases and all papers and records relating to such proceedings shall be kept in the office of the clerk of the court in a sealed file, which file shall be kept in a locked or sealed cabinet, vault or other container and shall not be open to inspection or copy by anyone, except upon court order for good cause shown."

Laws Governing Inheritance: Domestic Relations, Section 48-4-5. *Effect of order as to relations of parents and child and as to rights of inheritance; intestacy of adopted child.* "Upon the entry of such order of adoption, the natural parent or parents, any parent or parents by any previous legal adoption, and the lineal or collateral kindred of any such parent or parents, except any such parent who is the husband or wife of the petitioner for adoption, shall be divested of all legal rights, including the right of inheritance from or through the adopted child under the statutes of descent and distribution. . . ."

Author's Observations: William O. Morris stated, before the West Virginia Judicial Association on October 21, 1960, in a speech entitled, *Some Problems Relating to Adoptions in West Virginia and Recommended Changes:* "An examination of the statutes of the twelve states mentioned above [Virginia, Pennsylvania, Kentucky, Ohio, Maryland, Tennessee, North Carolina, South Carolina, Illinois, Delaware, New York and West Virginia] will disclose that only in West Virginia does the statute provide for an age differential between the petitioners and the child to be adopted."

The law he is speaking of is the following: Domestic Relations, Section 48-4-2. *Contents of petition; age of petitioner.* "The persons petitioning as aforesaid shall be at least fifteen years older than the child sought to be adopted. . . ."

William O. Morris further comments on this law: "Those who were responsible for this provision of the act must have been trying to insure that the normal minimum age difference between a natural parent and a child would be maintained in cases of adoption as nature has in part insured in the case of natural parent and child."

I do not disagree with laws regulating age differences to insure mature and responsible parents but disagree with the idea and usage of a term such as imitating "nature."

In a Report from the State Attorney General (page 194), a letter dated February 16, 1965, was directed to N.H. Dyer, M.D., M.P.H., State Director of Health. This letter was in response to Dr. Dyer's concern that there were instances where clerks were not furnishing the required information to the State Vital Statistics Department: ". . . some clerks are reporting that the name of the child at birth and the names of the natural parents are 'unknown.' A letter from C. Donald Robertson, Attorney General (prepared by Thomas B. Yost, Assistant), offered several interesting observations. 'It is readily admitted that, for various reasons, it is often preferable to some for the names of the natural parents to remain in blessed anonymity.' When a court clerk fails to report the natural name of the child and the names of the natural parents, or shows the same to be 'unknown' and the registrar of vital statistics is not satisfied that such names are in fact unknown, the registrar should refuse to issue a new birth certificate in the names of the adopting parties, for to do so would confuse the State's birth records by allowing one person to have two birth registrations."

This letter is only concerned with complication of the records, disregard for procedures, and interference with accurate statistics. There is no mention of falsifying records.

WISCONSIN

State Information Department:

State Capitol
Capitol Square
Madison, WI 53702
(608) 266-2211

State Agency:

Division of Community Services
Department of Health and Social
   Services
1 West Wilson St.
Madison, WI 53702

Court of Jurisdiction:

Circuit Court

Birth and Death Records:

Bureau of Health Statistics
Wisconsin Division of Health
P.O. Box 309
Madison, WI 53701

State office has partial records since 1814.

Marriage Records:

Bureau of Health Statistics
see address listed above

State office has records since April 1835.

Divorce Records:

Bureau of Health Statistics
see address listed above

State office has records since October 1, 1907.

Archives/Record Holdings:

State Historical Society of Wisconsin
University of Wisconsin
816 State St.
Madison, WI 53706

Department of Motor Vehicles:

Division of Motor Vehicles
Department of Transportation
255 Hill Farms State Office Bldg.
4802 Sheboygan Ave.
Madison, WI 53702
(608) 266-2233

Search and Support Groups:

Adoption Information and Direction **
P.O. Box 3397
Madison, WI 53704

CUB Representative, Cameron
CUB Representative, Milwaukee

Consult telephone directory or information operator, or write National Head-quarters, listed under Massachusetts, for current address.

> Master Search Clinic
> P.O. Box 3604
> Green Bay, WI 54303

State Reunion Registry: Wisconsin does not have a registry at the present, but one is being considered. Refer to Chapter 8 for a list of group registries.

Age of Majority: 18 years or older

Laws Governing Opening Records: Children's Code, Section 48.93. *Records Closed.* (1) "All records and papers pertaining to an adoption proceeding shall be kept in a separate locked file. No person shall have access to such records except on order of the court for good cause shown. . . ." (2) "All correspondence and papers, relating to the investigation, which are not a part of the court record, except those in the custody of agencies authorized to place children for adoption shall be transferred to the department and placed in its closed files."

Laws Governing Inheritance: Children's Code, Section 48.92. *Effect of adoption.* (2) "After the order of adoption is entered the relationship of parent and child between the adopted person and his natural parents, unless the natural parent is the spouse of the adopted parent, shall be completely altered and all the rights, duties and other legal consequences of the relationship shall cease to exist." (3) "Rights of inheritance by, from and through an adopted child are governed by Section 851.51."

Adoption in Wisconsin, a pamphlet written by the State Bar of Wisconsin: "The adopted child loses the right to inherit from or through its natural parents and relations under Wisconsin law. However, rights of inheritance are affected by wills, and generally the law of the state where the descendant lived determines rights of inheritance. Since inheritance rights of an adopted child may vary in different states and should be carefully guarded, if the adopted child has natural parents or relatives in another state, it is wise for adoptive parents to discuss this subject with their attorney."

Policies: *Summary of Survey Results on Post Adoptive Service to the Adult Adoptee and Open Adoption,* dated Spring 1980, taken by the Southern Regional Office, Adoption and Permanent Planning Section. *Summary:* The general trend of the responses was that changes in both legislation and adoption practice are needed. There is inconsistency in the interpretation of 48.93 (see "Laws Governing Opening Records") as witnessed by the split in policy regarding the release of nonidentifying information. There also seems to be significant sentiment to look at the possibility of a central registry or to re-examine the Minnesota statute. It was suggested that a statewide committee be formed to look at these issues and propose changes in the statutes.

WYOMING

State Information Department: State Capitol
Capitol Ave. at 24th St.
Cheyenne, WY 82001
(307) 777-7220

State Agency: Division of Public Assistance and Social
                                      Services
                                      Department of Health and Social
                                      Services
                                      Hathaway Bldg.
                                      Cheyenne, WY 82002

Court of Jurisdiction: District Court

Birth and Death Records: Vital Records Services
                                      Division of Health and Medical Services
                                      Hathaway Building
                                      Cheyenne, WY 82002

State office has records since July 1909.

Marriage Records: Vital Records Services
                                      see address listed above

State office has records since May 1941.

                                      County Clerk
                                      County where license was issued

Divorce Records: Vital Records Services
                                      see address listed above

State office has records since May 1941.

                                      Clerk of District Court
                                      County where divorce was granted

Archives/Record Holdings: State Library
                                      Archives and Records
                                      Supreme Court and Library Bldg.
                                      Cheyenne, WY 82001

Department of Motor Vehicles: Motor Vehicle Division
                                      Department of Revenue and Taxation
                                      2200 Carey Ave.
                                      Cheyenne, WY 82001
                                      (307) 777-7271

Search and Support Groups: ALMA Chapter, Riverton

Consult telephone directory or information operator, or write National Headquarters, listed under New York, for current address.

State Reunion Registry: Wyoming does not have a registry at the present. Refer to Chapter 8 for a list of group registries.

Age of Majority: 19 years or older

Laws Governing Opening Records: State House Bill No. 144, 1-726:4. *Petition for adoption of minor; by whom filed; requisites: confidential nature; inspection: separate journal to be kept.* (d) "The petition and documents filed pursuant to this section, and the interlocutory decree, if entered, and the final decree of adoption shall constitute a confidential file and shall be available for inspection only to the judge, or, by order of court, to the parties of the proceedings or their attorneys. . . . The court may order inspection of all or part of the confidential file in adoption proceedings only if it appears to the court that the welfare and best interests of the child will be served by the inspection."

Laws Governing Inheritance: House Bill No. 144, 1-726.14. *Effect of Adoption.* "Upon the entry of a final decree of adoption the former parent, guardian or putative father of the child shall have no right to the control or custody of the child."

NOTES

1. Deciding to Search

Page 2 For more information on the California lawsuit, interested adoptees and birthparents may refer to the complaint for declaratory relief filed April 3, 1981, in the Superior Court of the State of California for the County of Los Angeles, Case No. 0362120. The lawsuit was filed by attorney Howard M. Fields on behalf of ALMA and listed co-plaintiffs.

3 The complete text of Florence Fisher's remarks regarding the fundamental issue behind sealed adoption records can be found in her column "President's Message," *The ALMA Searchlight,* Autumn 1977, p. 1.

3 The insights on the court ruling in the New York lawsuit for open records comes from a May 13, 1981, letter to the attorney Howard M. Fields.

4 A fuller discussion of the generally confusing body of state laws regarding open records can be found in Mary Ann Jones, *Issues and Recommendations Regarding Sealed Adoption Records* (Newark, NJ: Child Services Association, 1977), p. 19, #1 notes.

5 The definition of nonidentifying information comes from Mary Sullivan, Task Force on Confidentiality in the Adoption Program—A Report to the California State Department of Health, Sacramento, CA, 1977, p. 24.

5 The case of Betty Chase was chronicled in an article entitled "Under 'Race' She Puts a '?'," *Los Angeles Times,* July 9, 1978, Metro Section, p. 1.

7 The complete text of James R. Carter's comments on the question of adoptee inheritance can be found in "Confidentiality of Adoption Records: An Examination," *Tulane Law Review,* vol. 52 (1977–78).

10 Sarah P. Collins's interpretation of the Freedom of Information Act and the Right of Privacy Act are from *Citizens' Control over Records Held by Third Parties* (Washington, DC: Congressional Research Service, Library of Congress Report No. 78-255), p. CRS-22.

12 The psychological harm felt by adoptees who lack a complete family medical and psychological history can be seen in the affidavits of Anita McCarthy and John Franklin Filippone, filed in support of the ALMA lawsuit in New York before the U.S. District Court for the Southern District of New York on May 23, 1977, reported in *The ALMA Searchlight,* Autumn 1977, p. 14.

12 The comments of Judge Wade S. Weatherford, Jr., on the relationship between needs and rights when considering opening adoption records can be found in "Report of the Governor's Commission to Study the Adoption Laws," issued by the State of Maryland, presented to the Governor and Legislature in 1980.

13 Concerning the stereotyping of relinquishing birthparents, see Edna Ewald, "Homecoming," *Good Housekeeping,* March 1981, p. 118.

14 Examples of similarities among long-separated siblings have appeared in the popular media. Among these are an article by Mel Jaffe entitled "Just One Big Happy Family Again," *New York Post,* January 30, 1981, p. 13, and an article by Phyllis Batelle entitled "Triplets and They Didn't Know It," *Reader's Digest,* May 1981, pp. 235–237.

14 Psychologist David Lykken's remarks about the scope of human behavior that might be genetically determined are found in Constance Holden, "Twins Reunited: More Than the Faces Are Familiar," *Science 80 Magazine,* November, p. 59.

2. Getting Moral Support

Page 22 The difficulties encountered when attempting to obtain information from agencies involved in adoption proceedings are mentioned in the affidavit of Katrina Maxtone-Graham, filed in support of the ALMA lawsuit in New York before the U.S. District Court for the Southern District of New York on May 23, 1977, reported in *The ALMA Searchlight,* Autumn 1977, p. 15.

27 The willingness to deal with any findings a searching adoptee or birthparent uncovers is expressed by Marilyn Louise Beck in an affidavit filed in support of the ALMA lawsuit in New York before the U.S. District Court for the Southern District of New York on May 23, 1977, reported in *The ALMA Searchlight,* Autumn 1977, p. 10.

36 The effect of the death of an adoptive parent and its ramifications to an adoptee's search are expressed in the affidavit of Roberta van Laven, filed in support of the ALMA lawsuit in New York before the U.S. District Court for the Southern District of New York on May 23, 1977, reported in *The ALMA Searchlight,* Autumn 1977, p. 12.

40 The statistics estimating the numbers of adoptee searchers in the United States come from an article entitled "Adoptees and Their Quest," *Washington Post,* February 6, 1978, p. a8.

5. Beginning to Search: Primary Sources of Data

Page 98 Former social worker Annette Baron's recollections of dealing with adoptees and birthparents seeking information are detailed in *A Time to Search* by Henry Ehrlick (New York and London: Paddington Press, 1977), p. 17.

104 The sample form authorizing release of medical information is based on form 712 given in the *Handbook of Law Office Forms* by Robert Seller Smith (Englewood Cliffs, NJ: Prentice-Hall, 1974).

108 The findings of the investigation into the Tennessee Children's Home Society are drawn from a report by Robert Taylor, Special Counsel on the Investigation of the Tennessee Children's Home Society, to J. O. McMahan, Commissioner of Public Welfare for the State of Tennessee (Nashville, TN: September 1950).

6. As the Search Progresses: Alternate Sources of Data

Page 134 The request pertaining to military records should be made on General Services Administration standard form 180.

146 The account of one searcher's use of the Social Security Administration to

locate another individual is chronicled by Hal Aigner in his book, *Faint Trails* (Greenbrae, CA: Paradigm Press, 1980). Mr. Aigner's book is available for $4.95 (plus $1.00 postage) from the publisher, located at 127 Greenbrae Boardwalk, Greenbrae, CA 94904.

REFERENCE SOURCES

The following list contains reference sources discussed in this book as well as others you might find useful in your search.

Access: The Supplementary Guide to Periodicals (New York: Gaylord Bros.), 1975 to present.

Androit, John L., *Guide to U.S. Government Publications,* 4 vols. (McLean, VA: U.S. Superintendent of Documents), 1978.

Ayer Directory of Publications (Philadelphia: Ayer Press), annual.

Binsfield, Edmund L., *Church Archives in the U.S. and Canada: A Bibliography* (The Archivist), 1958.

Blockson, Charles L., *Black Genealogy* (Englewood Cliffs, NJ: Prentice-Hall), 1977.

The Book of the States (Lexington, KY: The Council of State Governments), 1935 to present.

Books in Print (New York: R.R. Bowker Company), annual.

Child Welfare League of American Standards for Adoption Service (New York: Child Welfare League of America). Ask for latest edition of pamphlet.

Clare, Marcus, *A Canadian Guide for Adopted Adults in Search of Their Origins* (Vancouver, British Columbia: International Self-Counsel Press), 1979.

Code of Federal Regulations (Washington, DC: Government Printing Office), annual.

Collection and Use of Freedom of Information by the Social Security Administration (Social Security Administration). Pamphlet No. SSA-5000 at your local SSA Office.

County and City Data Books (Pittsburgh: U.S. Bureau of the Census, U.S. Department of Commerce), 1949 to present.

Cumulative Book Index (New York: H.W. Wilson Company), 1928 to present.

Directory of Special Libraries and Information Centers, 3rd ed. (Detroit: Gale Research Company), 1974.

Downs, Robert B., and Keller, Clara D., *How to Do Library Research,* 2nd ed. (Urbana: University of Illinois Press), 1975.

Editor & Publisher International Year Book (New York: Editor and Publisher), annual.

Encyclopedia of Associations (Detroit: Gale Research Company), 1980.

Everton, George B., Sr., *Handy Book for Genealogists,* 5th ed. (Logan, Utah: Everton Publishing), 1960.

Federal Registry (Washington, DC: Government Printing Office), daily.

Genealogical Records in the National Archives (Washington, DC: National Archives, Free Pamphlet #5).

Genealogical Sources Outside the National Archives (Washington, DC: The National Archives, Free Pamphlet #6).

Getting Yours: A Consumer's Guide to Obtaining Your Medical Records (Public Citizen's Health Research Group, Department P, 200 P Street, NW, Suite 708, Washington, DC 20036).

Greenfield, Stanley R., ed., *National Directory of Addresses and Telephone Numbers,* rev. ed. (New York: Bantam Books), 1979.

Handbook for Genealogical Correspondence (prepared by Cache Genealogical Library, Logan, Utah), 1963.

Hessletine, William B., and McNeil, Donald R., eds., *The WPA Historical Records Survey* (Madison: University of Wisconsin Press), 1958.

Index to U.S. Government Periodicals (Chicago: Infordata International), quarterly; 1974 to present.

Jacobus, Donald, *Index to Genealogical Periodicals*, 8 vols. (self-published), 1963.

Jones, Mary Ann, *The Sealed Adoption Record Controversy: Report of a Survey of Agency Policy, Practice and Opinions* (New York: Child Welfare League of America, Inc.), 1976.

Jones, Vincent L., *Family History for Fun and Profit* (Salt Lake City, Utah: Community Press), 1972.

Kirkham, E. Kay, *A Handy Guide to Record Searching in the Larger Cities of the U.S.* (Logan, Utah), 1974.

———, *Military Records of America* (Washington, DC: self-published), 1963.

———, *Simplified Genealogy for Americans* (Salt Lake City: Deseret Book Company), 1968.

———, *A Survey of American Church Records*, 2 vols. (Salt Lake City: Deseret Book Company), 1959.

Klein, Bernard, ed., *Guide to American Directories* (Coral Springs, FL: B. Klein Publications), annual.

Kupersmith, Nancy, "The Fight to Open Up Adoption Records," *Reader's Digest*, June 1978.

Lukowski, Susan, ed., *State Information Book* (Washington, DC: Potomac Books), 1977.

Martindale-Hubbell Law Directory (Summit, NJ: Martindale-Hubbell), annual.

Mitchell, Constance M., *Locating Books for Interlibrary Loan, with a Bibliography of Printed Guides Which Show Locations of Books in American Libraries* (New York: H.W. Wilson Company), 1930.

Mode, Peter G., *Source Book & Bibliographical Guide for American Church History* (Boston: J.S. Canner and Company), 1964.

The National Directory of State Agencies (Washington, DC: Information Resources Press), 1976.

The New York Times Index (New York: The New York Times), 1851 to present.

The Official Congressional Directory (Washington, DC: Government Printing Office), 1809 to present.

Patterson's American Education (Chicago: Educational Directories), 1904 to present.

Peskett, Hugh, *Discover Your Ancestors: A Quest for Your Roots* (New York: Arco Publishing Company), 1978.

Rabkin, Jacob, and Johnson, Mark, *Current Legal Forms with Tax Analysis* (New York: Matthew Bender & Company), 1980.

Readers Guide to Periodical Literature (New York: H.W. Wilson Company), 1905 to present.

Rillera, Mary Jo, *The Adoption Searchbook* (Triadoption Publications, P.O. Box 5218, Huntington Station, Huntington Beach, CA 92646), 1981.

———, *Natural Parents Documentation Guidebook* (self-published, P.O. Box 5218, Huntington Station, Huntington Beach, CA 92646), 1977.

Rottenberg, Dan, *Finding Our Fathers: A Guidebook to Jewish Genealogy* (New York: Random House), 1977.

Rubincan, Milton, and Staphenson, Jean, *Genealogical Research: Methods and Sources*, 2 vols. (Washington, DC: American Society of Genealogists), 1960.

Sheehy, Eugene P., *Guide to Reference Books* (Chicago: American Library Association), 1968 to present.

Sherick, L.G., *How to Use the Freedom of Information Act: FOIA* (New York: Arco Publishing Company), 1978.
Social Science Index (New York: H.W. Wilson Company), annual.
Stevenson, Noel C., *Search & Research* (Salt Lake City: Deseret Book Company), 1964.
Survey of American Census Schedules, 1790–1950 (Salt Lake City: Deseret Book Company), 1959.
Todd, Alden, *Finding Facts Fast: How to Find Out What You Want To Know Immediately* (New York: William Morrow), 1972.
Ulrich's International Periodicals Directory, 19th ed. (New York: R.R. Bowker Company), 1980.
United States Government Manual (Washington, DC: Government Printing Office), 1935 to present.
Vilardi, Emma M., *Handbook for the Search* (P.O. Box 5218, Huntington Station, Huntington Beach, CA 92646), 1978.
Westin, Jeane Eddy, *Finding Your Roots* (Los Angeles: J.P. Farcer), 1977.
Where to Write for Birth and Death Records, United States and Outlying Areas (Washington, DC: Government Printing Office, #PHS 80-1142), 1980. $1.50
Where to Write for Divorce Records, United States and Outlying Areas (Washington, DC: Government Printing Office, #PHS 80-1145), 1980. $1.50
Where to Write for Marriage Records, United States and Outlying Areas (Washington, DC: Government Printing Office, #PHS 80-1144), 1980. $1.50
Writer's Digest (9933 Alliance Road, Cincinnati, OH 45242). April 1981, advertisement on p. 69.

A READING LIST OF ADOPTION-RELATED BOOKS AND ARTICLES

The following is a list of books and articles on the subject of adoption and adoption records. Included here are personal accounts of those who have sought their birthparents or relinquished children.

Aigner, Hal, *Faint Trails,* Western States Edition (Paradigm Press, 127 Greenbrae Boardwalk, Greenbrae, CA 94904), 1980.
Baker, Nancy C., *Baby Selling: The Scandal of Black Market Adoptions* (New York: Vanguard Press), 1978.
Benet, Mary Kathleen, *The Politics of Adoption* (New York: Free Press), 1976.
Breasted, M., "Babybrokers Reaping Huge Fees," *The New York Times,* June 28, 1977, pp. 1, 11.
Buck, Pearl S., *Children for Adoption* (New York: Random House), 1964.
Burgess, Linda Cannon, *The Art of Adoption* (Washington, DC: Acropolis Books), 1976.
Campbell, Lee, *The Birthparents' Perspective* (Concerned United Birthparents, Inc. [CUB], P.O. Box 573, Milford, MA 01757).
———, *Understanding the Birthparent* (Concerned United Birthparents, Inc. [CUB], P.O. Box 573, Milford, MA 01757), 1977.
Dusky, Lorraine, *Birthmark* (New York: M. Evans and Company), 1979.
Ehrlick, Henry, *A Time to Search* (New York and London: Paddington Press), 1977.
Fisher, Florence, *The Search for Anna Fisher* (New York: Fawcett), 1973.
Freeman, J.T., "Who Am I? Where Did I Come From?" *Ladies Home Journal,* vol. 74 (March 1970), pp. 132–36.

Gallagher, U.M., "What's Happening in Adoption," *Children Today,* vol. 4, no. 6 (1975), pp. 11–13, 36.

Gaylord, C.L., "The Adoptive Child's Right to Know," *Case and Comment,* March–April 1976, pp. 38–44.

Goldstein, Joseph; Freud, Anna; and Sonit, Albert J., *Beyond the Best Interest of the Child* (New York: The Free Press), 1973.

Hulse, Jerry, *Jody* (New York: McGraw-Hill), 1976.

Kirk, David, *Shared Fate* (New York: The Free Press), 1964.

Lifton, Betty Jean, *I'm Still Me* (New York: Knopf), 1981.

————, *Lost and Found* (New York: Dial), 1979.

————, *Twice Born—Memories of an Adopted Daughter* (New York: McGraw-Hill), 1975.

McKuen, Rod, *Finding My Father, One Man's Search for Identity* (Los Angeles: Cheval Books/Coward, McCann & Geoghegan), 1976.

McTaggart, Lynn, "The Mexican Adoption Connection," *Family Weekly Daily Pilot,* September 7, 1980, p. 6.

Magnuson, James, and Petrie, Dorothea G., *Orphan Train* (New York: Fawcett), 1978.

Musser, Sandra Kay, *I Would Have Searched Forever* (Jan Enterprises, Box 268, Bala Cynwyd, PA 19004), 1979.

Pannor, Reuben; Massarik, F.; and Evans, B.W., *The Unmarried Father* (New York: Springer), 1971.

Paton, Jean M., *Adoption Portrayed in Books Published Between 1949 and 1977* (Orphan Voyage, 2141 Rd., 2300, Cedaredge, CO 81413).

————, *The Adopted Break Silence* (Cedaredge, CO: Life History Study Center and Jean Paton), 1954.

————, *The Discovery of Adoption, A Miscellany of Critical Observations* (Orphan Voyage, 2141 Rd., 2300, Cedaredge, CO 81413).

————, *Letters of Adoption* (Orphan Voyage, 2141 Rd., 2300, Cedaredge, CO 81413).

————, *Newspaper Accounts of the Orphan Voyage Program* (Orphan Voyage, 2141 Rd., 2300, Cedaredge, CO 81413).

————, *Orphan Voyage* (Country Press), 1968. This book was written under the name of Rutnena Hill Kittson. (Orphan Voyage, 2141 Rd., 2300, Cedaredge, CO 81413).

————, *They Served Fugitively* (Orphan Voyage, 2141 Rd., 2300, Cedaredge, CO 81413).

————, *Twenty-Three Years, A Compilation of the Coordinator of Orphan Voyage* (Orphan Voyage, 2141 Rd., 2300, Cedaredge, CO 81413).

Presser, S.B., "The Historical Background of the American Law of Adoption," *Journal of Family Law,* vol. 11 (1972), pp. 443–445.

Quinlan, Joseph and Julie, *Karen Ann: The Quinlans Tell Their Story* (New York: Doubleday), 1977.

Sanders, Patricia, and Sitterly, Nancy, *Search Aftermath and Adjustments* (self-published), 1981. (Pat Sanders, 20111 Riverside Dr., Santa Ana, CA 92707, or Nancy Sitterly, 1203 Hill St., Suffield, CT 06078.)

Sorosky, Arthur D., *The Adoption Triangle* (New York: Anchor Press), 1978.

Sorosky, Arthur D.; Baran, Annette; and Pannor, Reuben, "Opening the Sealed Record in Adoption: The Human Need for Continuity," *Journal of Jewish Communal Service,* vol. 51 (1974), pp. 188–196.

Triseliotis, John, *In Search of Origins: The Experiences of Adopted People* (London and Boston: Routledge & Kegan Paul), 1973.

Wishard, Laurie, and William R., *Adoption: The Grafted Tree* (San Francisco: Cragmont Publications), 1979.

A SEARCHER'S CHECKLIST

What follows is a checklist of information sources that have been referred to, although some have been treated at more length than others. Use it as an aid to developing leads in areas you've not yet covered. Use it as a record of sources you've referred to. While the listing here is extensive, it is not definitive—other sources may prove open to you. You yourself will decide how efficient your search turns out to be. Review carefully all information you receive, follow any new sources of information you discover, and always proceed in a positive manner.

Adoption Papers

____ Change of Name
____ Finalized Court Papers
____ Home Study Report
____ Petition to Adopt
____ Relinquishment Papers

Agency Records

____ Application to Adopt
____ Baptismal Certificate
____ Financial Agreements
____ Foster Homes
____ Home Study Reports
____ Medical Information
____ Petition to Adopt
____ Relinquishment Papers

Birth Records

____ Altered Certificate
____ Baptism Certificate
____ Christening Certificate
____ Original Certificate
____ Published Birth Notice

Cemetery Records

____ Obituaries
____ Interment Orders
____ Perpetual Care
____ Plot Records
____ Tombstones or Monuments

Census Records

____ City or County
____ State
____ Federal
____ School District
____ Soundex

Church Records

____ Birth Records
____ Baptism and Christening Records
____ Confirmation Records
____ Contributors List
____ Death Records
____ Marriage Records
____ Membership Rolls
____ Published Events or Yearbooks
____ Subscribers List
____ Sunday School Records
____ Tithe Records

City Directories

____ Haines Criss-Cross Directory
____ Polk Directory
____ Search Area Telephone Directory
____ Other (List:_____)

Court Records

____ Adoption Records
____ Change of Name
____ Citizenship
____ Relinquishment Records

Death Records

____ Burial Permit
____ Death Certificate
____ Obituaries
____ Probate Records
____ Published Accounts
____ Will

Divorce Records

____ Grant of Annulment
____ Index of Area Divorce Records
____ Published Accounts

Employment Records

____ Payroll Records
____ Profession or Trade
____ Union Membership
____ Work History

Engagement Records

____ Church Records
____ Newspaper Accounts

Estate Docket

____ Administrators
____ Executor(s)
____ Index to Probate Records
____ Will

Family Records

____ Correspondence
____ Insurance Records
____ Personal Recollections
____ Photographs

Genealogy

____ Genealogy Societies
____ Historical Societies
____ LDS Church Genealogy Records
____ Library of Congress
____ National Archives
____ Published Genealogies

Hospital Records

____ Admittance
____ Delivery Room
____ Medical Records
____ Nursery Records
____ Release Records

Immigration Records

____ Applications for Entry
____ Customs Records
____ Naturalization Papers
____ Passenger Lists
____ Passport Records

Land Records

____ Abstracts
____ Change of Title
____ Index to Records
____ Property Tax Lists

Licenses

____ Building
____ Business
____ Gun Registration
____ Hunting
____ Marriage
____ Professional
____ Trade
____ Vehicular

Marriage Records

____ Announcements
____ Application for License
____ Certificates
____ Church Records
____ Index to Public Marriage Records
____ Justice of the Peace
____ Licenses
____ Published Accounts
____ Wedding Announcements

Military Records

____ Death Rolls
____ Discharge Papers
____ Enlistment Records
____ Pension Records
____ Published Events
____ VA Records

Mortuary Records

____ Burial Permits
____ Burial Registers
____ Funeral Cards
____ Memorial Cards
____ Obituaries

Newspapers

____ Accomplishments Reported
____ Church Events
____ Club and Organization Events
____ Engagements
____ Graduations
____ Local History
____ Military Service Notes
____ Obituaries
____ Published Births
____ Published Deaths
____ Published Divorces
____ Published Marriages

Organizations

—— Fraternities
—— Honorary Societies
—— Professional Associations
—— Religious Groups
—— Social Clubs
—— Sororities
—— Trade Associations
—— Unions
—— Volunteer Organizations

Reunion Registries

—— ALMA
—— International Soundex
—— State Registries
—— Local Group Registry
—— Orphan Voyage
—— CUB Registry

School Records

—— Admissions Records
—— Alumni Records
—— Attendance Records
—— College or University
—— Diploma Lists
—— Directories

—— Graduation Records
—— Grammar School
—— High School
—— Private School
—— Published Events
—— Pupil Lists
—— School Census
—— Trade or Vocational School
—— Year Books

Trade Records

—— Labor Union
—— Magazines
—— Memberships
—— Newspapers

Vehicle Records

—— Boat License
—— Driver's License
—— Vehicle Registration

Voters Records

—— Index to Registration Records
—— Poll Books
—— Register of Voters
—— Voters Lists

SAMPLE LETTERS AND FORMS

Index